Don't Bank On It!

Also by
Craig R. Smith

Rediscovering Gold in the 21st Century:
The Complete Guide to the Next Gold Rush

Black Gold Stranglehold:
The Myth of Scarcity and the Politics of Oil
(co-authored with Jerome R. Corsi)

The Uses of Inflation:
Monetary Policy and Governance in the 21st Century

Crashing the Dollar:
How to Survive a Global Currency Collapse*

Re-Making Money:
Ways to Restore America's Optimistic Golden Age*

The Inflation Deception:
Six Ways Government Tricks Us...And Seven Ways to Stop It!*

The Great Debasement:
The 100-Year Dying of the Dollar and How to Get America's Money Back*

The Great Withdrawal:
How the Progressives' 100-Year Debasement of America and the Dollar Ends*

Also by
Lowell Ponte

The Cooling

Crashing the Dollar:
How to Survive a Global Currency Collapse*

Re-Making Money:
Ways to Restore America's Optimistic Golden Age*

The Inflation Deception:
Six Ways Government Tricks Us...And Seven Ways to Stop It!*

The Great Debasement:
The 100-Year Dying of the Dollar and How to Get America's Money Back*

The Great Withdrawal:
How the Progressives' 100-Year Debasement of America and the Dollar Ends*

*Works co-authored by Craig R. Smith and Lowell Ponte

Don't Bank On It!

The Unsafe World of 21st Century Banking

By Craig R. Smith

and Lowell Ponte

Foreword by Pat Boone

Idea Factory Press
Phoenix, Arizona

Don't Bank On It!
The Unsafe World of 21st Century Banking

Cover design by Dustin D. Brown, KrypticEye.com

Editing by Ellen L. Ponte

Portions of this book originally appeared in
the following projects by Craig R. Smith and Lowell Ponte:
Don't Bank on It! (2014 White Paper)
*The Great Debasement: The 100-Year Dying
of the Dollar and How to Get America's Money Back* and
Crashing the Dollar: How to Survive a Global Currency Collapse and
*The Great Withdrawal: How the Progressives' 100-Year
Debasement of America and the Dollar Ends.*
Copyright © 2010, 2011, 2012, 2013 and 2014 by Idea Factory Press.
All Rights Reserved.

Portions of this book originally appeared in
*The Uses of Inflation: Monetary Policy
and Governance in the 21st Century* by Craig R. Smith
Copyright © 2011 by Swiss America Trading Corporation
All Rights Reserved.

Library of Congress Data
ISBN Number 978-0-9898471-5-5
First Edition - September 2014

Idea Factory Press
2725 E. Mine Creek Road, #1028, Phoenix, AZ 85024
Tel. (602) 918-3296 * Ideaman@myideafactory.net

Updates, reviews and more are posted at
http://www.dontbankonitbook.com

Table of Contents

Foreword by Pat Boone vii

Introduction by Craig R. Smith 9

PART ONE – Banking's Evolution

Chapter One – Breaking the Banks 21

Chapter Two – Time Machines 47

Chapter Three – Fractured Reserve Banking 61

PART TWO – Politicizing Our Banks

Chapter Four – Dawn of the Fed 83

Chapter Five – Banking Left 105

Chapter Six – The Wars Against Tax Havens 135

Chapter Seven – Political Bank Robbers 153

PART THREE – The Choice

Chapter Eight – The Death of Banking (As We Know It) 179

Chapter Nine – A Future You *Could* Bank On 201

Epilogue: The Gamble 213

Footnotes 221

Sources 234

Dedication

To my wonderful wife and best friend
Melissa Smith, who makes me better
each day and raised our daughters
Holly and Katie to love the Lord
with all their hearts.
Also to my Pastor Tommy Barnett,
who taught me that doing the right thing
is always the right thing to do,
and to always hold onto the vision

Foreword
by Pat Boone

"Go to the ant, O Sluggard;
consider her ways, and be wise.
Without having any chief, officer, or ruler,
she...gathers her food in harvest."

– Proverbs 6:6-8

Thrift, saving, honesty and alertness are time-proven virtues, taught by the Bible. Another book also helped me learn the value of thrift: the little bank book of my first childhood savings account, which taught the rewards of saving today for tomorrow.

Today, however, government follows economist John Maynard Keynes' idea that saving is bad because the thrifty are not spendthrifts. In our spendaholic Progressive politicians' new Aesop fable, the lazy grasshopper is rewarded with free government goodies, and the industrious ant's savings are confiscated to pay for this.

In this book my long-trusted friend and advisor Craig Smith and former *Reader's Digest* Roving Editor Lowell Ponte explain why your bank account is now punished and discouraged with near-zero interest, yet is at risk of being looted in at least 20 different ways.

Thrift is still a great virtue, and saving is wise and rational if done right. Craig and Lowell show us how to reduce the huge and growing risks our bank accounts and the value of our dollar now face, and how to save our savings.

Pat

*"I believe that banking institutions
are more dangerous to our liberties
than standing armies."*

– Thomas Jefferson

*"Banks have done more injury
to the religion, morality, tranquility,
prosperity, and even wealth of the nation
than they...ever will do good."*

– John Adams

Introduction
by Craig R. Smith

*"Money amassed either serves us
or rules us."*

– Horace
Roman poet

Could the bank we trust to safeguard our money now be one of the riskiest places to put it?

I have known for years that strange and ominous things are happening to our banks and our other store of value, our dollar.

Yet even I was shocked recently when this hit close to home. Imagine this happening to you:

A friend told me that she had tried to withdraw $25,000 from her savings in cash at the local branch of a major bank where she has been a customer for many years. This was a friendly bank where smiling tellers greeted her by name.

This bank had always been delighted to accept her deposits. Suddenly, however, it refused to honor her request for a sizable withdrawal.

Worse, a teller patronizingly demanded that she explain why she was trying to take out this money – as if she were a child who needed their permission or approval, or a note from her father.

My friend was stunned. This was *her* money, not the bank's, she had always assumed. And what she intended to do with her own money was none of this bank's business.

However, not until the following day, when she returned with a lawyer, did the bank allow her to withdraw this money from her own account.

When we looked into this, we discovered that more and more such bank refusals are happening, and that what my friend experienced is merely one telltale sign of many frightening risks now emerging in our banks, currency and economy.

"Capital Controls"

In January 2014, Stephen Cotton walked into the British building where he had banked for 28 years, a branch of London-based giant HSBC that calls itself "The World's Local Bank." He filled out a withdrawal slip for 7,000 Pounds [approximately $11,000] he owed to his mother. [1]

The bank refused to let Mr. Cotton have money from his account. It literally demanded a letter from his mother. It also refused to let him withdraw lesser amounts equivalent to roughly $7,500 or $6,000. The bank at last let him take the equivalent of $4,500 from his savings, but refused to let him withdraw any more that day. Customers had not been informed of these arbitrary new rules that HSBC quietly imposed in November 2013.

"You shouldn't have to explain to your bank why you want that money," said Cotton. "It's not theirs, it's yours."

Alas, under today's laws he is mistaken. As we shall explain, your deposits in certain key ways belong to the bank. What you "own" is a deposit receipt, an IOU for what the law now sees as the bank's "unsecured asset."

"All these regulations which have been imposed on banks allow enormous interpretation," Member of Parliament Douglas Carswell told the BBC in a January 24, 2014 story. "It basically infantilises the customer. In a sense your money becomes pocket money and the bank becomes your parent."

"We have an obligation to protect our customers, and to minimize the opportunity for financial crime," an unapologetic HSBC spokesman told the BBC.

[HSBC, which is by some measures the world's largest bank, in December 2012 agreed to pay a $1.92 Billion fine in a money-laundering case in the U.S. This record fine did not alter the bank affiliate HSBC Securities (USA) Inc.'s position as one of 21 privileged "Primary Dealers" of the Federal Reserve Bank of New York.]

If the $121 Billion on deposit in HSBC's dwindling 248 American branches disappeared because of theft or cybercrime, reimbursing account holders could cost the government's Federal Deposit Insurance Corporation (FDIC) as much as one-fifth of its entire theoretical capability to insure all deposits in U.S. banks – a capability, at maximum, only about one-fourteenth of the at least $7 Trillion of FDIC-insured bank accounts.

The FDIC, even with the promised help of the Fed and the U.S. Treasury, cannot under present arrangements insure the safety of more than about 7 percent of U.S. private bank accounts in a major financial crisis.

HSBC depositors can be required to "provide evidence" that they will spend it in an HSBC-approved way before they can withdraw their OWN money - or they may find it frozen. We warned readers to expect this in our 2013 book *The Great Withdrawal.*

Assumed Risk

Worse yet, evidence is mounting that U.S. banks have plans to do the same kind of thing in the name of "protecting" depositors from the rising threat of cyber attacks, identity theft, global economic disruption and other risks.

JPMorgan Chase Bank sent a letter informing many business customers that "starting November 17, 2013: You will no longer be able to send International wire transfers" and "Your cash activity limit...will be $50,000 per statement cycle, per account." These changes, the letter said, "will help us more effectively manage the risks involved with these types of transactions."

"So...JPM is now engaged in the risk-management of ATM withdrawals?" asked *ZeroHedge.com* in an October 16, 2013 article that published a copy of the bank's letter. "Reading between the lines, this sounds perilously close to capital controls to us...." [2]

"[H]ow long," asked *ZeroHedge*, "before the $50,000 limit becomes $20,000, then $10,000, then $5,000 and so on, until Business Customers are advised that the bank will conduct an excess cash flow sweep every month....?"

As its frightening letter went viral on the Internet, Chase rushed to deny that it was implementing "capital controls" and reined in its new policy. Its "derisking" policy, said Chase, had caused an "Overreaction" among savers.

"Liquidity Hoarding"

This letter might be a tiny foretaste of the kinds of contingency plans at JPMorgan Chase – and at the handful of other giant banks that control more than half of all American bank deposits – for swiftly locking down capital controls on all accounts the instant the government so commands.

Our banks and money are being manipulated to serve the same political agendas. We should be thinking of our banks and our dollar as our two intertwined ways we can save – and others can expropriate – the fruits of our labor.

At the top of every piece of paper money in your wallet are the words "Federal Reserve Note," the name of the central bank that oversees the bank with your accounts. As we will show you, your bank and your money are in a very real sense one, and this is something that needs to change if we wish to save our independence and liberty.

The banks know that they are far less secure, in many ways, and far more at risk than they can openly admit.

Their insecurity was one of the causes of the economic near-collapse of 2007-2008 and resulting Great Recession that has given us the slowest recovery in American history – slower even than the Great Depression.

Before this crisis, banks routinely lent money to one another. If one bank had an unusual number of withdrawals, for example, other banks would promptly prop up its capital reserve with overnight loans.

However, when this crisis struck, the large banks were frightened and stopped lending to one another. Federal Reserve economist Jose Berrospide described their reaction as "liquidity hoarding" because they were unsure whether other banks would remain solvent and were afraid of losing their own assets and lines of credit. [3]

Some of these banks had been called "Too Big To Fail," but they watched as the Federal Reserve and U.S. Treasury let one TBTF bank, Lehman Brothers, go bankrupt without throwing it a financial lifeline.

The Fed and Treasury would later lock the heads of America's biggest banks in a room and, as the story goes, not let them leave until all had agreed to accept huge bailout loans that would remove any doubts about their liquidity.

When push came to shove, however, the major banks ceased lending to one another because they know how unsure today's banks and capital really are.

The risk that all of us take by lending our money to the banks – in the form of bank deposits – is huge and getting bigger.

This risk comes not only from computerized bank robbers but also from many other places, including the very people and entities we trust to protect what we have deposited in our bank.

The expression "you can bank on it" means that something is secure, a sure bet, reliable.

Nevertheless, during the 2008 crisis, when some of our largest banks were asked to put their own money behind one another, their actions have spoken more loudly than any words that they were afraid to "bank on" America's banks.

Small regional banks have relatively limited access to lending, yet in past recessions 70 percent of all new jobs that made recovery possible came from America's small to medium-sized regions.

In this book we will show you what banks know, and why, despite near-record recent profits, they continue to behave with what appears to be uncertainty, apprehension and fear.

Vulnerable Targets

My co-author has a relative nearly 90 years of age whose bank account and credit cards have repeatedly been looted by identity thieves and hackers who have made off with thousands of dollars.

"It used to be so simple," she says, shaking her head. "I never had to worry about such things."

This senior citizen, sometimes distracted by pain medication and a back problem, grew up in a world where people were more trusting and hence less guarded about sharing information.

Decades ago, people seldom worried about a restaurant waiter carrying off their credit card, where its information could be copied and sold.

And for those who are new to computers, when an email says you have won a prize, your first response is not necessarily to avoid clicking on a link or attachment that might infect your computer with a spy program.

"I was surprised when helping her to find out how little information a hacker or identity thief might need," says Lowell. "Her checking account was successfully accessed by an offshore crook who was using her account number and her routing number to pay *his* bills. Both numbers are printed at the bottom of every check that we use."

No wonder that modern digital bank robbery is now epidemic.

A Vault Beneath Manhattan

Some 80 feet beneath the Federal Reserve Bank in Manhattan is its gold vault, said to be in America second only to Fort Knox, Kentucky in the quantity of gold it holds.

Not all this gold is American. Some was deposited for American safekeeping by foreign governments.

During the Cold War, as a precaution against Soviet invasion, West Germany deposited a portion of its gold, approximately 1,536 metric tons, in the New York Federal Reserve Bank's vault.

Germany also made deposits in London, Paris and Frankfurt, altogether totaling worldwide 3,391 tons, officially the second largest gold reserves in the world, after America's.

When Germany in late 2012 asked to withdraw a mere 84 tons of its gold from the Fed, it was told that this would take at least 7 years. By mid-2014, only 5 tons of Germany's gold have been sent from the New York Fed to Frankfurt. [4]

According to the German news magazine *Der Spiegel*, a secret report by Germany's Federal Audit Office "noted that the Federal Reserve Bank of New York refuses to allow the gold's owners to view their own reserves." [5]

In June 2014, the German government announced that it will leave its gold in the New York Fed's "safe hands." [6]

"The Americans are taking good care of our gold," said a spokesman for Chancellor Angela Merkel's Christian Democratic coalition. "Objectively, there's absolutely no reason for mistrust." [7]

However, there is reason to wonder why major banks, from my friend's bank to the New York Fed, are discouraging depositors from withdrawing their money or gold.

This, perhaps needlessly, feeds speculation and uncertainty that have already prompted other nations – the Netherlands and Finland among them – to wonder if they should also withdraw their gold stored at no cost by the Fed.

If the New York Fed has Germany's gold, why not just give it to them?

Has the Fed rehypothecated this gold, using another nation's gold as fractional-reserve collateral in secret financial arrangements it does not want made public?

This Un-Bank Book

The book in your hands will take you on nine thought-provoking journeys into the past, present and future perils of banking to show why it is no longer logical or wise to put most of your money in unsafe bank accounts.

In **Chapter One**, we might still think of ourselves as living in the Wild West of steel safes and bank robbers like Jesse James, but even the James-Younger Gang was defeated in its most famous attempted heist by their ignorance of a new technology.

We, almost 140 years later, live in a very different, almost-cashless society where our money increasingly exists merely as flickering electronic impulses inside computers and global networks. We show how Jesse James today could not steal your savings or identity, yet hackers and cyber warriors might be able to rob you within milliseconds from the far side of the world.

Chapter Two explores how banking and money evolved together as two intertwined depositories of value, and how the universal money of gold and silver was transformed into government-issued debased coins and paper bills that rulers to this day continue to manipulate to rob their citizens.

Chapter Three shows how the looting of private bank accounts by English kings led to fractional-reserve banking, the fragile and unstable way our banks work today. This lucrative innovation has added a huge, sometimes-fatal amount of risk to modern banking. It, more than anything else, is why our banks now undergo "stress tests," tests that if scored honestly would usually be graded "F" for Failure.

Chapter Four reveals how the unstable economy caused by fractional-reserve banking was used to justify the imposition of the Federal Reserve System in 1913. The Fed's real aim, as members of Congress warned, was to centralize political power over our banks and currency. We will show how the internal contradictions of Federal Reserve policies have today trapped America's banks and economy in what we call the "Fed Paradox."

Chapter Five exposes how the abuse of the regulatory power over banking led to the near-collapse of our economy in 2008, caused the Great Recession, produced the boom and continuing bust in housing, and is giving us a slower, sicker "recovery" than even what followed the Great Depression.

Chapter Six looks at how the U.S. Government is extending its regulatory and taxing power over the entire world banking system. We look at the 2013 take-down of one island tax haven and a government official's declaration that these tactics are a "template" for how private bank accounts will be seized elsewhere in the near future. America's July 1, 2014 strong-arm move to crush small tax havens around the planet should be an ominous warning that the exits are being closed because savers might soon be trying desperately to escape from their bank accounts here.

Chapter Seven reveals how the world's money-hungry governments are planning to take – and already *are* secretly taking – your bank deposits. We show you the Obama Administration's sinister "Operation Choke Point" and other grabs for power over our banks. We will show how the government may be plotting to confiscate IRAs, 401(k)s, and other retirement accounts "for your own good," as has already been happening in other countries.

And we will look at the coming "world wealth tax" that, its advocates make clear, will almost certainly happen through a surprise simultaneous seizure of bank accounts in the United States and around the world.

Think you are safe from such expropriation of your savings because you are not wealthy? By world standards, the *average* American income is in the top 1 percent of incomes planet-wide. The advocates of this surprise global tax at the International Monetary Fund and elsewhere assume that merely *having* a bank account likely means that you are rich and ought to be targeted to have your wealth redistributed.

Chapter Eight shows the choice we face over banking's future. Banks as we have known them are about to disappear in the cashless global society that is dawning.

We will explore how the nationalization of our banks could happen, and what a future of the government politically and ideologically controlling all money and credit could be like. We are already far closer to this Orwellian future than most Americans know.

Chapter Nine offers an alternative that you *could* bank on that combines old-fashioned security and sound money with convenient advanced technologies. In this brighter potential future that you can choose, honest money returns as a store of value, prosperity reawakens, and you might even become your own banker with your own gold standard.

Here we shall meet a former Harvard University economics professor who recently withdrew nearly a million dollars from his personal account at a major bank because of the high risk he now sees in the giant banks that control more than half of American accounts.

Our Epilogue summarizes the 20 reasons our investigation has found as to why it no longer makes logical sense to keep most of your money deposited in a bank account. We also suggest ways to diversify and protect your money against the breakdown of the old banking system and dollar that is now inevitable....a question only of when, not if.

It also challenges you to TEST what we have found out about the kind of 21st Century bank you now trust with your money. The results of this test might frighten you. It could certainly open your eyes.

However, before proceeding you should know two things:

After reading this book, you will never again be able to see your bank, or the U.S. Dollar, as you did before.

You are about to take a journey of ideas and information that crosses thousands of years and many lands.

Fasten your seatbelt. It's going to be an eye-opening and surprise-filled ride.

Craig R. Smith

German children play with stacks of money during the hyperinflation period of the Weimar Republic, 1922.

Photo: Courtesy of RareHistoricalPhotos.com

"BRAVO! In Craig Smith and Lowell Ponte's newest book, DON'T BANK ON IT! they have successfully torn down the facade of America's most deceptive financial institution - modern mega-banks - and yet somehow also made it interesting, understandable and actionable reading.

- **DR. MICHAEL SAVAGE**
Host, The Savage Nation

PART ONE
Banking's Evolution

Chapter One
Breaking the Banks

"Banks are an almost irresistible attraction
for that element of our society
which seeks unearned money."

— **J. Edgar Hoover**
Former Director
Federal Bureau of Investigation

**Banking and Money, our intertwined ways of storing value, are entering
a disembodied, digital future of great convenience but greater danger.
We have bet our economy – indeed, our entire civilization – on a system
of computers and networks to protect our savings that has never stood
the test of time. This system can be hacked or robbed by cyber crooks,
or potentially destroyed in a heartbeat by a digital "Pearl Harbor"
attack launched from half a world away by Chinese, Russian or Islamist
cyber warriors. We are taking a huge gamble and urgently need to
reduce this risk to our banks.**

On September 7, 1876, eight men on horseback rode quietly into Northfield,
Minnesota, 40 miles south of Minneapolis. They had come a long way to make a
bank withdrawal.

Among them were Jesse James and his older brother Frank as well as Cole
Younger and his brothers Bob and Jim, along with a few comrades.

The outlaws came to Northfield for political as well as mercenary reasons. They
had been Confederates who in their native Missouri fought with Quantrill's
Raiders, using guerrilla tactics of pillage and looting.

The bank in Northfield was rumored to be one of the richest west of the
Mississippi. And Adelbert Ames, a former Union general and Republican

Reconstruction Governor of Mississippi, and his father-in-law, radical Republican Congressman Benjamin Butler, had money in this bank. Both men were hated by many Southerners.

At precisely 2 pm, Jesse and Frank and Bob Younger walked into the First National Bank of Northfield, drew their side arms, and demanded that its safe be opened.

Acting cashier Joseph Lee Heywood told the robbers that the safe had a chronometer and could not be opened for any reason. True, the safe had an impressive time-lock, but the robbers never noticed that it had not been set. The safe with more than $15,000 inside could easily have been opened.

A passerby saw through the bank windows what was going on inside before being threatened by the other gang members standing guard outside. He walked down the street several feet, then began running and shouting: "Get your guns, boys! They're robbing the bank!"

The James-Younger gang hesitated, then ran for their horses. Two were cut down by lethal citizen gunfire from nearby windows and balconies. Jesse and Frank somehow escaped without a scratch and got away, but a badly-wounded Cole Younger and the rest were soon captured.

It was a historic turning point of sorts, as the most famous of old-fashioned bank robbers were defeated by their ignorance about new-fangled banking technology.

This bloody day lives on in legend, the stuff of Hollywood movies such as 1972's "The Great Northfield Minnesota Raid" and 1980's "The Long Riders." In reality, the raid failed, and their take from this bank robbery was only $26.70. [8]

Cashless in Stockholm

A strange new age in banking and money is dawning.

Imagine the James-Younger gang today trying to rob a bank on the cutting edge of this new age, a modern bank in Stockholm, Sweden.

The cowboys enter the bank, draw their six-shooters and demand the bank's money.

They do not know that weapon detectors have sent an automatic alarm to local police, who are already closing in while watching them via the bank's security cameras.

The robbers do not know that the bank's doors have already quietly locked behind them, preventing their escape. But none of these things are what makes this bank different.

"We have no dollars or Krona," the bank manager calmly tells them. "We are a cashless bank in a cashless community. I am sorry to tell you that nobody here has any money, because no one here uses what you call money anymore."

"What kind of trick is this?" snaps Jesse James. "People deposit their money here. This is a bank. So give me your money right now, or we'll start shooting."

"You win," says the manager as he hands James his wallet. The veteran robber eagerly opens it to find nothing but a few plastic cards smaller than playing cards.

"Here's *my* money," says a young assistant manager, holding up the glowing screen of a smart phone.

"You are welcome to steal these things," the manager says, "but you will have no way to turn them into the kind of money you seek. Only the rightful owner can do that."

"Well, then, we'll hold you hostage until you get us money," says Jesse James.

"Jesse, look around at the windows," says Cole Younger. "My guess is that there are 50 soldiers out there carrying some kind of fancy rifles who have this bank surrounded."

"You can take us hostage – and we will cooperate, because the Stockholm Syndrome is familiar to us," says the bank manager with a smile, "but the authorities will not give you money nor let you escape. You will either die in a shootout or spend the rest of your life in prison. But you do have a way out...."

"How?" asks Frank James.

"You obviously are crazy. You've just tried to rob a bank that everybody knows has no money. In our enlightened society, we do not punish crazy people. Throw down your guns, surrender, and you will be freed and given psychological counseling by our wonderful welfare state. Chances are, the government will give you disability cards of your own so you can buy things. The reindeer steaks at the railway station restaurant are delicious."

"I'm not sure if this is a dream or a nightmare, or if you're crazier than we are, but I don't want another gunfight with Swedes like in Northfield," says a bewildered Cole Younger as he lets his gun fall to the floor.

"Money, Money, Money"

Welcome to Tomorrowland. The cashless society is almost a reality in Sweden. Only three percent of transactions there are done using cash, and most of these are small – for cups of coffee or snacks.

Fully 97 percent of transactions in Stockholm now happen via credit cards, smart phones, checks or other means of transferring disembodied money that now exists almost entirely as flickering digital signals inside computer circuits.

Whole towns in Sweden now accept no cash, according to Associated Press. A 2012 CBS report showed a church in which the collection plate has been replaced by a credit card machine for ethereal parishioner donations.

One outspoken supporter of the new cashless world is musician Bjoern Ulvaeus, whose first name initial is the second "B" in the superstar Swedish pop group ABBA.

Ulvaeus co-wrote their hit song "Money, Money, Money," which tells us that everything "must be funny....always sunny, in the rich man's world." And he should know, because ABBA sold more than 380 million albums and singles worldwide.

"I can't see why we should be printing bank notes anymore," says Ulvaeus. [9] Going cashless has advantages, starting with zero risk of catching a cold or flu from touching paper money that has passed through many dirty hands.

In this almost-cashless society you might have less to fear from ordinary pickpockets and purse snatchers, who without your fingerprint or other biometric identifier might find it difficult to tap into your accounts or credit.

Old-fashioned bank robberies are now rare in Sweden because, as the James-Younger gang discovered, there is almost no cash to steal from banks or individuals in a nearly-cashless society.

However, while on-the-spot bank heists are getting harder, banks that depend on computers to store and oversee their accounts digitally can be looted, and customer identities and money stolen, by unseen cyber crooks with very long fingers half a world away.

"Cybercrime in Sweden has gone from 3,304 cases in 2000 to 20,000 in 2011," reported Wallace Henley. [10]

The new age of banking and currency, as this book will reveal, in many ways puts your money at much more risk than ever before in human history.

A modern criminal gang can steal not only what you saved in past years but also your present financial identity and future credit. Stagecoach robbers used to demand "your money or your life." Today's cyber criminals can, in a very real sense, rob you of both at the same time.

Cyber Heists

Over the last two decades financial cyber attacks have grown in size, frequency and impact - often targeting banks, financial services, military and government agencies – and the world's two billion Internet users, who reportedly already suffer $1 Trillion annual losses to cybercrime. [11]

According to security expert John Watters of iSight Partners, cybercrime already puts more money into criminal pockets than the trade in all illicit drugs. "Cyber Attacks Are the 'New Normal' for the Financial Services Industry," says the *Wall Street Journal.*

"A concerted cyber-attack could potentially paralyze financial markets. One of the problems with electronic trading is that it is very time dependent," says Ashley Jellyman, head of information assurance for UK telecommunication group BT. "When you press 'Sell Now' and nothing happens, you have got a problem."

"Attacks on the U.S. financial industry that nobody has ever seen before resulted in 15 of the largest U.S. banks being offline for a total of 249 hours in 2013," reports NBC News.

"How prepared are the financial markets for a cyber attack?" asks *TheBanker.com.* Not prepared enough, according to bank researchers.

"A white paper from the Depository Trust and Clearing Corporation, one of the world's largest post-trade services operators, identified cyber attacks as one of the most substantial threats to financial stability ... cyber attacks could have a huge financial and reputational impact, and severely damage market integrity," reports *efinancialnews.com.*

More than 100 million Target customers recently discovered their private credit card information is no longer private.

Citigroup, Wells Fargo, Chase, Bank of America, U.S. Bank, American Express, Chicago Mercantile Exchange, PayPal ... the list of bank and financial service cyber attacks just keeps growing daily.

And worse yet, many security breaches may not even have been discovered. In its 2014 Security Report, Cisco Systems said that every corporate or government computer network it has studied shows signs of hacker attacks.

Retailer Neiman-Marcus' computer network, say experts, apparently had a hacker's bug in it doing damage for at least nine months before the invading program that raided confidential customer information was discovered.

We know that during the Cold War era of spies and counter-spies, it was common for one side to plant "mole" agents in the other's agencies. These agents could remain dormant for years, even decades, doing nothing until an order activated them. Government agencies, corporations and banks could already have dormant "mole" programs undetected in their computer networks. Hackers and foreign agents can activate such moles from far away at an opportune, coordinated moment to bring down entire major banks or our banking system.

The six biggest "Too Big To Fail" banks hold, among them, more than half of all American bank accounts. If one of these banks is brought down, the consequences for the U.S. economy could be dire.

Banks doubtless contain backup files of their data, but if mole programs are well enough concealed they have probably been duplicated into such backup files as well and might alter or destroy those files, too.

Our government, economy and society have become totally dependent on centralized computer networks to move, record and safeguard our transactions and even our individual and company identities. What will happen when an enemy finds ways to unplug – or, perhaps worse, to pour vast amounts of false information into – our computer systems?

Financial Warfare: The New Battleground

"This is America's new battle space. The doctrine of mutually assured destruction or the notion of taking on our military even after years of prolonged challenges is not something that enemies are even thinking of engaging in anymore. It's all about cyber attacks, attacking the financial and national infrastructure - that's the frontier," reports *SiliconAngle*.

"Every minute, of every hour, of every day, a major financial institution is under attack," reports the *London Telegraph*. "Attacks are not limited just to theft and can take the form of denial of service assaults on a bank's online operations to prevent customers from accessing their accounts."

"Intelligence leaders said for the first time that cyber attacks and cyber espionage have supplanted terrorism as the top security threat facing the United States," reports Reuters. "The annual economic loss from cyber attacks is in the tens of billions of dollars."

"Cyber war isn't the future; it's already here," warned *Time* Magazine investigative reporter Lev Grossman in July 2014. "It's business as usual. In this war, the battlefield is everywhere, bugs are the weapons," and hackers who make and sell such computer-invading digital bugs "are arms dealers." [12]

China, Russia and the Middle East dominate the news as the launching points of cyber attacks.

"Retired Army General Keith Alexander, who formerly headed both the NSA [National Security Agency] and U.S. Cyber Command, has called China's ongoing electronic theft of American intellectual property 'the greatest transfer of wealth in history,'" reported Grossman. [13]

"A private U.S. computer security company issued a study accusing a secretive Chinese military unit of being behind hacking attacks on a wide range of American industries," says Reuters. The Chinese People's Liberation Army has, by one expert estimate, 125,000 cyber warriors who work full-time at hacking into Western computer systems.

This may be one of the reasons why, according to IBM's security division, the *average* American company's computers in 2013 faced 16,856 attacks. [14]

The risks since 2008 have grown far larger as the digital interconnections of companies and their customers have grown exponentially, as have the numbers and skills of potential attackers. The largest "Too Big To Fail" banks have grown by 37 percent since 2008, becoming "Much Too Big To Fail."

In their book of modern strategy, *Unrestricted Warfare*, Chinese People's Liberation Army Colonels Qiao Liang and Wang Xiangsui wrote: "a single man-made stock market crash, a single computer virus invasion, or a single rumor or scandal that results in a fluctuation in the enemy country's exchange rates or exposes the leaders of an enemy country on the Internet, all can be included in the ranks of new-concept weapons." [15]

The "Internet of Things"

Liang and Xiangsui warn cryptically that in the kinds of future cyber attacks they envision: "Some morning people will awake to discover with surprise that quite a few gentle and kind things have begun to have offensive and lethal characteristics." [16]

By 2020, our world could have 50 billion items in what has been called the "Internet of Things," as tech expert Patrick Tucker recently told the Pew Research Center.

Futurist Jeremy Rifkin in his 2014 book *The Zero Marginal Cost Society* sees the "Internet of Things" technology as one path to a future where many things, from college education to entertainment, will cost nothing. The problem is that this technology will also replace humans in millions of jobs on the way to the "eclipse of capitalism" that Rifkin welcomes. And long before it eclipses capitalism, the "Internet of Things" might help usher in a new Dark Age of vulnerability and breakdowns.

As depicted in a popular television commercial, in the near future people will be able to pick up a cell phone and remotely lock the doors of a distant home, check the temperature and amount of milk in its refrigerator, raise the thermostat or switch on the air conditioner, turn off faucets, switch on a dishwasher, check the smoke alarm, direct a flat floor-scurrying vacuum to start cleaning, set a recording on the DVR, pre-heat the oven or slow cooker, and do dozens of other things.

This dawning age of the "smart house" will be possible because more and more appliances, door locks and other things are becoming available with computer brains built into them. Those computer circuits, either via wiring or varieties of Wi-Fi, are able to give information and take commands via the home's central computer or telecommunications system.

The danger is that anything with such computer chips and interactivity can be hacked. If you can remotely tell your back door to lock, a sophisticated hacker can command your back door to unlock.

A Backdoor To Your Bank Account

Worse, since this Internet of Things usually links to and from your computer system, it might, despite precautions to prevent this, become a backdoor into your computer, and through your computer to your bank account.

One refrigerator has already been found that contained a built-in bug so that when connected into a family computer system, the refrigerator was programmed to hack that computer and become a channel through which cyber crooks could extract confidential financial, banking and other data such as passwords and pin numbers. [17]

Many were surprised in early 2014 when Microsoft announced it would no longer be patching any newly-discovered holes in its aging XP operating system. Many were shocked to learn that more than half of Automated Teller Machines (ATMs) in the United States run via XP and might now be more vulnerable to cyber theft.

People immediately grasped the threat to their bank accounts with ATMs, but they have not yet understood a similar fast-emerging threat from cyber criminals who might find an Open Sesame path to tunnel into your bank account via your home refrigerator or even you new highly-computerized car.

Just imagine speeding along a highway in a "driverless car" 10 years from now when, suddenly, hackers or cyber warriors half a world away take control of your car's computer. Imagine this someday soon happening to millions of such cars at the same time.

Perhaps this is what Liang and Xiangsui were seeing – a day when almost everything, from children's toys to microwave ovens to cars, will be remotely controllable by computer chips and therefore be hackable.

Even more ominously, scientists keep working on creating interfaces between computers and the human brain. Some researchers already speculate that the natural human brain itself is "hackable." If in the future we routinely merge our minds with computers, we all may be as hackable as the things now being connected and commanded via the Internet of Things.

The Great Firewall

The Chinese bring at least two things to the age of cyber warfare that we need to learn:

The first is what the great Chinese military strategist Sun Tzu taught 2,500 years ago in *The Art of War:* that war is not waged only with soldiers and arms on a small battlefield; it is also waged by recognizing that *everything* is the battlefield. Victory comes from undermining an opponent's logistical systems, perceptions, values, morals, faith, culture – and economy.

The second is that depending only on computer firewalls to protect our data and systems could be a fatal error.

The Chinese know something about walls. They built the Great Wall of China to protect themselves against attack and invasion by horse-riding nomads from the grasslands of Asia.

The Great Wall in all its branches may have been more than 5,500 miles long. Millions were mobilized to build it over centuries at vast cost in treasure and human life, with untold thousands of soldiers, prisoners, peasants and child laborers buried anonymously in the fill dirt between its inner and outer walls. (The Chinese believed that the restless ghosts of the Great Wall's dead would ward off evil spirits.)

Despite this enormous investment, at critical moments in its history the Great Wall simply failed to protect China from invasion.

As Cambridge University historian Julia Lovell recounts in her book *The Great Wall: China Against the World, 1000 BC – AD 2000*, Mongol Manchus and others discovered that they did not need to overcome the wall and its defenders militarily. Given the morals of many in Chinese culture, these invaders merely needed to bribe the Great Wall's gatekeepers to unlock and open the doors so their armies could pass through. [18]

Our culture has already produced Edward Snowden, who, apparently for his own moral and ideological reasons, copied and divulged to foreigners many of the most sensitive secrets of America's National Security Agency.

The gatekeepers of the computer systems at our largest banks hold security keys that might allow sophisticated foreign or domestic hackers to steal billions of dollars – or potentially to cause trillions of dollars' worth of chaos in the U.S. economy.

Would you risk your life savings by betting that none of these bank gatekeepers would ever accept a bribe? Or be swayed by personal or ideological motives? With billions or even trillions of dollars and the outcome of a power struggle for world dominance at stake, how big a bribe might these gatekeepers be offered by a foreign government such as China?

Truth be told, you are betting your bank deposits on this risk right now....and being paid near-zero in interest by your bank for taking this gamble.

The Cyber Crescent

On March 28, 2013, the American Express website went offline for hours during a distributed denial of service attack by the Izz ad-Din al-Qassam group. These attacks are part of a larger trend of disruptive and destructive attacks on financial institutions by politically motivated groups.

CNN is one of several media giants hacked by the Syrian Electronic Army (SEA). CNN's Facebook and Twitter accounts tweeted: "DON'T FORGET: Al Qaeda is Al CIA da. Funded, armed and controlled." SEA has already hacked The Associated Press, the *Washington Post*, and President Barack Obama's official Twitter account.

The *London Daily Telegraph* reported on how Osama bin Laden successor Ayman al-Zawahiri planned to attack the United States:

"'We should bleed America economically by provoking it to continue in its massive expenditure on its security, for the weak point of America is its economy, which has already begun to stagger due to the military and security expenditure," he said, according to SITE, a jihadist monitoring group. "America is not a mythic power and the Americans, after all, are humans who can be defeated, felled and punished.'"

"Zawahiri urged the Islamic world to 'abandon the dollar and replace it with a currency of other countries that are not taking part in the aggression against us.' He also said that Muslims should refuse to buy goods from America and its allies, as such spending only helped to fund U.S. military action in Muslim lands." [19]

In October 2012 the U.S. Secretary of Defense Leon Panetta admitted that "the threat from cyber attacks and a future attack on the country's critical infrastructure could have an effect similar to the Sept. 11 terrorist attacks of 2001," reports *Computerworld.* Secretary Panetta referred to such attacks as a potential "Pearl Harbor."

Stuxnet *Redux*

The United States and Israel in 2009 created what may be the first advanced cyber war weapon, a computer worm known as Stuxnet. Planted in computers regulating centrifuges that Iran was using to enrich radioactive material to nuclear weapon grade, this worm caused subtle malfunctions. Experts believe that by altering their spin, Stuxnet destroyed 20 percent of those centrifuges and slowed Iran's acquisition of atomic bombs by a few years.

When Russia sent troops into Ukrainian Crimea in early 2014, its waves of troops were preceded by massive cyber attacks designed to disable military, governmental and other computer networks in Ukraine. Officials suspected that the cyberwar weapon unleashed on them is "Ouroboros," also known as "Snake," a Russian modification of the Stuxnet worm.

These digital attacks were intended to blind and cripple the command, control and communications computer programs of the smaller nation and its citizens, as well as their economic infrastructure such as banks. [20, 12]

Stuxnet's destructive potential, has been captured and re-targeted on the West. China launched a spy computer bug in 2009 called Aurora that attacks the vulnerabilities of Microsoft's Internet Explorer. A Russian hacker created a kit called Blackhole to devastate personal computers. Hackers in 2011 stole RSA's SecuriD code, a tool used by, among other companies, Bank of America. [21]

A massive arms race is growing rapidly between those who craft such weapons and those trying to defend against them.

In past World Wars, attackers needed costly weapons. Today, hacker and cyber warfare attacks can be launched relentlessly using computers that can be dirt cheap. The effectiveness of such attacks may be decided by the sophistication of the attacker, or by an Achilles Heel weakness defenders failed to notice when creating our giant systems out of billions of lines of computer code...or by sheer luck.

The bottom line is that every single American citizen, including the President, is vulnerable to this new form of cyber financial warfare. The U.S. Defense Secretary and Homeland Security Director have warned us. The question now is not *if*, but *when* the next successful attack will occur....and how many of the centralized systems we depend upon will be damaged or shut down.

"Game Plan" To Crash The Dollar

We have been writing about the increasing threat of economic and cyber warfare in our last three books, *The Inflation Deception, The Great Debasement and The Great Withdrawal.*

America in September 2008 suffered a financial "Pearl Harbor," an internationally-launched coordinated computerized attack designed to drain overnight trillions of dollars from our most important financial institutions.

The resulting panic persuaded federal lawmakers to approve vast emergency bailout funds for banks, brokers and key corporations.

This remarkably-timed attack and resulting economic confusion persuaded voters to renew the liberal Democratic control of Congress and to elect a charismatic but unknown and untested anti-capitalist radical community organizer as president.

As we laid out in detail in *The Inflation Deception*, according to Defense Department consultant Kevin D. Freeman, this attack was the culmination of three coordinated assaults that began in 2007 with "a speculative run-up in oil prices that generated as much as $2 Trillion of excess wealth for oil-producing nations, filling the coffers of Sovereign Wealth Funds, especially those that follow Shariah Compliant Finance."

Oil prices soaring to $147 per barrel devastated the American economy, already vulnerable from the housing boom hitting a ceiling and the negative economic influence of a new and imperious Democratic Congress.

"The rapid run-up in oil prices," wrote Freeman in his 2009 analytic study *Economic Warfare: Risks and Responses: Analysis of Twenty-First Century Risks in Light of the Recent Market Collapse,* "made the value of OPEC oil in the ground roughly $137 Trillion (based on $125/barrel oil) virtually equal to the value of all other world financial assets, including every share of stock, every bond, every private company, all government and corporate debt, and the entire world's bank deposits." [22]

Economic Terrorism

"This means that the proven OPEC reserves," wrote Freeman, "were valued at almost three times the total market capitalization of every company on the planet traded in all 27 global stock markets."

The second phase of this assault on U.S. financial entities began in 2008 with a series of "bear raids" against companies such as Bear Stearns and Lehman Brothers and seemed clearly coordinated to collapse the companies.

These raids struck not only at Lehman Brothers, but also at other companies with their own vulnerabilities such as Merrill Lynch, which was also being thought of by Bank of America head Ken Lewis as a company he wanted to own. "The bear raids were perpetrated by naked short selling and manipulation of credit default swaps, both of which were virtually unregulated," wrote Freeman. "The short selling was actually enhanced by recent regulatory changes...." [23]

The Russian Bear?

"The source of the bear raids has not been traceable to date due to serious transparency gaps for hedge funds, trading pools, sponsored access, and sovereign wealth funds," wrote Freeman.

"What can be demonstrated, however, is that two relatively small broker dealers emerged virtually overnight," he wrote, "to trade 'trillions of dollars worth of U.S. blue chip companies. They are the number one traders in all financial companies that collapsed or are now financially supported by the U.S. Government. Trading by the firms has grown exponentially while the markets have lost trillions of dollars in value.'"

In March 2014, days after Russian forces invaded Crimea after knocking out Ukraine's military computers and other key computer networks, newly-revealed footprints provide evidence as to who was behind the 2008 assault.

BBC Business Editor Robert Preston authored an article titled "Russia 'Planned Wall Street Bear Raid'." In it he tells of the unaired portion of an interview he did with Henry Paulson, who in 2008 was U.S. Secretary of the Treasury.

Secretary Paulson told Preston that Russia had approached the Chinese to propose a "joint pact" that both nations dump selected U.S. bank securities on the market with the intent of increasing "the turmoil on Wall Street – presumably with a view to maximizing the cost of the rescue for Washington and further damaging its financial health." China, Paulson told Preston, chose not to do this. [24]

"Financial Jihad"

The risk of phase three of this attack could involve "a potential direct economic attack on the U.S. Treasury and U.S. Dollar....," wrote Freeman.

"A focused effort to collapse the dollar by dumping Treasury bonds has grave implications including the possibility of a downgrading of U.S. debt forcing rapidly-rising interest rates and a collapse of the American economy," Freeman wrote. He also noted that authorities had recently seized counterfeit U.S bonds with "a face value of $134 billion."

A year before Freeman's original study, the American Center for Democracy published a detailed analysis, *The Fifth Generation Warfare*, of what its analysts Dr. Rachel Ehrenfeld and Alyssa A. Lappen identified as the risk, tactics, strengths and weaknesses of what they called "Financial Jihad." [25]

As evidenced by Freeman's study for the Department of Defense, the Pentagon is acutely concerned about the prospects for economic warfare against the United States. [26]

The Pentagon has also been "war gaming" possible scenarios of social breakdown caused by an economic collapse. One of these war games was "Unified Quest 2011." [27]

Financial analyst James Rickards, in his 2014 book *The Death of Money: The Coming Collapse of the International Monetary System*, writes that some modern terrorist groups may be so sophisticated that, through intermediaries, they now invest in ways that will become profitable because of attacks they are about to make.

Rickards was involved in a CIA study codenamed Project Prophesy, begun in April 2002 shortly after the 9-11 attacks, that sought and in at least one instance found a way to anticipate coming terrorist targets by detecting unexpected bursts of targeted investment. [28]

"Just as our reliance on critical infrastructure has grown, so have the threats," said Deputy Assistant Secretary of Defense for Cyber Policy Robert J. Butler in testimony before the Senate Committee on Homeland Security and Governmental Affairs in May 2011. [29]

America's staggering debt remains the "single biggest threat to our national security," warned Admiral Mike Mullen, chairman of the Joint Chiefs of Staff in April 2011. It weakens our capabilities, makes us more fragile and vulnerable, and makes others in the world perceive us as a world power in decline. [30]

Our "Flash Crash" Culture

On May 6, 2010, the New York Stock Exchange suffered what came to be called "the Flash Crash," when the Dow Jones Industrial Average plummeted unexpectedly by nearly 1,000 points in only minutes.

A single Sell order valued at approximately $4.1 Billion purportedly set off a cascade of computerized buy-and-sell programs around the world that are designed to respond immediately, and without consulting human beings, to key changes in market prices. As each major trading computer reacted, it could have triggered programmed reactions in similar computers. [31]

Some of these systems use High Frequency Trading (HFT) that today can launch trade decisions, buy and sell orders, in mere thousandths of a second or less. This, according to critics, allows traders who have paid millions for this razor-thin advantage-in-time to detect incoming stock purchases; frontrun and automatically buy that stock before the competing slower order gets processed; and sell the stock a fraction of a second later to the slower order at a slightly higher price. [32]

Such are the systems, with their risk of triggering buy or sell cascades around the world, that are being used in today's merging worlds of high-tech investing and high-money banking.

Intelligence, Artificial

Future historians, however, might focus on a *different*, smaller "flash crash." Looking backward, this may have been the start of what caused the financial collapse that would change our civilization forever.

It happened on Leap Year Day, February 29, 2012, a relatively quiet Wednesday on the New York Stock Exchange.

Suddenly, a "violent sell-off in stocks…seemed to start at exactly 10:00 AM" Eastern Time, recounted *Business Insider* reporter Sam Ro. "[T]he supernatural speed of the sell-off had traders thinking two words: Artificial Intelligence." [33]

One who thought this was Art Cashin, the veteran director of floor operations for

UBS Financial Services, a subsidiary of giant United Bank of Switzerland. His *Cashin's Comments* the next morning said:

"Algo My Way By Myself Or Open The Pod Doors, HAL...As noted, the instantaneous nature of the selloff...raised lots of questions.... Those questions prompted an intriguing hypothesis....that [the just-released speech by Federal Reserve Chairman Ben Bernanke] had been instantly parsed by a computer using Artificial Intelligence."

"You wouldn't need much Artificial Intelligence to see...quickly and clearly" that Bernanke's speech described improving employment in the economy, which would shift Federal Reserve concern to the other half of its dual mandate, from jobs to "worrying about inflation and a firm dollar," wrote Cashin. Such a shift could re-value many stocks and trigger both market buying and selling.

"So was the selloff started by someone's version of HAL 9000 [the soft-spoken yet murderous spacecraft computer in Stanley Kubrick's 1968 movie "2001: A Space Odyssey," whose three-letter name HAL was a one-letter backstep from computer company IBM]?" asked Cashin. "We don't know for sure. There are said to be such experiments on trading desks at hedge funds and elsewhere. And, it certainly fits the action to a tee." [34]

This is no longer your father's financial world of slow, thoughtful individual banking and stock buying. By 2011, 73 percent of market trading was already algorithmic, done via machines and exotic programmed computer algorithms. [35]

In 1987 the average share of stock was held by one owner for approximately two years. By 2011 it was held for only 22 seconds. And this churn is getting faster and faster. [36]

By 2011, "a company announced the ability to execute trades within nanoseconds," wrote Cris Sheridan of *FinancialSense.com.* "According to *Wikipedia*, 'One nanosecond is to one second as one second is to 31.7 years.' Just let that seep in for a moment. How many millions of trades can be made in one second? Too many. Although speed isn't a substitute for intelligence, in terms of trading, it's a pretty good proxy." [37]

For years computer scientists tried to teach computers to comprehend the English language and to glean business data from world news, creating early business decipherment programs to do this such as "Ripper," "Shredder, "Rebellion" and "You Don't Know Jack."

A.I.-pocalypse Now

Today's Artificial Intelligence (A.I.) computers can sift key investment information 24 hours a day from the world's vast digital news and data flow. Not only can they read business news but also write the data they analyze into business news stories key-worded to be easy for other A.I. computers to read -- and to use to make, buy and sell investment decisions in tiny fractions of a second, without necessarily consulting humans. [38]

We have encountered and empowered a superior alien intelligence of our own making. The science fiction stories about the dangers of this are many. In "2001," HAL's programming prompts him to defend the space mission by killing all but one of the very astronauts he supposedly was programmed to protect and serve.

In the 1956 movie "Forbidden Planet," we learn of an extraterrestrial civilization that was destroyed by an Aladdin-like computer they built to fulfill their every wish; too late, they realized that it also automatically fulfilled the nightmarish destructive wishes from their minds' primitive subconscious.

More than fiction, Artificial Intelligence frightens some of today's brightest scientists and engineers. Elon Musk, the genius behind PayPal, SpaceX and Tesla electric automobiles, fears that A.I. could potentially prove to be "more dangerous than nukes." Astrophysicist Stephen Hawking warns that A.I. could destroy humankind. [39]

"One can imagine such technology [Artificial Intelligence] outsmarting financial markets, out-inventing human researchers, out-manipulating human leaders, and developing weapons we cannot even understand," wrote Hawking and three scientific colleagues in a May 2014 article. "Whereas the short-term impact of AI depends on who controls it, the long-term impact depends on whether it can be controlled at all." [40]

Are we creating super-predator rivals that could out-compete and replace us? Could we become merely an evolutionary step to the next dominant life form on planet Earth, A.I. computer machines? Look at what is now happening in the stock market.

"Shaping" Markets, Marginalizing Investors

"For decades, professional investment advisors have continued to teach reliance on 'value investing' and 'buy-and-hold' as long-term guides to successful investment. [But] technology may now have overridden such investment concepts," we are told in *The Marginalizing of the Individual Investor*. [41]

This analysis, Sheridan tells us, is published "by the global think tank International Economy, whose editorial board includes...former and current presidents of the European Central Bank, George Soros, Martin Feldstein, and various Federal Reserve chairmen.

"High-frequency trading platforms are focused solely on ramping up speed and volume so as to maximize tiny gains per transaction," *Marginalizing* continues. "Computerized algorithms that are momentum-sensitive are increasingly high-frequency trading-driven, raising serious doubts about traditional concepts of how markets should work."

"Investment strategies based on fundamentals such as a company's long-term performance have been swept aside by high-frequency trading algorithms hunting for inefficiencies in daily pricing and super arbitrage opportunities," *Marginalizing* continues. "In so doing, they open investors to a new form of risk that has not been accounted for in most 'buy and hold' asset allocation models."

"In effect," individual traders are confronted with overwhelming momentum-driven forces that are unrelated to performance of individual businesses," writes *Marginalizing*. "A 'fair price' may exist, but high-frequency traders are not seeking fair prices – they are focused on immediate profit...."

"Unfortunately," warns *Marginalizing*, "high-frequency trader interaction with computerized algorithms of large-cap financial institutions is providing opportunities for high-speed, virtually undetectable market manipulation. Where there is opportunity to 'shape' the market for advantage, it is likely that such opportunity will be exploited."

Are our A.I. computers and official policies already rigging our stock markets, banks and currency? Where is this self-driving vehicle taking us?

The choice being offered to us is to lose the value of our money in bank accounts, or to lose our money in risky, potentially-rigged stock market casinos where giant broker-banker partnerships own the biggest, fastest computers. Government lets all this continue because it shakes down the banks and brokers that have our money and shares their "take." We need to create our own choice that benefits and protects us.

Progressive Collectivism

Today's automated computer programs, some pundits suspect, have put the modern computer-driven global stock markets and investment banks on a hair trigger, not unlike liquid-fueled nuclear missiles of the early 1960s that were to be launched at the first sign of preemptive enemy missile attack because military planners believed they had to "use it or lose it." Only with the development of solid fuel rockets and invulnerable hardened missile silos did this hair trigger policy change.

Our weakening economy and the U.S. Dollar are becoming more vulnerable because, as Robert Butler warned, we rely on ever-more-centralized systems.

Decentralizing our technologies would make America much less vulnerable to high-tech terrorism and breakdowns. What left-liberals condemn as "urban sprawl," combined with local self-reliance, would make us much harder for terrorists to attack and shut down. [42]

America's ruling Progressives, however, are ideologically committed to forcing more and more centralized control onto every aspect of life in the United States. Decentralization and self-reliance would make Americans too independent, too free, and those on the Left are eager to replace individual liberty with collectivist control.

These centralized systems of control are making our economy and society vastly more vulnerable to many kinds of "flash crashes," inadvertent or deliberate, in the technological systems on which we depend. We have invested our fate in systems whose vulnerabilities we clearly do not fully know or comprehend. Could this be the Achilles Heel of our civilization, the fatal weak spot that brings it down?

In October 2010, Russian hackers nearly took over the NASDAQ stock exchange in what may have been their attempt to pirate its secret computer programming. [43] In August 2014, evidence emerged that Russian hackers have amassed 1.2 billion sets of computer user names and passwords. [44]

Credit Card Blackout

On May 20, 1998, North America was devastated by a storm – not only the usual hurricanes and tornados, but a storm in space caused by the heavy eruption of charged particles from our Sun. As these particles battered our planet, they caused our protective magnetic field to buckle inward and our irradiated atmosphere to expand outward.

Overhead, one of our most important communications satellites, PanAmSat's Galaxy IV, malfunctioned. We suddenly learned how dependent our earthly technologies have become on such things.

News wire feeds were disrupted, as was CBS' ability to broadcast its network programs nationwide. Suddenly 80 percent of pagers in America, including those used by emergency personnel, stopped working for the first time in 35 years.

Many drivers needing to fill their vehicle gas tanks were unable to. Without the satellite to link their automated gas station card reader to a distant computer, credit cards could not be approved for purchases. Many ATMs also stopped working.

By 2013, thieves had learned how to use stolen credit cards by first climbing onto the roof of a store, and then by covering its small satellite antenna card verification uplink with a sheet of ordinary aluminum foil. Many merchants, if digital verification is slow, will simply allow a card to be used for purchases of a few hundred dollars or less. Many pay the price if the card proves to be invalid.

In 1998, within hours of the Galaxy IV malfunction, another satellite was repositioned in orbit and began taking up the slack. After seven hours, things began to return to normal. [45] What would happen if merchants and banks suddenly stopped accepting *your* credit cards – for hours, days or potentially much, much longer?

Black Swan

In his book *The Black Swan*, New York University mathematician Nassim Nicholas Taleb explains that some events are highly improbable, yet cause catastrophic consequences when they happen. [46] Consider one such *Black Swan* that scientists believe happens on average once every 150 years...but that in theory could happen at any time.

The day is September 1, 1859. In his office a telegraph operator sits down at the most advanced technology of the time. As he reaches for his Morse code key, a spark like a small bolt of lightning leaps from the key to his hand, painfully shocking him.

Miles away, another telegraph office mysteriously catches fire. Along the telegraph wire strung outside, people that night are frightened to see sparks jumping to nearby metal. They had believed the telegraph was safe.

Throughout the United States and England, telegraphs either ceased working or, oddly, continued to work even when disconnected from their power source.

Scientists now call what happened that day a "Carrington Event," named for amateur British astronomer Richard Carrington, the first that noontime to observe a solar flare, a huge Coronal Mass Ejection on the face of the Sun. This fast-moving blast of charged particles 17.6 hours later slammed into Earth's magnetic field, causing wild electromagnetic effects.

The 1859 event lit up the night in North America with auroras as far south as Hawaii and the Caribbean, so brightly that people could read newspapers by this rare visit of the Northern Lights. In the Rockies, miners were awakened by the light and began preparing breakfast, thinking sunrise was approaching. In Australia and parts of Asia, Victorian telegraph systems were knocked out for two days. [47]

Closer Than You Think

Imagine such a Carrington Event today causing voltage surges through almost everything in your world that has wires, including our national power grid, computers, cars, cell phones, GPS and other satellites, military and banking computer systems and all the other electronic marvels we have made central, essential and almost second-nature in our civilization.

How much damage could another Carrington Event cause? In 2013 the insurers of Lloyds of London and Atmospheric and Environmental Research (AER) in the United States jointly estimated the current cost to the world economy of such an event today to be $2.6 Trillion, more than half the annual budget of the U.S. Government. [48]

The real cost might be much higher. Such a solar storm could fry power system transformers around the world, and this could take months, even years or decades, to replace at enormous cost. Are you prepared for the social and economic devastation of months without power, of watching your TV and computer by candlelight? Or of not being able to withdraw your money at the bank?

"A major electrical blackout can produce a loss of access to funds," writes engineer James A. Marusek. "Credit card processing, bank transactions, ATM withdrawals, check validation, payroll disbursement, and even cash registers are dependent on the availability of electrical power. This problem can be compounded by the loss of key satellites that form part of the conduit for transmitting financial data." [49]

Such problems can be caused by natural events, as well as human error and deliberate attack. Russian hackers have devoted much effort to probing America's national power grid – which in the past has caused two major Northeastern power blackouts via the simple failure of a single relay or circuit breaker setting off a cascade effect. The People's Republic of China has been developing both giant laser cannons and high-speed rockets designed to destroy satellites in orbit.

Another Carrington Event might fry the huge computers of stock trading, banking, welfare and taxation, or crash Belgium-based SWIFT, the Society for Worldwide Interbank Financial Telecommunications.

Truth is, we will have at most only hours, or perhaps only mere minutes, of warning to shut down and protect such things as best we can. We do not know how much damage a Carrington Event today could do to our digital-dependent world.

This is a Black Swan, a rare risk, so why worry? The National Aeronautics and Space Administration (NASA) wanted you to know that on July 23, 2012 the Sun exploded with an event bigger than Carrington, two super-sized mass coronal ejections only minutes apart.

Had this happened one week earlier, the solar blast would have hit Earth as we sped around our year-long orbit, but with much more destructive energy than the 1859 event. Truth be told, such solar ejections may not be rare, and Earth is a duck in our Solar System's cosmic shooting gallery.

A similar threat to our computer-dependent civilization could be EMP (Electro-Magnetic Pulse) from, e.g., a small 3-5 kiloton terrorist nuclear device lifted to 110,000 feet above America's heartland via a simple weather balloon. Its detonation theoretically could in an instant fry computer chips, circuits and power grids in a circle more than 800 miles across.

Such a blast east of Cleveland might wipe out electronics from Chicago, Toronto and Indianapolis to New York City, Philadelphia and Washington, D.C. Above Dallas, it could wreck computers as distant as Houston, Austin, San Antonio, Tulsa, Little Rock and Baton Rouge. Triggered above Tallahassee, it might devastate computers from Miami to Tampa and Orlando, and as far away as Atlanta, Nashville and New Orleans. Detonated east of Santa Barbara, California, it might scramble computer brains from San Diego and Los Angeles to San Francisco and Silicon Valley, and from Las Vegas and Reno potentially to as far away as Phoenix. Above Seattle, such a blast could also take out computers in Portland, Oregon, and Vancouver, British Columbia, as well as computerized companies Microsoft and Amazon. In Europe, such a blast above Frankfurt,

Germany could crash computers from London and Paris to Copenhagen, Zurich, Milan and Berlin. Such terrorist attacks could also massively disrupt government and banking electronics in all these places.

A single EMP attack might reach even farther, perhaps coast to coast, according to an August 2014 *Wall Street Journal* article and interview by former CIA Director R. James Woolsey. We explored the terrorist EMP risk to the military, banks and our economy in *The Great Debasement*. [50]

The lesson to take from this is that you have ways to protect your money. It can be just as safe as it was for people in pre-computerized 1859. Since the bank is paying you almost zero interest, you have little to lose by making your money safe….but you may have an enormous amount to gain.

However, if you fear more down-to-earth threats, note that a Russian hacker group known as "Energetic Bear" has been spreading a Stuxnet-like virus named "Dragonfly," which the computer security company Symantec has been studying since 2012. This computer bug is designed to disrupt electrical grids, petroleum pipelines, and even wind turbines. It has infiltrated utility systems in much of the U.S. and Europe and has the potential to sabotage infected systems. [51]

Safety Net

The very idea that became the Internet began when the U.S. military considered how to build a computer system that could not easily be shut down – and recognized that decentralization was the key. They saw that a network of many small, independent computers linked together through multiple crossing points and nodes like a spider web would be much harder to disrupt than a network that operated through one giant centralized command computer.

This kind of individualistic decentralization of power was the same idea America's Framers sought to build into our society and Constitution. And this is what the collectivist "Progressive" politics of the past 100 years have sought to eradicate.

Under today's collectivist government systems, the risk that a "flash crash" could cascade into a massive crash of the dollar and economy therefore grows bigger every day.

If the weakening U.S. Dollar and our financial institutions have been targeted for disruption and destruction by global power brokers and terrorists, then it would be prudent to move a portion of our personal investments and money out of their bull's-eye. This saving remnant should be converted into something with value that will survive – and even grow in the wake of an economic collapse.

We first introduced Freeman and his findings about the concerted attacks on America's financial institutions in detail in our 2011 book *The Inflation Deception*. These attacks, including an assault only weeks before the 2008 elections, played a key role in electing President Barack Obama.

Three-Stage Crack-up

In January 2014 a new book, *Game Plan: How to Protect Yourself from the Coming Cyber-Economic Attack* by Freeman, provides additional confirmation (from a Defense Department insider) of an international plan to bring down the dollar as the world's reserve currency. [52] The pattern he now sees, past and future:

Stage 1 occurred 9-11-2001. Islamic terrorists targeted the World Trade Center buildings with the goal of slashing the financial jugular vein of America. The attack successfully closed the U.S. stock, bond and money market trading for six days. Assets would be frozen.

Stage 2 occurred 9-15-2008. Research now confirms that Arab Sovereign Wealth Funds leveraged their $2 Trillion windfall from oil price profits to conduct a $20 Billion "bear raid" on some of America's major financial institutions. Merrill Lynch, Bear Stearns, Fannie Mae, Freddie Mac and ultimately Lehman Brothers were devastated, and Lehman went bankrupt. This plunged the U.S. into a housing collapse and deep recession, which our nation still suffers from today.

Stage 3 will be a "bear raid" on the U.S. Dollar. It is no secret the Arabs, Russians and Chinese share the goal of replacing the U.S. Dollar as the world's reserve currency. Their ultimate goal is to introduce a new gold-backed Russian Ruble and Chinese Yuan/Renminbi during the next U.S. or global panic. The dollar would be frozen.

The coming bear raid on the U.S. Dollar could take many forms, including a staged cyber attack on the five major U.S. banks, closing down bank account access, another "flash crash" on Wall Street, or targeting America's power grid or water supplies. Our vulnerability to a major cyber attack keeps growing daily.

Our enemies' goal is to create a major financial panic that would discredit the U.S. and our already-debased dollar, which has lost 98 percent of its purchasing power since the Federal Reserve was created in 1913. The Fed's original mandate was, and is, to protect the dollar's value.

Our enemies' goal is for American citizens and foreign trading partners to begin shunning the U.S. Dollar all at once in favor of a new currency with a more trustworthy store of value and gold backing.

A cyber attack on the U.S. Dollar could happen at any time - without warning. Therefore, holding significant wealth in stocks, bonds and banks has never been riskier.

Technologies such as bank time-locks on safes made old-fashioned theft more difficult, but in the emerging cashless digital world technology may be making banks easier to rob than ever before.

And if what you keep in your bank's safe or safe-deposit box is denominated in dollars, you are already being robbed of your money every day by a technique that does not even need to know who you are or where you hide your money.

No bank safe, however strong or secure, can protect your dollars from this kind of robbery -- but knowing what to do might, as we shall show you.

Chapter Two
Time Machines

" 'You mighty city of Babylon! In one hour your doom has come!
The merchants of the earth will weep and mourn over her
because no one buys their cargoes anymore...' "

" 'In one hour such great wealth has been brought to ruin!....
No worker of any trade will ever be found in you again....
Your merchants were the world's important people.
By your magic spell all the nations were led astray.' "

– The Bible
Revelation 18 (NIV)

**Banking was born near Babylon almost 5,000 years ago and in
key ways has scarcely changed. Clay records still exist of named banker
families, employees and customers, ancient loans and debts still awaiting
collection. We discover how humankind came to bank on grain, then
silver & gold, and then mere paper. We learn how banking and money
got their names.**

From the dawn of our time, humans have sought time machines.

We have searched for the fabled Fountain of Youth, and for thousands of years have
paid dearly for pills and potions that promise to hold back the wrinkles a bit longer.

Knowing that "you can't take it with you," we have prayed for a way to transmit
it on ahead to wherever we are going.

Banks and money are time machines.

We have created and reinvented both banks and money as ways to preserve, protect
and carry into the future the purchasing power we have in our hands today.

Real money, in addition to being a medium of exchange and unit of account, is a "store of value" that we hope can stop time...or at least slow it down until we can spend what we have earned to satisfy our needs and dreams.

Banks have been storehouses of money and other valuables, so you might think that banks began as a place to store money.

In fact, the first banks began *before* what we now call money was invented.

Seed Banks

In the Middle Eastern land we know as Iraq – which ancient Greeks called Mesopotamia, the fertile crescent of land "between the rivers" Tigris and Euphrates – pagan temples several thousand years ago began providing storage space where farmers could deposit their seed for next year's planting.

These first "seed banks" were protected by both the king and the temple's pagan deity. This helped safeguard against theft by humans, and perhaps to a lesser degree against hungry rodents and insects.

Grain was a valuable commodity in the ancient world and was used in exchange.

One of the earliest units of Biblical money – the Shekel, still used as the name of Israel's currency – began in Mesopotamia around 3,000 B.C. as both a unit of value and a measure of barley, which among Israelites later became a measure of silver.

The Bible repeatedly tells people to use "honest weights and measures" in such exchanges, not two sets of scale weights or cups rigged to favor either the buyer or the seller.

To this day, one measure of certain precious metals from antiquity is the "grain," roughly the weight of a single grain of wheat.

Babylon Bankers

Travel 62 miles south of modern Baghdad along the Euphrates River and you will find the ruins of Babylon, which in 600 B.C. was the richest, most prosperous city on Earth.

At its heart were terraces that held lush plants, some from hundreds of miles away, one of the Seven Wonders of the Ancient World known as the "hanging gardens of Babylon."

Ceremonial processions in the ancient city passed through the Ishtar Gate, named for a regional fertility goddess. The gate was faced with blue-colored bricks crafted to produce a giant and colorful billboard of animals – lions, aurochs, and the mythical one-horned, dragon-like Mushushshu.

Large portions of these original bricks were long ago spirited away to museums in cities such as Berlin.

During his brief rule in Iraq, Saddam Hussein had craftsmen build a reduced-size reproduction of the Ishtar Gate to promote tourism. Envisioning his place in history, Hussein had his own name baked into the back of every imitation blue brick so it could be read millenniums hence by future archeologists.

The Ten Lost Tribes of Israel had been conquered by the Assyrian Empire, marched into exile, and vanished into history.

The Assyrian Empire itself was then defeated by the Babylonian Empire, which went on to conquer Israel's two surviving tribes and march them off into captivity in 597 B.C.

"By the rivers of Babylon, there we sat down," wrote the Psalmist. *"Yea, we wept, when we remembered Zion. We hanged our harps upon the willows in the midst thereof. For there they that carried us away captive required of us a song; and they that wasted us required of us mirth, saying, Sing us one of the songs of Zion. How shall we sing the Lord's song in a strange land? If I forget thee, O Jerusalem, let my right hand forget her cunning." [53]*

Because the Babylonians kept elaborate records on durable clay tablets, we have detailed accounts of the Babylonian Murashu family banking firm. These records, which reflect many of the methods in today's banking, show Jewish-like Semitic names such as "Jacob" among banking employees and customers under early Persian rule. [54]

Such names should not surprise us. The founding patriarch of the Jewish people was Abraham, who came originally from "Ur in the Chaldees," a Sumerian city in southern Mesopotamia.

Early in the Babylonian exile "we surprisingly encounter at least two full-fledged Jewish banks operating there – the banking houses of Murashu and Egibi," reported a study, *The History of Jewish Banking*, by the Manfred and Anne Lehmann Foundation in New York City. "Many cuneiform tablets evidencing their money lending transactions and bearing Jewish names have been preserved." [55]

The experience was transformative. Those taken in chains to Babylon were Hebrews or Israelites. Those freed and sent home by King Cyrus of the Babylon-conquering Persian Empire in 538 B.C. felt a new post-exilic identity as Jews, descendants largely of the tribe of Judah.

Rulers Rob Money's "Store of Value"

The rulers of Middle Eastern kingdoms began making coins of gold or silver nearly 4,000 years ago, then quickly learned and employed the tricks of stealing back for themselves part of the value from their own coins.

A typical king would call in and melt down his nation's old coinage, dilute its precious metal with cheaper base metal, then issue new coins to honor himself or a local pagan deity.

Such kings reimbursed the old coins of their subjects with these new debased coins, as if the value of the two were the same. The kings then pocketed whatever diverted pure gold or silver, or however many additional coins containing precious metal, that such re-minting let them get away with, leaving their subjects to wonder where their king got all his new wealth.

Rulers, then as now, were eager to siphon off whatever of value that their people earned. These rulers, however, were furious and punished it as a crime when others clipped or filed off bits of precious metal from rough-edged royal coins or made their own counterfeits by melting, further diluting, and then recasting the king's coinage.

Worse than a Highwayman

Human greed and deceit have always been with us. The debasement of money we call inflation, however, according to Nobel laureate economist Milton Friedman, is always the result of an act of government or an official central bank.

"Governments are inherently inflationary," wrote free market economist Murray Rothbard in his classic book *What Has Government Done to Our Money?* [56]

"Bankers know that history is inflationary," wrote Christian socialist historian Will Durant, "and that money is the last thing a wise man will hoard."

By "money" Durant apparently meant government fiat currency, which is indeed something that wise people distrust.

"Throughout history, governments have been chronically short of revenue," wrote Rothbard. "The reason should be clear: unlike you and me, governments do not produce useful goods and services that they can sell on the market; governments...live parasitically off the market and off society. Unlike every other person and institution in society, government obtains its revenue from coercion, from taxation." [57]

Taxation has limits, noted Rothbard, because beyond a certain level it prompts people to revolt against their rulers, as happened in colonial America.

Oppressive taxation also gives people incentives to flee, or to hide what they have, or to become a lot less productive when the fruits of their labor are taxed away.

"If taxation is permanently short of the style of expenditure desired by the State," wrote Rothbard, "how can it make up the difference? By getting control of the money supply, or, to put it bluntly, by counterfeiting."

"On the market economy, we can only obtain good money by selling a good or service in exchange for gold, or by receiving a gift," wrote Rothbard. "The only other way to get money is to engage in the costly process of digging it out of the ground."

"The counterfeiter, on the other hand, is a thief who attempts to profit by forgery," Rothbard wrote; "e.g., by painting a piece of brass to look like a gold coin."

Such a government counterfeiter passing off money with no productivity behind it "is more sinister and more truly subversive than [a] highwayman" who cheats a single victim, wrote Rothbard, "for he robs everyone in society, and the robbery is stealthy and hidden, so that the cause-and-effect relation is camouflaged."

Fixing Prices

Accompanying such government inflation is a repeating pattern of coercion, as Robert Schuettinger and Eamonn Butler lay out in their book *Forty Centuries of Wage and Price Controls: How NOT to Fight Inflation.* [58]

Over and over, for nearly four thousand years, rulers have debased their money. At first, their subjects accept this money and by doing so are robbed of a portion of what they sell to the ruler and his retainers.

The people then recognize, sometimes slowly and other times quickly, that the ruler's money has less value than it claims. Merchants begin to raise their prices denominated in the king's money. Workers demand more coins for a day's work. The ruler then responds with laws requiring the populace to use only his money.

Such laws are usually accompanied by political denunciations of businesspeople for raising their prices out of greed and making "windfall profits," of the worker for holding society for ransom by demanding higher wages, and of others for speculation or lack of patriotism when they resort to barter or other varieties of exchange that circumvent using the king's debased money.

The next traditional ruler response, ancient and modern, has been some variant of wage and price controls.

Ten pounds of turnips used to cost one coin. The king – who has debased and pocketed half the valuable metal that these coins used to contain – now commands, through criminal penalties, that merchants continue to sell their turnips at the old price.

The merchants' response for forty centuries has been to offer smaller, cheaper turnips to retain their profit margin – or to stop selling turnips at all.

The king is always praised for his "price control" law in defense of the people, and for his crackdown on greedy, gouging businesspeople, until the people realize that no turnips can actually be bought in the marketplace anymore at any price.

"If you think health care is expensive now," wrote journalist P.J. O'Rourke, "wait 'till you see what it costs when it's free."

Goddess of the State

Ancient Romans also used their temples as banks. Overlooking the forum was the temple of Rome's protector goddess of the state, Juno Moneta, whose name means "advisor" or "warner."

Juno Moneta's squawking sacred geese, legend told, had saved Rome by warning the city's military commander of the approach of hostile Gauls.

Her temple for four centuries was also the site where Rome's silver coins were minted. Moneta thus came to be the origin of our words "mint" and "money."

By the time of the Emperor Nero (54-68 A.D.), the mint had moved, and many Romans were storing their money in private banks. Under Nero's reign over a Roman Empire remarkably similar to our own bureaucratic welfare state, the debasement of government coinage began.

Rome's private deposit bankers were called *argenarius* because their business was *argentum*, silver. (This is also the namesake of the South American nation Argentina.) Rome's moneylenders made their living by exchanging the coins of its many foreign visitors for the empire's legal tender from the Imperial Mint.

These moneymen did their business in closed courtyards, where traditionally they sat on a long bench called a *bancu*, the origin of our word "bank."

By Rome's Third Century A.D., wrote one historian, "as a result of mounting inflation, widespread hoarding of specie, and sharply reduced revenues, the emperors resorted to reckless adulteration of the imperial coinage to meet their military and administrative costs."

"As a result, distrust of new currency was widely manifested, by individuals as well as by banks. Ultimately the government refused to accept its own coinage for many taxes and insisted on payment in kind." [59]

Nervous Bankers

As one Roman emperor overthrew another in an ongoing series of coups, "banks were understandably hesitant to accept the coinage issued by the usurpers."

Historians know this from a surviving official letter ordering banks to accept the coins of two such short-lived emperors, and from public emergency decrees setting forth the punishment for dealing in black market money. [60]

The debased Roman *Denarius* coin disintegrated from inflation, and merchants and workers demanded many more of them in exchange for what they were selling. In 301 A.D. the Emperor Diocletian issued his famous Edict on Maximum Prices requiring citizens, on penalty of punishment or even death, to accept at face value Roman imperial currency. Penalties applied to those who bought as well as sold at a higher price than the Edict allowed.

Diocletian's Edict has survived. It laid out precise maximum prices that could be charged in *denarii* for various weights of grain and other foods, types of wine, lumber, wool and silk, job wages, shipping costs, as well as matters as small as how much a Notary could charge for putting his seal on a document (10 *denarii*) or what veterinarians could charge for trimming an animal's hooves (6 *denarii*). [61]

Even as Diocletian's fixed prices were being chiseled into stone for all to read, the *denarius* was losing value by the day because the government was taking more and more precious metal content out of it.

The Cost of Leading

One wonders if President Richard Nixon consulted Diocletian's Edict for the guidelines used in his own 1970s wage and price controls, or if Mr. Nixon studied what had happened to powerful empires that cut the gold anchor of their money, as he did in August 1971.

Since World War II, the U.S. Dollar has been the world's reserve currency. When Mr. Nixon severed the dollar's gold anchor, however, he cut the world financial system adrift from monetary stability.

The dollar's rapid decline was causing so much inflation and uncertainty around the globe that in 1979 the "world's other central bank," the International Monetary Fund (IMF) created by the 1944 Bretton Woods monetary agreement, attempted to improve matters.

The IMF began issuing its own "currency" known as SDRs, Special Drawing Rights, that initially were pegged at one SDR equals one dollar. The IMF in 1979 "flooded the market with 12.1 billion SDRs to provide liquidity as global confidence in the dollar declined," writes economic analyst James Rickards in his 2014 book *The Death of Money*. [62]

SDRs do not circulate like ordinary money. They have traded among the IMF and the central banks of various nations as a reserve currency that makes such banks more solvent. In 1979 SDRs were being used as "paper gold" to take pressure off the weakening dollar by helping stabilize an uncertain global economy.

"In August 2009 the IMF once again acted as a monetary first responder and rode to the rescue with a new issuance of SDRs, equivalent to $310 Billion, increasing the SDRs in circulation by 850 percent," writes Rickards. By then, however, SDR value was based not on the weakening dollar but on a "basket of currencies" from major nations.

With junkie spendaholic political leaders, the U.S. and its currency will continue to decline as we keep creating money not by working but by reproduction.... merely printing more and more trillions of dollars. The debate among economists increasingly is not whether the dollar will remain the global reserve currency, but, rather, what will replace it. Will it be a new Chinese Renminbi, a new version backed by the gold China has been accumulating? Will it be the IMF's SDR, with value based on a basket of currencies that will include the dollar but not be dominated by it?

It has not been easy to lead the global economy since World War II. As Belgian-American economist Robert Triffin observed in 1960 in his famous Triffin's Dilemma, America makes the world prosperous by running deficits, buying more from other nations than we sell them. Running perpetual deficits, however, over time undermines world confidence in the dollar, the world currency, and produces instability.

This has been particularly challenging when other nations, especially in Europe, could afford lavish welfare states from what they saved by letting our taxpayers provide their national defense.

Inflation's Golden Antidote

Succeeding Emperors of the Western Roman Empire followed the socialist price-control path to its logical conclusion. Those who refused to grow food or perform other essential tasks for imperial wages were forced to do such jobs for the empire, and to sell the fruits of their labor at regulated prices. This downward debasement slide of money by a weakening Rome became the road to serfdom, not unlike the road we are traveling down today.

In 301 A.D., however, the Emperor Diocletian also issued very limited numbers of a new coin called the *Solidus* (Latin for "solid") that later became Rome's golden antidote to inflation. Each solidus was one-sixtieth of a Roman Pound of pure gold, about 5.5 grams, worth 1,000 *denarii*.

In 312 A.D. the Roman Emperor Constantine replaced Rome's earlier gold coin the *Aureus* with the *solidus*, defined as 1/72nd of a Roman pound (4.5 grams) of pure gold. It became the most reliable coin in human history.

Most people recall learning that the Roman Empire fell around 476 A.D. This is only half true. Constantine, who gave Christianity the standing to become the imperial state religion, had split the Roman Empire into Western and Eastern halves. The Western half fell in 476 A.D.

The Eastern Half of the Roman Empire, with its capital Constantinople – now called Istanbul in Turkey – was renamed the Byzantine Empire and did not fall until 1453 A.D., less than 40 years before Columbus reached the New World.

Byzantium for many centuries avoided the dark and medieval feudal stagnation of serfdom in the West. The Eastern Empire was cosmopolitan, successful and rich. Only in its latter days of fighting Islam did its taxes become so high that a few in its empire actually welcomed Muslim armies as liberators.

Coining Soldiers

The Eastern Empire's longevity came in part from its money. Constantine's *solidus* retained its weight and gold purity for six centuries, was then briefly debased, and then reissued again in a purer form.

This reliable gold coin – the medium in which imperial taxes had to be paid – came to symbolize the wealth, power and stability of Byzantium throughout Europe, Asia and Africa.

Then as now, the integrity or debasement of a nation's money carries a powerful message about how honorable and reliable that nation and its government are.

Byzantium's government frequently re-minted new *solidi* from old, not to debase or siphon off their gold content as most other governments had done for centuries, but to give the impression that fresh, new gold was always pouring in to enrich and empower the Christian Byzantine Empire.

The Islamic Caliphates, to demonstrate their own merit, minted gold coins that resembled Constantinople's. Both the Muslim coins and Byzantine *solidi* were widely used in international trade and nicknamed Bezants, a name that evoked Byzantium.

Our word "soldier" originally comes from Byzantium's gold *solidus*, a coin used during the late Western and long-enduring Eastern Empire to pay Roman Legionnaires. [63]

The word "soldier" thus originally implied that someone worthy of this title is as solid, valuable, reliable, strong and trustworthy as the Byzantine gold *solidus* coin that is its namesake.

Our word "salary" likewise comes from a Roman soldier's pay, from his regular ration of salt (*sal* in Latin).

Faith in Paper

As it did in the West and Near East, money in the Far East transformed societies.

"Money is a spiritual thing," wrote Chinese scholar Lu Bao around 300 A.D. in his discourse *The Money God*:

"It has no rank yet is revered; it has no status yet is welcomed."

"Where there is money," he wrote, "danger will turn to peace and death will give life."

"Where money slips away, honour will turn to baseness and life will give death."

"They say 'Money holds power over the spirits,'" wrote Lu Bao. "If that is true, just think of its power over men!" [64]

Several peoples had previously used individual paper contracts signed from one person to another as a medium of exchange, often with the formal imprimatur of banking agents. Romans as early as a century before Jesus used written *praescriptiones* to transfer a promise of money or credit. Even earlier, India used paper bank notes called *adesha* to transfer money.

By the 3rd Century A.D., the Persian Sassanid Empire used letters of credit called *chak*, and six centuries after that the Muslim Abbasid Caliphate of Baghdad used similar paper money transfer documents called *sakk*. *Chak* and *Sakk* are probably the root name and idea behind your personal bank checks.

Song Money

While much of Europe faced the Dark Ages, China's Song Dynasty invented paper and, by the 7th Century A.D., what we think of as paper money.

Using wood block printing, the Song at first produced what amounted to promissory notes that could be redeemed for metallic coins. When coin copper ran short, the government began issuing paper that simply took the place of hard money.

By 1175 A.D. China's government was operating at least four factories in different cities to churn out paper money. One of these factories, records show, employed 1,000 workers.

In some ways this paper currency was remarkably modern. By 1107 A.D., it was printed on a special paper with intricate designs and six different colors of ink to make counterfeiting difficult.

In other ways, the early Song notes seem odd to us today. Distinctly different paper notes were printed for use in specific regions of China. Each note carried a time limit of three years, which meant that this currency could not be saved, hoarded or hidden from the tax collector for a longer period than that. Each note was like a sales coupon that had to be used by its expiration date.

Sometime around 1268 A.D. the Southern Song Dynasty began printing a single China-wide currency convertible to gold or silver, but by then the Song's days were numbered. This dynasty, as it turned out, had its own expiration date – with destiny.

Mongol Money

By 1279 the Song's last defenders were defeated by Mongol troops of the grandson of Genghis Khan, Kublai Khan, and his Yuan Dynasty. Kublai at first printed the restricted currency used by the Song, but the Yuan soon created a flood of currency, not backed by metal yet without time limits on when it could be spent.

The Mongol ruler required his subjects to accept his currency at face value.

"The Chinese government confiscated all gold and silver from private citizens and issued them paper money in its place," writes anthropologist Jack Weatherford in his book *The History of Money: From Sandstone to Cyberspace.*

"Even merchants arriving from abroad had to surrender their gold, silver, gems, and pearls to the government at prices set by a council of merchant bureaucrats."

"The traders then received government-issued notes in exchange," writes Weatherford.

Dough for the Devil

Marco Polo, a Venetian merchant who visited Mongol-ruled China, "saw clearly that this system of paper money could work only where a strong central government could enforce its will on everyone within its territory," writes Weatherford. [65]

Inflation began rising as succeeding rulers enjoyed the royal prerogative of manufacturing money. The Chinese took to calling paper money "wind money" because its value could so easily and quickly blow away.

When a ruler can have all the money he desires simply by printing it, how long will he or she resist this temptation? How long could you if you had the power to conjure vast amounts of money?

To this day, many Chinese ritually burn a paper imitation currency called "Hell Money" as a way of sending spending cash to deceased loved ones in the afterlife. It is usually sent to hell, because presumably nobody needs money in heaven.

By 1455 the Ming Dynasty, to stabilize its economy, banished paper money and curtailed most international trade.

Risky Banking

In the Renaissance Italian city-states such as Florence, powerful new banking families such as the Medici were using paper to facilitate business by conveniently transferring wealth between cities and even between countries.

Monarchs in this innovative new age had their own court bankers.

Meanwhile, a strange new way of banking by the gold dealers of London and the Netherlands was beginning to sow seeds that have grown into how we bank today.

The place where you bank almost certainly uses this kind of banking.

The United States became independent as this brave new banking was sweeping the Western world, and we have been profoundly shaped by its influence.

It has made some individuals wealthy and some nations prosperous, yet plunged others into economic crisis and depression.

However, say some economists, this is a highly risky and unethical way of banking that has led to today's destabilized national and global economy.

These economists believe that today's banking, as well as today's currency, will always cause major dangers and should be replaced.

This odd banking is a time machine that perilously moves our fortunes up and down, but not necessarily forward. In the next chapter we shall discover why.

Chapter Three
Fractured Reserve Banking

*"The business cycle arrived in the Western world
in the latter part of the Eighteenth Century.
It was a curious phenomenon, because
there seems to be no reason for it,
and indeed it had not existed before."*

– Murray Rothbard
Economist and Historian [66]

After losing their trust in government to safeguard their money, merchants in London turned to private goldsmiths who were inventing a new kind of banking. This surprising innovation can be profitable, which is why your bank uses it today. It is also inherently risky, and a cause of recessions and depressions. Your bank account is at increased risk at this very moment because of it.

On a bright summer day in July 1640, the merchants of London awoke to learn that the money they had deposited for safekeeping in the Royal Mint was gone. King Charles I had simply expropriated 120,000 Pounds' worth of bullion entrusted to the Mint, including most of their deposits.

In January 1672, his son King Charles II seized the cash of London's bankers deposited in the Exchequer, the government's "bank to bankers." This king in one surprise blow – a surprise except to His Majesty's cronies, who withdrew their deposits days earlier – confiscated nearly 1.33 million Pounds' worth of coins and bullion. [67]

The revenue-hungry government was clearly a threat to private money and property. To escape the king's greedy clutches, merchants turned to the goldsmiths of London, prosperous private craftsmen who already had sophisticated ways to store and protect silver and gold.

For a nominal fee, goldsmiths would safeguard deposits of silver and gold – or so their customers who walked away with a receipt for their deposits might have thought.

These goldsmiths, however, were ingenious profit-seeking merchants themselves. Perhaps they knew what William Shakespeare wrote in his poem *Venus and Adonis*:

> *"Foul cankering rust the hidden treasure frets,*
> *But gold that's put to use more gold begets."*

With gold that used to be entrusted to the government now filling their vaults, the goldsmiths thought of a surprising, even shocking, idea that transformed global banking – an idea your bank almost certainly uses today.

What Possible Harm?

Washington University economists Stuart Greenbaum and Anjam Thakor describe this fundamental transformation:

> *"It gradually dawns on the goldsmith that it is not really necessary to have a unit of gold for each outstanding receipt. This idea must have come as a revelation, an epiphany.*
>
> *"To be sure, the strait-laced would recoil at the idea of issuing more receipts than one had gold, but if no one ever withdraws the gold, then what possible harm?*
>
> *"The naughty possibility of printing extra warehouse receipts changed the world. This discovery was the banking equivalent of the Newtonian Revolution, every bit as important to banking as gravity was to physics." [68]*

The late Emory University business finance Professor George Benston once surmised that England's goldsmiths

> *"...came to realize that the people to whom they had given receipts for gold they held for safekeeping were using the receipts as money.*
>
> *"...But when the receipts were used as money, only a fraction was redeemed at any one time, permitting the goldsmiths to lend out the 'surplus' gold. Thus, they engaged in fractional-reserve banking.*

"...Furthermore, competition among goldsmiths led to their paying interest rather than charging fees for the safekeeping service." [69]

Element of Risk

This new kind of banking, however, *could* do great harm. Sometimes the borrower was unable to repay the gold he had borrowed. Sometimes the original depositor or a person to whom he had traded his deposit receipt came asking for the gold.

Gold merchants would try to have on hand at least a fraction of the gold they were supposed to have – a fraction that if only a few came to make withdrawals would be sufficient to cover the gold merchant's obligation.

Whenever depositors began to feel that their gold might be at risk, any serious sign of instability or trouble at the gold merchants' bench or in society would be taken as a storm warning.

Not only war but also mere rumors of war could trigger what today we call "a run on the bank," in which many depositors rush to demand the return of their gold at once, before the limited supply held by the gold merchants ran out.

This introduced an element of risk that had not existed before. Depositors had little reason in the past to doubt that all the precious metal they put in a bank would be there, because in old-fashioned banking the deposits were not being lent out.

When people know at the outset that they are putting their money into a bank that will be unable to return all deposits at once, the depositor wonders what other depositors are going to do if economic bad news arrives.

Such fractional-reserve banking creates not a sense of security, as we might hope that money in the bank would bring, but of insecurity. If even a few neighbors rush to remove their deposits from such a bank, this can trigger the herd inside our heads to become part of a stampede. It taps into the same group instincts one sees in a stock market panic or a lynch mob.

Because fractional-reserve banking adds this risk of bank runs to the economy, it makes a society more vulnerable and unstable. It has the potential to turn every rumor or problem into a crisis.

The greatest risk here is always the quality of a loan's collateral. The best collateral not only holds its value but also is readily available. Imagine being a banker using the gold from a "demand deposit," which the depositor can demand back at a moment's notice, and lending this in a 30-year mortgage on a home that termites might devour or an Act of God might destroy before the loan is paid off. The banker is often thus expected to borrow "short" from depositors in order to lend "long." This is one of many reasons why banking is an inherently risky business.

Drug of Choice

Despite its terrible risk and potential downsides, however, most American and other modern banks do fractional-reserve banking. The reason is because for those willing to believe, it is a powerful drug, an economic stimulant to which we have become addicted. Leaving it would for many cause painful withdrawal symptoms.

Fractional-reserve banking, remember, is magic. Give the goldsmith a dollar, he lends it to someone else, and he gives you a receipt.

This is an early version of what economists call a "multiplier effect." The borrower now has in hand a real dollar. The goldsmith has a debt obligation from the borrower that is worth a dollar plus interest, which he can treat as an asset. And you have a receipt that can be redeemed for a dollar, plus a smaller amount of interest, that you can treat as an asset.

What had been one dollar has, at least briefly, multiplied by more than three times. Everyone is richer, at least until the piper must be paid. This multiplication of "wealth" stimulates the economy.

In today's economy, one dollar on deposit permits a large fractional-reserve bank to lend approximately $10. The bank is thus literally allowed to create, if not print, money and earn interest on all of it.

The Bank of Ponzi

Economist Murray Rothbard saw fractional-reserve banking as a Ponzi scheme, or as a sleight-of-hand trick through which a merchant or banker collects interest by lending out money that apparently is owned by somebody else. [70]

As you might expect, the courts were eventually asked to decide who actually owns the money. A British court ruled that such money does not belong to the depositor or to the borrower.

When you deposit money into a fractional-reserve bank, the court held, the bank actually becomes the *de facto* owner of an unsecured loan or asset you have given it. The receipt or passbook that you walk away with and think of as evidence of "your" bank account is instead an IOU.

The goldsmiths of London thus began an evolving, expanding legal transformation that continues to unfold in many complex ways.

A Different Smith

In 1776 Adam Smith, in his founding work of capitalist theory *The Wealth of Nations*, addressed what today we call fractional-reserve banking.

The Bank of England had been established 82 years earlier, in 1694, as the second oldest central bank in the world. (Sweden's Sveriges Riksbank had been founded in 1668.) It adopted some of the fractional-reserve banking methods of the goldsmiths, and it helped make possible more stable banks that the king did not loot, at least not in the ways Charles I and Charles II had done.

Smith had witnessed 30 years of the effects of a central bank in Scotland and was impressed, if a bit surprised:

"The business of the country is almost entirely carried on by means of the paper of those different banking companies, with which purchases and payments of kinds are commonly made," wrote Smith. "Silver very seldom appears...and gold still seldomer."

Smith concluded: "That the trade and industry of Scotland...have increased very considerably during this period, and that the banks have contributed a good deal to this increase, cannot be doubted." [71] He saw the positive side of fractional-reserve stimulus, not the negative side when people lose faith in its illusion of increase and then rush to withdraw their deposits.

Smith did not call himself an economist, because in 1776 a different and revealing term was used to describe his field. What we now call economics was in Adam Smith's time called "Political Economy," a recognition of the dominant role the king and government played in the marketplace.

New World Money

America's Founders fought our revolution with paper money because we had been cut off from British currency. The experience made them determined that a free and strong American Republic must be built on solid, not paper, money.

During the American Revolution, the cash-starved Continental Congress did what most modern governments do. Lacking sufficient money, it recruited the printing press as a weapon to conjure paper money out of thin air. And American banks created their own magic money via the new fractional-reserve banking.

When our War for Independence began, America's 13 former colonies and their 2.4 million people had in circulation money equivalent in value to around 12 Million Spanish Dollars – only 5 Spanish Dollars, on average, for every man, woman and child. New York delegate Gouverneur Morris proposed that the Congress fund the war by printing a paper Continental currency denominated in dollars.

In 1775, Congress printed $6 Million of the new currency, increasing money in the colonies by 50 percent in one year.

In 1776 the Continental Congress issued $19 Million more, then another $13 Million in 1777, $64 Million in 1778, and an astonishing $125 Million in 1779. "There was no pledge to redeem the paper, even in the future," wrote economist Murray Rothbard in his *History of Money and Banking in the United States*, "but it was supposed to be retired in seven years by taxes levied pro rata by the separate states."

"The retirement pledge was soon forgotten," wrote Rothbard, "as Congress, enchanted by this new, seemingly costless form of revenue, escalated its emissions of fiat paper."

Paper Hangers

Within five years, these lawmakers wallpapered America with $225 Million of this unbacked paper, putting nearly 19 dollars in circulation for every one at the start of the Revolution – an increase in paper money of almost 2,000 percent.

As historian Edmund Cody Burnett observed, "such was the beginning of the 'federal trough,' one of America's most imperishable institutions."

The cheaply-printed bills were easy to counterfeit by the dishonest – and by the British, who flooded the rebel states with more millions of fake Continentals to undermine popular support for and trust in the Revolution.

The supply of these notes quickly outpaced demand, and as Economics 101 teaches, the value of these scraps of paper plummeted.

Revolutionary soldiers were paid in Continentals. When farmers or merchants refused to accept the inflated paper currency for food or supplies the Continental Army needed, their goods were sometimes "impressed" and they were forced to accept the devalued paper as payment.

When the first Continental dollars were issued, Americans were willing to exchange them for silver dollar coins at 1 or 1.5 to one. A year later it took three Continentals to buy such a coin. By December 1779 the exchange rate had fallen to 42 to one. By December 1781 a dollar coin fetched 168 of the paper bills.

Imagine the price of potatoes at your local market rising in only six years from $1 per pound to $168 per pound, and you get some idea of how soldiers and merchants felt about the value of being paid with America's first fiat paper currency.

By 1779, the Continental Congress sold the first of what eventually would be $600 Million worth of a parallel currency, loan certificates, that after the war became part of the young nation's debt. These, too, quickly lost value and within a year were exchanging for silver dollars at 1/24th of their face value. Americans took to saying of the devalued paper that even the cheapest things were "not worth a Continental."

Making Bank on America

During the last years of the Revolutionary War, a wealthy Philadelphia merchant named Robert Morris became, in Rothbard's description, the "virtual economic and financial czar of the Continental Congress."

Morris pushed through a measure to make taxpayers redeem part of the national debt, debt that had seemed worthless and been sold to speculators by ex-soldiers and merchants for pennies on the dollar. This harvested a fortune for speculator friends of Mr. Morris.

Contrary to the decentralist, states' rights-oriented Articles of Confederation, wrote Rothbard, Morris pushed for creation of "a strong central government, the power of the federal government to tax, and a massive public debt fastened permanently upon the taxpayer."

Above all, Morris wanted to create America's first commercial and central bank. This Bank of North America, headed by Morris himself, would be privately owned and modeled on the Bank of England.

This new entity, chartered by Congress and opened in 1782, was America's first "fractional-reserve" bank, authorized to create money by making loans based on the reserves of customer deposits...a use of other people's money that, according to Rothbard, would likely be a criminal offense in any profession other than modern banking.

Bankopoly

Bank of North America notes were by law privileged to be legal tender for paying all duties and taxes in the new nation, with value on a par with precious metal coin.

"[N]o other banks were to be permitted to operate in the country," wrote Rothbard. "In return for its monopoly license to issue paper money, the bank would graciously lend most of its newly-created money to the federal government to purchase public debt and be reimbursed by the hapless tax- payer."

"The Bank of North America was made the depository for all congressional funds," wrote Rothbard. "The first central bank in America rapidly loaned $1.2 million to the Congress, headed also by Robert Morris."

Beyond this bank's base in Philadelphia, Americans soon noticed that it appeared to be printing more paper currency than the government had metal coin to redeem.

As his political power waned, Morris repaid most government money held by his bank, ended his role as America's first central banker, and had his bank re-chartered by the State of Pennsylvania. America's first financial czar slipped quietly into history.

Reviving the Dollar

For the Framers who shaped the United States Constitution, which in 1787-89 replaced the star-crossed Articles of Confederation, their experience with inflated paper money, debt, taxation, sneaky speculators, greedy politicians and manipulative bankers left a life-long bad taste in their mouths and distrust in their hearts and minds.

For more than 100 years, popular distrust of a national bank kept America off the easy downward path that almost all other major nations have now taken.

America's winding, ascending path took us away from paper fiat currency of our Revolution and lifted us to a brief Golden Age of astonishing prosperity based on genuine, solid money.

It has been a difficult journey, however, during which the U.S. Dollar died and was brought back to life in various incarnations.

Today, in the early 21st Century the dollar has reached the last of its cat-like nine lives. It might continue as a ghost or virtual or Zombie currency. Its fast-approaching next fall, however, will end its final incarnation as tangible currency.

Forging Solid Money

The Constitution gave Congress the enumerated power in Article I Section 8 "To coin Money, regulate the Value thereof, and of foreign Coin...." In Article I Section 10 it denied states the power to "coin money" or "make any Thing but gold and silver Coin a Tender in Payment of Debts..."

Naively, James Madison deemed this sufficient to keep American money honest. He assumed that future generations would honor the Founders' standard that government could never give itself any power not explicitly permitted by the Constitution, which gave the government no power to issue paper fiat currency.

The Constitution's Article I Section 8, alas, did give Congress the power "To borrow Money on the credit of the United States."

"I wish it were possible to obtain a single amendment to our Constitution," wrote Jefferson in 1789. "I would be willing to depend on that alone for the reduction of the administration of our government to the genuine principles of its Constitution; I mean an additional article, taking from the federal government the power of borrowing."

Piggish Bank

"Paper money has had the effect in your state that it will ever have, to ruin commerce, oppress the honest, and open the door to every species of fraud and injustice," wrote George Washington in 1787 to a constituent in Rhode Island.

The Father of our Country knew full well the threat that paper fiat money could pose to the new republic.

Yet while Jefferson served as President George Washington's Secretary of State, the President's young protege Alexander Hamilton, our first Secretary of the Treasury, eagerly planned and created the First Bank of the United States, modeled on the Bank of England.

Hamilton argued that the fledgling nation had a "scarcity" of gold and silver, and that economic growth depended on issuing paper money.

Congress established this new bank in February 1791 with a 20-year charter. The government owned 20 percent of this bank, with the rest owned by private investors.

The new bank's notes were to be redeemable in, and kept at par with, gold and silver, which in the impractical theory of a bimetallism standard were to have a fixed exchange value to one another. This gave the paper money a quasi-legal tender status.

The new money was to be invested in the assumed federal debt and in subsidy to manufacturers. Sound familiar?

"The Bank of the United States promptly fulfilled its inflationary potential by issuing millions of dollars in paper money and demand deposits, pyramiding on top of $2 million in specie [gold and silver]," wrote Rothbard.

Money Changers

"The result of the outpouring of credit and paper money by the new Bank of the United States was an inflationary rise in prices....of 72 percent," Rothbard continued. In addition, "speculation in government securities and real estate values were driven upward," along with a spawn of new commercial banks in the states.

"If the American people ever allow private banks to control the issue of their currency, first by inflation, then by deflation, the banks and corporations that will grow up around [the banks] will deprive the people of all property until their children wake up homeless on the continent their fathers conquered," Jefferson continued.

The issuing power should be taken from the banks and restored to the people, to whom it properly belongs," Jefferson concluded.

"History records that the money changers have used every form of abuse, intrigue, deceit, and violent means possible to maintain their control over governments by controlling money and its issuance," said Jefferson's protege President James Madison.

"If the debt which the banking companies owe be a blessing to anybody, it is to themselves alone, who are realizing a solid interest of eight or ten percent on it," wrote Jefferson to a friend in 1813.

Conjuring with Money

"As to the public, these companies have banished all our gold and silver medium, which, before their institution, we had without interest, which never could have perished in our hands, and would have been our salvation now in the hour of war; instead of which," wrote Jefferson, "they have given us two hundred million of froth and bubble, on which we are to pay them heavy interest, until it shall vanish into air."

"We are warranted, then," Jefferson continued, "in affirming that this parody on the principle of 'a public debt being a public blessing,'[as Alexander Hamilton said]...is...ridiculous. [T]he truth is, that capital may be produced by industry, and accumulated by economy: but jugglers only will propose to create it by legerdemain tricks with paper."

"If Congress can do whatever in their discretion can be done by money, and will promote the general welfare, the government is no longer a limited one possessing enumerated powers, but an indefinite one...," wrote James Madison in 1792.

"Of all the contrivances for cheating the laboring classes of mankind, none has been more effective than that which deludes them with paper money," warned Daniel Webster.

The Second Bank

The First Bank of the United States lost popularity, and Congress withdrew its Charter in 1811. Soon, however, the U.S. plunged into the War of 1812, which put the young nation in what Rothbard described as "a chaotic monetary state, with banks multiplying and inflating...checked only by the varying rates of depreciation of their notes."

In 1816 Congress chartered a Second Bank of the United States. Like its predecessor, the new bank was a private corporation with one-fifth of its shares owned by the government.

This Second Bank of the United States was authorized to create paper currency, purchase a large chunk of the national debt and receive U.S. Treasury deposits.

"From its inception, the Second Bank launched a spectacular inflation of money and credit," wrote Rothbard. "Outright fraud abounded...especially at the Philadelphia and Baltimore branches....It is no accident that three-fifths of all the bank's loans were made at these two branches."

The resulting huge expansion of money and credit "impelled a full-scale inflationary boom throughout the country," wrote Rothbard. What followed were the Panic of 1819 and America's first crash and depression by 1820 as speculative bubbles in real estate and manufacturing burst.

The Second Bank survived the crisis, of which economic historian William Gouge wrote: "The Bank was saved, and the people were ruined." Again, does this today sound familiar?

Crippled by Populism

"The United States...is highly crisis prone," write Columbia University Business School Professor Charles Calomiris and Stanford Professor Stephen Haber in their 2014 book *Fragile by Design: The Political Origins of Banking Crises and Scarce Credit.* [72]

"It has had major banking crises in 1837, 1839, 1857, 1861, 1873, 1884, 1890, 1893, 1896, 1907, the 1920s, 1930-33, the 1980s, and 2008-09. That is to say, the United States has had 14 banking crises over the past 180 years!"

"Canada, which shares not only a 2,000 mile border with the United States but also a common culture and language, had only two brief and mild bank illiquidity crises during the same period, in 1837 and 1839, neither of which involved significant bank failures."

Why have American banks been so fragile and unstable, while banks in Canada have seemed reliable and rock solid?

Calomiris and Haber believe that a country's banks reflect its political culture. Banks strike deals with those in power.

In Canada, they write, its banks reflect its conservative, consensus-driven parliamentary system. This has produced mostly banking that sticks to business and generally is not the pawn nor bankroller of partisan agendas. From the beginning, Canada had only a handful of large, well-financed banks that spread branches across the country.

The United States, by contrast, has been "crippled by populism," they write.

For almost 170 years, from the 1810s until roughly 1980, American banking has been shaped or heavily influenced by what Calomiris and Haber describe as "a durable alliance between small 'unit bankers' (operating banks with no branches) and agrarian populists (farmers who distrusted corporations of nearly every type, as well as the elites that controlled them)."

This populist alliance successfully resisted for a century the imposition of a Bank of England-like elitist central banking system of the sort our first Secretary of the Treasury Alexander Hamilton tried to establish.

"The fact that a coalition of farmers and small bankers was able to dismantle the banking institutions that had been set up by Alexander Hamilton, and that it was then able to establish an inefficient and unstable alternative that endured for more than 150 years, implies that something about this coalition was woven into the fabric of America's political institutions," write Calomiris and Haber.

Unlike Canada, America prior to World War II mostly had many small banks, including many that were not well funded and hence fragile. These banks, however, often had near-monopoly status in the town or region where government permitted them. They – as well as most potential competitors – were prohibited from interstate, or in many cases even intercity, banking.

As a result, these banks could charge high rates for loans because government protected them from competition. In a pre-Internet age, locals often had no idea what a mortgage could or should cost.

Local bankers and their allies in government made money from this system, write Calomiris and Haber. But these isolated small banks outside major centers such as New York City lacked the resources to meet the needs of, or to attract, large companies.

Even now, of the world's "strongest" 20 banks as analyzed by Bloomberg for 2013, America has only two banks on the list: Citigroup ranked 9th and JPMorgan Chase ranked 15th. Canada, by contrast, had 5 banks on the Bloomberg list, China 4 (including one Hong Kong bank), Singapore 3 and Sweden the same as the U.S. with 2 banks among the top 20. [73]

In 1913 Progressive President Woodrow Wilson signed into law a powerful central banking system, the Federal Reserve; but for the seven decades thereafter, even the Fed would accommodate elements of this powerful political populist coalition's entrenched system of banking.

The Bank War

Out of the 1820 Depression's bitter fruits emerged the anti-central bank movement that in 1828 elected President Andrew Jackson, a popular General who won the Battle of New Orleans against the British during the War of 1812 – and who would command a battle to destroy the Second Bank of the United States.

"The Jacksonians were libertarians, plain and simple," wrote Rothbard. "Their program and ideology were libertarian; they strongly favored free enterprise and free markets, but they just as strongly opposed special subsidies and monopoly privileges conveyed by government to business or to any other group."

"In the monetary sphere, this meant the separation of government from the banking system," he wrote, "and a shift from inflationary paper money and fractional reserve banking to pure specie [gold and silver] and banks confined to 100-percent reserves."

As President, Jackson succeeded in lowering tariffs and, wrote Rothbard, "for the first and probably the last time in American history, paying off the federal debt."

"A Den of Vipers"

"I too have been a close observer of the Bank of the United States," said Jackson in an 1834 speech. "I have had men watching you for a long time, and am convinced that you have used the funds of the bank to speculate in the breadstuffs of the country."

"When you won, you divided the profits amongst you, and when you lost, you charged it to the bank," said President Jackson. "You are a den of vipers and thieves. I have determined to rout you out, and by the Eternal I will rout you out!"

Or, as liberals put it today, the "banksters" personally pocketed the profits and "socialized" the losses, sticking taxpayers with the bill.

Jackson withdrew government funds from the Second Bank and eventually brought it down. And when the brief economic depression of 1837 followed, the country began widespread use of Mexican silver coins as our working currency.

America's economy quickly recovered. This shows once again the ability of *real* money to stimulate recovery. Real money gives people confidence that what they earn and save will retain its value, that they cannot be robbed by politicians or Federal Reserve bankers debasing paper money with a printing press to cheat those who save and lend.

Prior to the creation of the Federal Reserve, American economic crises tended to be numerous but usually short in a vibrant economy with vigorous recuperative powers. Since 1913, when the Fed was created to manipulate America's money supply, we have seen the Great Depression and the ongoing Great Recession, downturns from which recovery has been slow and painful.

Because of the Jacksonian movement – the free enterprise origin of what today has metastasized into a very different and more collectivist Democratic Party – America would do without a controlling central bank for the next eight decades.

The central bankers at last came to power in 1913 and soon got even, as we noted in *The Inflation Deception*:

"The Federal Reserve and the government welfare state cynically took their revenge by putting paper-money-hating Andrew Jackson's face on the $20 bill and Jefferson's face on Food Stamps to lend their legitimacy to both pieces of fiat paper that Jefferson and Jackson would repudiate were they here today."

Decentralized Banks

Without a national central bank, Americans turned to local and regional banks. When government currency was in short supply, people bought, sold and saved by using the paper notes issued by usually-small private banks.

This was risky for savers because government regulations typically confined such banks' lending to a single state or even town, meaning that these banks could quickly run out of money and collapse if customers panicked and started withdrawing their savings.

Such bank runs were all too common in the young republic, because one of the things our banks had adopted from England was the risky system of fractional-reserve banking.

A major cause of collapse for many such banks, however, was not customer demands for their money.

State governments "required banks to collateralize their notes by lodging specified assets (usually state government bonds) with state authorities," according to University of Georgia economist George Selgin and George Mason University economist Larry White.

"[C]lusters of 'free bank' failures were principally due to falling prices of the state bonds they held," write Selgin and White, "suggesting that the bond-collateral requirements caused bank portfolios to become overloaded with state bonds."

Or as economist Robert P. Murphy explained in *The Politically Incorrect Guide to Capitalism*, "government regulation actually unbalanced the banking system."

Government demands that banks buy large quantities of debased state bonds could push otherwise-solvent banks off a cliff. Then as now, with today's President Obama-Fed Chair Janet Yellen deliberate inflation, innocent savers continue to pay the price for greedy politicians who squeeze banks to extract government spending money.

Some banks developed solid reputations for safety, and their private "currency" promissory bank notes, akin to today's private bank traveler's checks, were widely accepted beyond their states' boundaries.

As we noted in a previous book, during the years before the War Between the States, the $10 note issued by the Citizens' Bank and Trust Company of New Orleans, chartered in 1833, may have been the most popular and trusted paper currency in many Southern states.

Because its customers included Louisiana Cajuns, Creoles and other French-speaking Americans up and down the Mississippi River, this $10 bank note in one corner carried the large letters "DIX," French for ten.

These bank notes were quickly nicknamed Dixies, and the Southern states where they were in wide circulation came to be called "the land of Dixies," or Dixieland, or simply Dixie. [74]

Bankrolling a War

When war between the states came in 1861, both the Union and Confederacy lacked sufficient gold and silver to pay for it. Both began issuing huge amounts of unconvertible paper money.

The Union called its paper fiat money "Greenbacks," because of their color, the same color as our fiat paper money today.

The U.S. Government insisted that Greenbacks were genuine money. It paid Union troops in this paper fiat currency. Greenbacks, however, cannot even be called true legal tender because for some of its own taxes – especially tariffs – the Federal Government refused to accept payment in Greenbacks. It insisted on payment in gold.

Following the war, the victorious U.S. Government was eventually willing to redeem these Greenbacks for a small amount of gold. By then, millions had been traded to speculators here and abroad for pennies on the dollar. Those speculators became big winners when fractional gold redemption became law.

Confederate money went the way of the paper money of America's first confederacy under the Articles of Confederation – the Continental paper used to fund the American Revolution. Many Confederate "graybacks" ended their days as wallpaper lining the rooms of homes.

Farmers and other creditors knew that Greenbacks kept being printed in huge quantities and therefore continued to lose value. This meant that Greenbacks were easy money. They could be borrowed and spent for a known purchasing value, then later repaid with cheaper, inflated Greenbacks.

By the 1870s a new Greenback Party arose, largely in the West and upper Midwest, that urged government to print lots more of this cheap paper money that benefited debtors and shortchanged creditors.

The Greenback Party's supporters despised gold as money precisely because it did not lose value, and therefore gave them no way to cheat lenders by repaying debts with debased paper money worth less in purchasing power than what was originally borrowed.

Poor Gold

The Greenback Party, however, soon made common cause with Western and Midwestern populists who wanted more abundant silver, "the poor man's gold," to be the Federal Government's main coinage. The amount of silver in the economy at the time was increasing, so its supply-and-demand value was decreasing.

Bimetallism had always posed problems, as first the California Gold Rush of 1849 and later major silver strikes caused the market price of one metal or the other to vary. By 1870 it was clear that the nation should pick either silver or gold as the basis for defining the value of the U.S. Dollar.

The nation elected gold advocate candidates, including Republican President William McKinley, and what followed were by monetary standards the most prosperous four decades in American history.

Speculators still caused marketplace disruptions and brief panics. Politicians still pandered for the votes of "Silverites" with laws that continued silver subsidies and coinages, and this caused investors to worry whether America would abandon gold and retreat to a debased silver standard.

Nevertheless, for more than 40 years Americans enjoyed the security of knowing that what they earned and saved in the form of gold was not losing value as paper fiat money always has done. During these years Americans' hard work was secure against government debasement of their money.

Roosevelt the First

After McKinley's 1901 assassination, Americans suddenly found that the reins of government had been passed to his 42-year-old Vice President Teddy Roosevelt. Roosevelt had been the aggressive, Progressive reformist Governor of New York and media-lionized national hero who led a combat group known as the Rough Riders in Cuba during the Spanish-American War.

This first President Roosevelt would set forces in motion that led to the end of America's Golden Age. Soon the value of the U.S. Dollar would be put under the control of the monetary wizards at a mysterious and secretive, all-powerful central bank that now shapes our world.

These Progressives would crucify humankind not upon a cross of gold, as Presidential candidate William Jennings Bryan said, but upon a double-cross of paper and the fractional-reserve banking whose amplified swings of boom and bust have been used to justify imposing European-like political control over our economy.

"My friend, in this land of the free you need fear no tyrant who will spring up from among the people," said Bryan in his "Cross of Gold" speech at the 1896 Democratic National Convention. "What we need is an Andrew Jackson to stand as Jackson stood, against the encroachments of aggregated wealth."

The Centralization of Banking

Because of Presidents Jefferson and Jackson and the coalition of small bankers and agrarian populists, banking in America remained largely decentralized.

"What united them were strongly held views about the plight and moral superiority of the common man, who they believed deserved access to land and credit," write Calomiris and Haber. "What united their agrarian populist followers was a deep suspicion of big city businesses and businessmen, which they viewed as a threat to their way of life."

"In 1914 there were 27,349 banks in the United States, 95 percent of which had no branches!" they write.

Yet, as we shall see, over the next 100 years the world of American banking, like the rest of our society, would be fundamentally transformed. Just before New Year's Day 1914, the centralization of American banking began.

PART TWO
Politicizing the Banks

Chapter Four
Dawn of the Fed

*"The process by which banks create money
is so simple that the mind is repelled."*
— **John Kenneth Galbraith**
Money: Whence It Came, Where It Went

**The Federal Reserve System and its 12 private banks were needed,
said supporters, to get politics out of America's banks. The Fed was
also to act as a banker of last resort to protect an economy of Booms
and Busts caused by highly risky fractional-reserve banking. Instead of
depoliticizing our banks and currency, the Fed has turned into a fourth
branch of government, and the Fed chair is now in some ways even
more powerful than the President of the United States.**

The United States needed its own central bank like England's, argued Progressives
during the first decade of the 20th Century.

Such a bank would free the nation's money supply from partisan political
manipulation, they said, as the Bank of England purportedly had done.

Above all, they claimed, having our own central bank would regulate America's
money supply and prevent economic downturns like the Panic of 1907.

However, the 1907 downturn was not caused by a faulty money supply. It happened
because the President of the Knickerbocker Trust Company failed in his attempt
to corner the copper market. The resulting situation led the National Bank of
Commerce to announce that it was no longer accepting checks from Knickerbocker,
which set off a bank run of customers demanding their money back.

One major trigger of this typical, short-lived 13-month recession, as economist
Murray Rothbard understood, was fractional-reserve banking, which had made the

American economy susceptible to uncertainty, fear, panic and bank runs. Yet none of the central bank advocates called for an end to fractional-reserve banking.

What the central bank supporters apparently wanted was that the United States become more like Europe, with a way to expand the economy and government through an "elastic" inflationary money supply that let borrowers repay their debts with cheaper money.

Their problem was that America's economy was on a classic gold standard, which made our money self-regulating and without any need for a central bank to second-guess the free market. In an age of Progressive enthusiasm, the gold standard was keeping conservative and capitalist values in the saddle.

The central bank boosters' moment came in 1912, when a Republican split vote between former President Theodore Roosevelt and incumbent President William Howard Taft led to the election of Progressive Democratic President Woodrow Wilson.

The Fed Fix Is In

In 1913, under Wilson, a new cartel of 12 private central banks called the Federal Reserve would be authorized to begin turning America's gold into paper – and soon use that paper fiat currency to reshape and rule the United States through chronic inflation.

The Fed was devised in secret, and secrecy concerning its back room transactions and agreements has always been the Fed's preferred mode of operation.

The Fed's enabling legislation provided that American dollars, which until 1913 had 100 percent gold backing, now the new Federal Reserve Notes had only 40 percent "fractional reserve" gold backing.

Many Republicans in Congress were convinced that the Fed was designed to dethrone the gold standard and empower redistributionist Progressives such as the Silverites who wanted easy money, cheap credit that could be repaid with devalued dollars, and government spending unchecked by gold.

One lawmaker who opposed the Fed's creation was conservative Republican and longtime Massachusetts Senator Henry Cabot Lodge – whose son also became a Senator and, in a losing 1960 race, Vice President Richard Nixon's vice-presidential running mate.

"The [Federal Reserve Act] as it stands seems to me to open the way to a vast inflation of the currency," Lodge prophetically warned in 1913.

"I do not like to think that any law can be passed," said Lodge, "that will make it possible to submerge the gold standard in a flood of irredeemable paper currency."

"Inflation and Deflation Work Equally Well"

Another fierce opponent was Swedish-born Minnesota Republican Congressman Charles A. Lindbergh, father of the later-to-be-famous aviator.

"This [Federal Reserve] Act establishes the most gigantic trust on Earth," said Rep. Lindbergh.

"When the President signs this bill, the invisible government by the Monetary Power will be legalized," he said. "The people may not know it immediately but the day of reckoning is only a few years removed.... The worst legislative crime of the ages is perpetrated by this banking bill."

In 1913 Lindbergh authored *Banking and Currency and the Money Trust*.

In 1917 he published *Why Is Your Country At War and What Happens to You After the War and Related Subjects*, in which he argued that international financial interests had dragged America into World War I for their own benefit. In 1918 government agents destroyed its printing plates.

"The financial system....has been turned over to the Federal Reserve Board," wrote Lindbergh. "That board administers the finance system by authority of....a purely profiteering group."

"To cause high prices, all the Federal Reserve Board will do will be to lower the rediscount rate..., producing an expansion of credit and a rising stock market," wrote Lindbergh. "Then when...business men are adjusted to these conditions, it can check...prosperity in mid career by arbitrarily raising the rate of interest."

The Federal Reserve, warned Rep. Lindbergh, "can cause the pendulum of a rising and falling market to swing gently back and forth by slight changes in the discount rate, or cause violent fluctuations by a greater rate variation and in either case it will possess inside information as to financial conditions and advance knowledge of the coming change, either up or down."

"This," he continued, "is the strangest, most dangerous advantage ever placed in the hands of a special privilege class by any Government that ever existed."

"The system is private, conducted for the sole purpose of obtaining the greatest possible profits from the use of other people's money," said Lindbergh. "They know in advance when to create panics to their advantage. They also know when to stop panic."

"Inflation and deflation work equally well for them," Lindbergh warned, "when they control finance."

When he died in 1924, Lindbergh had left the Republican Party and joined the Minnesota Farmer-Labor Party to run for Governor as its standard-bearer.

"Moneyed Vultures"

Voices reminiscent of President Andrew Jackson's continued to challenge America's new national bank. In a 1932 speech, the longtime chairman of the House Banking and Currency Committee, Representative Louis McFadden (R-Pennsylvania) looked back on almost two decades of America's experience having our currency controlled by the Federal Reserve:

"[W]e have in this Country one of the most corrupt institutions the world has ever known. I refer to the Federal Reserve Board and the Federal Reserve Banks, hereinafter called the Fed."

"The Fed has cheated the Government of these United States and the people of the United States out of enough money to pay the Nation's debt," said Congressman McFadden. "The depredations and iniquities of the Fed has cost enough money to pay the National debt several times over."

"This evil institution has impoverished and ruined the people of these United States, has bankrupted itself," said McFadden, "and has practically bankrupted our Government. It has done this through the defects of the law under which it operates, through the maladministration of that law by the Fed and through the corrupt practices of the moneyed vultures who control it."

"Some people think that the Federal Reserve Banks are United States Government institutions. They are private monopolies which prey upon the people of these United States for the benefit of themselves and their foreign customers; foreign and domestic speculators and swindlers; and rich and predatory money lenders."

"In that dark crew of financial pirates there are those who would cut a man's throat to get a dollar out of his pocket," Congressman McFadden continued; "there are those who send money into states to buy votes to control our legislatures; there are those who maintain International propaganda for the purpose of deceiving us into the granting of new concessions which will permit them to cover up their past misdeeds and set again in motion their gigantic train of crime."

McFadden's views are harsh. Yet they are the views of a professional banker, past Treasurer and President of the Pennsylvania Bankers' Association, and, as we noted above, a Member of Congress who from 1920 until 1931 chaired the House Banking and Currency Committee.

Politicizing Money

The rationalization for creating the Federal Reserve was that it got politics out of decisions about America's money supply. Such decisions would henceforth be made objectively by non-politicians who are uninvolved in the partisan buying and selling of votes. The Fed's bankers would be free to do what is best for the country, not the party in power at the moment.

The Fed was supposed to give us separation of money and state because, despite its name, the Federal Reserve is scarcely more a part of the Federal Government than is the private shipping company Federal Express.

"The Federal Reserve Banks are not federal instrumentalities..." said the ruling in *Lewis v. United States*, 9th Circuit Court in 1992.

The United States Budget in 1991 and 1992 affirmed in passing: "The Federal Reserve banks, while not part of the government...."

The trouble was, and is, that the Fed's seven-member Board of Governors is regarded as a Federal Government agency. Its members are appointed by the President of the United States and consented to by the U.S. Senate for staggered 14-year terms.

Out of these seven, the President appoints the Fed Chair, currently Janet Yellen, and Vice Chair, currently Stanley Fischer, former Governor of the Bank of Israel, and can reappoint them to a succession of four-year terms.

Rural to Urban Power Shift

The Federal Reserve was not the only change imposed in 1913 by the new Progressive President Woodrow Wilson. Two constitutional amendments would also radically transform the federal design of America's Framers.

The 16th Amendment enacted in 1913 allowed the creation of a Progressive income tax, meaning a tax that confiscated far more from the rich than from others. Karl Marx and Friedrich Engels in their 1848 *Communist Manifesto* proposed such an income tax as one of 10 ways to destroy capitalism.

As the Fed began squeezing gold out of the dollar, the new income tax required citizens to pay their taxes in dollars. This forced Americans to keep working for dollars.

Marx and Engels also proposed among their 10 ways to eliminate the business middle class, the bourgeoisie, that government have monopoly control over all banking and credit. The imposition of a dominant central bank, the Federal Reserve, was a giant step towards this collectivist goal. As the Fed's power has grown, fulfillment of this Marxist objective has arguably moved closer.

America's Framers created two legislative bodies, the House and Senate, as America's Congress. The House, directly elected every two years by the people, was to be the voice of the people. The Senate was not elected by the people, but by the legislatures of the various states, each of which chose two Senators with staggered six-year terms.

The Framers wanted the Senate to represent state interests and be loyal to individual states. This was anathema to populists who wanted popular opinion and the pressure of its causes to prevail.

The 17th Amendment enacted in 1913 replaced legislative selection and created direct election of Senators. This effectively turned states into giant congressional districts with fixed boundaries that could not be gerrymandered. The six-year term of Senators made them a bit less subject to populist enthusiasms, but to win election and re-election Senators would now have to win the votes of the people, not just a small elite of state lawmakers.

The 17th Amendment shifted power in the country away from rural districts where the power of local bankers often held sway, and shifted it towards cities, where bigger bankers, commercial interests and different values predominated.

Much Indebted

The new Progressive era in 1913 brought another transformative change. It allowed the interest paid to bankers and other lenders to be deducted from one's income tax.

This change gave people an incentive to borrow and spend, especially since debts could ultimately be repaid with inflation-devalued dollars. It began to hook people on the "politicians' disease" – addiction to borrowing, spending and debt.

This tax deductibility of interest was not limited only to home mortgage interest. We can remember when the interest charged on one's credit card was deductible, which certainly stimulated Americans to charge things.

This deductibility originally applied to everything, and, only after more than seven decades, was restricted to mortgages by the 1986 tax reform. Politicians by then were tired of giving people back billions in what could have been tax revenues.

Those politicians, however, were afraid to touch the home mortgage interest deduction, knowing that this could cause a public revolt. Millions had been able to afford their houses, borrowers believed, only because of this tax break.

Homeowners instinctively understood that their home values would plummet if the mortgage interest deduction vanished – because fewer potential buyers would be able to afford their home. Few looked at the flip side of this – that in fact they were paying much more for their home because its bank mortgage interest was deductible. This made homes and mortgages desirable as one of the few big tax breaks available to little people.

The American Dream has long included a home of one's own. The dream grew for decades as home prices kept climbing after World War II, reaching stratospheric heights by around 2005.

Many ignored this dangerous housing bubble because it was easy to borrow from your home equity, using it as an ATM, or for a new home whose ever-growing market value seemed like a sure-thing investment. Its rise was inevitable, the saying went, because "they aren't making any more land."

Looking back, some are stunned by how hypnotic home ownership had become. For many it may be a malinvestment; they would be happier renting rather than investing 30 years of steep mortgage payments to be owner of an expensive-to-maintain, high property-tax home.

Yet when the government gives a large tax deduction for something, however dubious as an investment, this will attract investors tired of paying high taxes.

The higher the interest cost of a home mortgage, the bigger the tax deduction. It was a fool's paradise exploited not only by American dreamers but also by Progressive ideologues.

Levitating the Market

The Fed originally had one mandate – to protect the value and stability of the nation's money. In 1979 it was given a second mandate – to carry out monetary policy that produces full employment.

Some analysts now say the Fed has taken upon itself a third mandate – to boost, or in the words of one financial pundit, to "levitate" – stock market prices.

In a November 4, 2010 *Washington Post* Op-Ed column, then-Fed Chairman Ben Bernanke nearly said as much. Of the Fed's Quantitative Easing II (QE II) commitment to inject another $600 Billion into the economy that had been announced a day earlier, Bernanke wrote:

> "Stock prices rose and long-term interest rates fell when investors began to anticipate the most recent action.... And higher stock prices will boost consumer wealth and help increase confidence, which can also spur spending. Increased spending will lead to higher incomes and profits that, in a virtuous circle, will further support economic expansion." [75]

Three years later, a study by the McKinsey Global Institute showed that the Fed's stimulus programs produced results that, as the *New York Times* reported, "haven't been distributed equally." [76]

Low interest rates made government and giant private borrowers the big winners from Fed stimulus. They are still making bank savers the big losers. Easy money enriched many stock market speculators in the casino of Wall Street, which has gone up while the real business economy wallowed or declined.

Bernanke and his successor as Fed Chair, Janet Yellen, apparently do watch the market and consider whether their policy decisions will depress or "juice" stocks. Their decisions can have both economic and political consequences.

Does it go too far, as *Forbes* columnist Charles Biderman wrote in 2013, to say that "The Fed is helping to rig the stock market"? [77]

"[T]he Fed creates $4 Billion a day and eventually some of that money goes into equities," wrote Biderman. "And that, of course, helps keep stock prices elevated. So it doesn't matter that we are having major problems with the underlying economy and markets that normally would depress stock prices...."

"It seems that the Fed is willing to keep stock prices elevated, so the Obama administration can keep spending trillions of dollars that really don't exist," wrote Biderman. "How long can this go on? At some point gravity wins out. For now, equity inflows continue. Let's see what happens when the inflows stop."

The Pusher Fed

Easy money has always been a feelgood drug, a hallucinatory and addictive drug. One problem with addictive substances is that the user requires an ever-increasing dose to get the desired effect. The Fed has been a pusher, willing and able to give the stock market its needed fix of easy money.

We know this. In 2010, when Fed Chair Ben Bernanke acknowledged that his policy was intended to help boost stocks, the market was around 13,000. After four years of relentless Fed stimulus, the asset-inflated stock market bubble has been around 17,000 – four thousand points higher, despite a lackluster economic recovery that is slower even than that following the Great Depression.

The stock market has been high on and addicted to a drug that most economists know is now doing more harm than good. [78] The Fed is trying to switch to other stimulants, such as risky Reverse Repo manipulation of the economy [79], while causing as few painful withdrawal symptoms as possible. And these monetary doctors are attempting this during an election year, probably with more conjured stimulus money ready if the market starts to fall back towards post-easy-money depression.

A few commentators have suggested that Ms. Yellen's Fed may have a fourth unspoken mandate – to make the economy seem as good as possible in the months leading up to November 2014 and November 2016.

While the 2014 election-year politics stymied political agreements among the majority-Republican House of Representatives and Democrat-controlled Senate and White House, the Federal Reserve has involved itself in so many government activities that critics say it has become more like a "Fourth Branch of Government," a "Central Planner," than a politically-neutral Central Bank.

"The Fed has crossed a bright line," warned University of Chicago Booth School of Business Professor John H. Cochrane in August 2012. By imposing stress tests on banks, lending directly to non-banks such as insurance giant AIG, and acting as a regulator, the Fed has greatly expanded its power beyond monetary policy.

The Fed was supposed to have independence from undue political influence as a central bank that dealt only in monetary policy. As Fed tentacles intrude into realms of congressional political power, including regulatory and fiscal policy matters, the Fed cannot expect elected politicians to let it usurp their areas of authority without a response, Cochrane argues.

From its point of view, the Fed might see itself much as the federal courts did vis-a-vis civil rights. When political gridlock and political fear thwart congressional and presidential response to important issues, the Fed, like the courts, may feel tempted to fill the policy power vacuum created when politicians do nothing.

And power may be going to the Fed's head – or heads. During years of Quantitative Easing, the Fed acquired a $4.3 Trillion portfolio balance sheet, up by $3 Trillion since the near-economic meltdown of 2008.

According to University of Dallas Professor Mike Cosgrove, to deal with this monster the Federal Reserve, incredibly, is considering whether to pay banks up to $100 Billion per year *not* to lend to main street businesses. [80]

Instead of today's 0.25 percent that the Fed pays in interest for bank excess reserves, it might boost this to as much as 2 percent or even more to give banks an incentive to lend their money to the Fed itself instead of to other customers. From the banks' point of view, lending to the Fed is a zero-risk proposition that soon might pay well....the opposite of the high-risk, zero reward deal you now get for lending your money to your bank in the form of a deposit.

This, the unproven theory goes, might give the Fed "an equivalent function of what the federal funds rate did before QE," a new way to regulate the economy.

The more likely result, Cosgrove warns, is that the Fed could make economic growth even slower while losing control over inflation expectations – a formula that could lead to a variety of economic problems.

How would you feel after learning that your business cannot get a bank loan because the Fed is paying America's banks not to lend to small businesses? Where does this potentially currency-wrecking, job-destroying policy fit amid the Fed's first two mandates?

Principalities and Powers

To complicate this further, when Democrats controlled both houses of Congress prior to the 2010 midterm elections, they through the Dodd-Frank law created a new agency, the Consumer Financial Protection Bureau (CFPB) to regulate lenders. The funding for CFPB was by law to come directly from the Federal Reserve.

The biggest power of Congress is in its control of government purse strings. Circumventing congressional power to cut the funds of this new agency set a precedent for establishing a whole new level of government that cannot be held accountable by the people's elected lawmakers. This is one of many recent expansions of power for the Federal Reserve.

The CFPB, its critics warn, can assert regulatory power over literally every kind of commercial transaction in the U.S. economy, including lending and other bank and bank-like activities. In theory, by enforcing its power and dictates over more and more businesses, this new bureau could quickly grow into the most powerful single regulatory agency in our government.

Without being able to control CFPB's budget, Congress might be powerless to prevent this agency from metastasizing into a partisan or ideological monster able to devour the entire free marketplace.

Historians might look back on the creation of the CFPB as the day our constitutional republic of limited government, held in check by elected representatives of the people, died. This alien mutant agency may be the Progressive prototype for how they intend to transform us into a post-Constitutional, post-free market America.

By Their Fruits

The Bible says that we should judge a tree by its fruits. What financial fruits have nearly 100 years of Fed meddling with America's money supply produced?

You can see where the Fed has taken us with a glance at the Federal Reserve Notes most people now call money. When the Fed began, a $50 gold certificate included the words "Will Pay to the Bearer on Demand $50," making it clear that this piece of paper was merely a promissory note held in lieu of real money, genuine money being a fixed and convertible quantity of physical gold.

Before the Fed became overseer of America's money, the economy rose and fell, with dollars slightly gaining or losing purchasing power. Overall the dollar grew in strength and value, so that what cost $100 in 1829 could be purchased for only about $64 in 1913.

The gold dollar was not only a reliable store of value, but also an excellent investment in an appreciating asset.

Prior to the Fed, stock market panics (often triggered by speculators and corner-the-market schemes) and runs on banks (especially before bank accounts were insured) happened. The economy was resilient, however, and markets usually bounced back quickly to reach new highs.

Down Goes the Dollar

After the Fed began to tighten its stranglehold over our money, the path of the dollar has been almost entirely downhill through inflation. Today's inflated dollar has the purchasing power of only two 1913 pennies, a scant 2/100ths of the 1913 dollar.

During World War I President Woodrow Wilson effectively took the dollar off the classic gold standard by making it more difficult to convert dollars into gold.

After World War I the United States quietly transferred nearly $1 Billion in gold to Great Britain as a gesture of personal friendship between central bankers, a gesture American consumers paid for in lost dollar value, in inflation.

During most of the 1920s, concluded economic historian Murray Rothbard, the Federal Reserve did not tighten money and bring on the Great Depression as used to be believed. On the contrary, the Fed encouraged inflation to help devalue the dollar in order to make Great Britain's Pound more valuable and ease that nation's return to a gold-exchange standard.

The personal friendship between a top Fed executive and a British policymaker that produced this Britain-boosting tilt in U.S. monetary affairs is discussed in Liaquat Ahamed's 2009 bestseller *Lords of Finance: The Bankers Who Broke the World.*

The high price Americans paid for this Fed debasing of their currency for Britain's benefit provided little of lasting help to us. In 1931 the British Government abandoned the gold standard and has not returned to it.

Conservative Republican Presidents Warren G. Harding and Calvin Coolidge brought America back quickly from a sudden sharp recession in 1920-21 by slashing government spending and the size of the Federal Government.

These conservatives were succeeded by Progressive Republican Herbert Hoover, who as head of a global relief organization funneled food aid to Bolshevik regions of the Soviet Union, which helped prevent the collapse of its Marxist dictatorship. Hoover was invited by Woodrow Wilson to be the Democratic nominee for President, but refused. Hoover declared that he did not favor *laissez-faire* (free market) capitalism, and instead advocated an economy run by voluntary partnerships between government and corporations.

Under Herbert Hoover, the same Federal Reserve System that had expanded America's paper money supply during the 1920s suddenly contracted the money supply during 1929's fever of Fed-stimulated margin stock buying. Unwise Fed manipulation of the money supply, Rothbard argued, is what tanked the Stock Market and plunged America into the Great Depression in 1929.

The Fed's and Hoover's ill-advised attempts at economic engineering, as Milton Friedman and Anna Schwartz later documented, turned what probably would have been just another short recession into a Great Depression that government interference in the economy made worse and prolonged for more than a decade.

FDR's Gold Grab

Among Progressive President Franklin D. Roosevelt's first acts as President in 1933 was to issue Executive Orders making it illegal for ordinary Americans to own gold bullion, and confiscating people's bullion gold coins (but not coin collectors' numismatic gold coins). Other 20th Century rulers reportedly would outlaw gold ownership – among them Hitler, Mussolini, Stalin and Mao.

In the U.S., bullion was forcibly exchanged for Federal Reserve currency at just over $20 per Troy ounce of gold.

Immediately after this expropriation, FDR arbitrarily raised the official exchange rate of gold to $32 per Troy ounce, then ultimately to $35 per ounce, with government immediately pocketing the value difference to fund his welfare programs and public works projects.

By Executive Order, FDR also outlawed what had become traditional in business contracts – a "gold clause" specifying that the amount to be paid was either in U.S. Dollars or a particular quantity of gold, whichever at the time of payment had greater market value.

These gold clauses in effect secured payment of contracts in either of two different kinds of "money," one of which the government prior to FDR could not control. (The 1857 Coinage Act forbade using foreign gold or silver coins as legal tender.)

Under FDR, Americans also saw passage of the Banking Act of 1933 and its provision that came to be known as the Glass-Steagall Act, after its two Southern Democrat sponsors, Senator Carter Glass of Virginia and populist Congressman Henry B. Steagall of Alabama.

Two Kinds of Banking

Glass-Steagall separated commercial from investment banking. Investment banks could be involved in a variety of investing activities. Commercial banks could not, because Congress did not wish to allow commercial bankers to speculate with what were now government-insured accounts protected by the new Federal Deposit Insurance Corporation. Investment banks have no access to government-insured deposits.

This confined local commercial banks to offering low-risk small business loans and mortgages to neighbors they knew, and to buying and selling bonds and other fixed-income securities for their own accounts. This was precisely what most Southern and Western populists such as Congressman Steagall wanted, and where commercial banks would stay for almost the next four decades.

Contrary to what many believe, Glass-Steagall was *not* repealed in 1999 by the Gramm-Leach-Bliley Act. Insured banks are still prohibited from underwriting or dealing in securities. What was repealed in 1999 were the Glass-Steagall provisions that had prohibited commercial banks from being affiliated with investment banks engaged in underwriting and dealing in securities. [81]

"Although investment banks could take more risks than insured banks and had much higher leverage, the investment banks that got into trouble in the [2008] crisis – Lehman Brothers, Bear Stearns, and Merrill Lynch – were not affiliated with any of the insured banks that had major losses," writes Peter Wallison of the American Enterprise Institute. [82]

"[T]hese investment banks got into trouble," writes Wallison, "not by taking greater risks than insured banks but by buying and holding the same [wrongly graded] AAA-rated MBS based on subprime and other low-quality mortgages.... If Glass-Steagall had never been amended in 1999, the financial crisis of 2008 would have happened exactly as it did."

While nations with freer economic systems rapidly recovered from the Great Depression, the United States under Roosevelt's Progressive collectivist policies wallowed in prolonged high unemployment and a stagnant economy.

Pearl Harbor and World War II empowered FDR to conscript unemployed men into the military. Approximately two out of every three American soldiers in this war were drafted, and more doubtless joined the Navy, Marines or Coast Guard to avoid conscription into the Army.

The wartime economy regimented us into a command economy, complete with rationing and austerity on the home front. Rosie the Riveter and many thousands of other women became skilled factory workers. America, a manufacturing superpower, went back to work.

America still had a work ethic. War production healed us and restored our optimism and self-confidence. Recovery was expected and therefore happened.

By war's end, America's ratio of debt to Gross Domestic Product was at least 122 percent, by some measures even deeper in debt than we are today at close to 100 percent.

Sole Superpower

The United States was still standing, with its factories and cities intact while the world's other once-powerful nations had been knocked to their knees and were severely damaged, weakened and impoverished.

The steps taken at this history-turning moment, as America became a nuclear superpower, continue to shape our world today.

The 1944 treaty called the Bretton Woods agreement provided that the United States Dollar would continue to be pegged at $35 per Troy ounce of gold, a convertibility redeemable mostly by European central banks. Other major nations in turn agreed to peg their currencies to the dollar, thereby creating what was supposed to be at least the faint shadow of the pre-World War I gold standard.

What we called a gold standard, however, was actually the European pre-war "gold-exchange standard." To turn dollars into gold, central banks had to bundle thousands of dollars and in exchange receive gold bars too heavy to carry in a purse or pocket.

This new "gold exchange standard" was impossible for most ordinary people to use. One could no longer take twenty $1 bills to the local bank and swap them for a $20 gold piece as under the pre-Fed gold standard. This did not matter to average Americans anyway, because the prohibition against their owning gold remained law until the mid-1970s, after the Bretton Woods gold anchor ended.

Out of Bretton Woods came two enduring institutions: what today we call the World Bank, by custom run by an American, and the International Monetary Fund or IMF, supposedly the world's "lender of last resort" and "other central bank," by custom headed by a European.

The Secret Tax

The United States has done a slow-motion version of using inflation as a *de facto* tax for a long time.

In 1945 Beardsley Ruml, the Chairman of the Federal Reserve Bank of New York, reportedly delivered a remarkable speech before the American Bar Association in which he declared: "The necessity for a government to tax in order to maintain both its independence and its solvency is...not true for a national government."

"Two changes of the greatest consequence have occurred in the last twenty-five years which have substantially altered the position of the national state with respect to the financing of its current requirements," said Ruml.

"The first of these changes is the gaining of vast new experience in the management of central banks," he said.

"The second change is the elimination, for domestic purposes, of the convertibility of the currency into gold."

FDR's prohibition of gold ownership by Americans meant that U.S. citizens could no longer seek a safe haven here against inflation by converting their paper dollars into gold bullion.

Ruml's speech, published in the January 1946 issue of the quarterly journal *American Affairs*, offered a surprising new vision of what taxes "are really for."

The primary purpose of federal taxation listed by Ruml is "As an instrument of fiscal policy to help stabilize the purchasing power of the dollar."

The implication of Ruml's speech is that government can fund itself merely by printing as much money as needed. Indeed, the *American Affairs* article was titled "Taxes for Revenue Are Obsolete."

The newly-printed dollars produced out of thin air acquire their value, in effect, by devaluing the old dollars that people have earned and saved through their productive efforts.

To prevent a blaze of high inflation or hyperinflation from burning up the entire value of every dollar in circulation, new and old, taxes are used to selectively claw back money from targeted individuals, groups and industries.

Tax policy, said Ruml, will "express public policy in the distribution of wealth and of income, as in the case of the progressive income and estate taxes....[and] in penalizing various industries and economic groups...[and] to isolate and assess directly the costs of certain national benefits, such as highways and social security."

Ruml Touches You Today

Ruml, incidentally, touches working Americans' lives every payday. This Progressive advisor to Presidents Herbert Hoover and FDR devised income tax "withholding" that deducts money from each paycheck before you receive it.

Before Ruml's withholding became Internal Revenue Service policy in 1942, only around seven percent of Americans actually paid income tax – and many of those who did felt the tax's pain acutely.

Americans were deceptively told that if they signed up to have their taxes withheld, the government would not require most of a year's tax payment from them. In fact, government did collect such tax via withholding without requiring them to write a check.

The government has loved tax withholding from the beginning. It collects money almost immediately from taxpayers. It creates a paper and now-computerized trail of who is paid how much by whom, and establishes witnesses involved on both sides of every income transaction.

Best of all from the government's point of view, income tax withholding takes money almost invisibly from workers – and leaves many euphorically grateful to Uncle Sam for their tax refund.

All that such tax refunds mean, of course, is that people overpaid to avoid tax penalties, and gave government an interest-free loan of their money for up to a year.

As President Ronald Reagan and other withholding critics have argued, citizens should be required to write one huge check to the IRS every year so that taxes hurt. This, they argue, would give citizens a more realistic sense of their relationship to government than does paying steady, unnoticed withholding taxes out of every paycheck all year long.

For an even better sense of taxation, paying this one huge annual check to the IRS should be required one day before election day, when you vote for the politicians who are taking and spending your money. Tax day should not be as the politicians set it up, with April 15 as far away as possible in the calendar from November election days.

Colossus

Do Progressive policies – from the income redistribution of the income tax and welfare state to the easy money policies of the Federal Reserve – deserve credit for American preeminence in the world following World War II?

Not according to quasi-Marxist French economist Thomas Piketty, whose 2013 Progressive best-seller *Capital in the 21st Century* concludes that U.S. success following the war was an outlier, an unusual event, not evidence of inherent American superiority. [83]

Piketty sees America's few decades of success as the result of American factories and power remaining intact while the rest of the world had to rebuild. Almost any nation with any economic system could have held sway, he argues, if given the advantaged position America then enjoyed.

We, of course, take a more optimistic view of American Exceptionalism and its potential for success when not held down by policies that divert our capital resources, discourage our investors and achievers, and dampen what Keynes called our "animal spirits" and enthusiasm.

Stimulant or Depressant?

The Federal Reserve's policies have amply demonstrated one thing that we predicted. It tested John Maynard Keynes' hypothesis that the business cycle could be flattened by central bank or government injections of money into the economy during the low part of the cycle.

We predicted that in the Great Recession that began in 2008, following Keynes' prescription would produce an "anti-stimulus" because by increasing the risk of inflation it would cause businesses to invest and hire less, not more. History has shown that we were right. Even a veteran economist with the St. Louis Federal Reserve acknowledged that the stimulus made things worse, not better.

Perhaps because capitalists have usually co-existed with government, Keynes assumed that political tinkering could fine-tune the marketplace into optimal prosperity, a perpetual springtime without recessions or depressions. Defying the law of unintended consequences, Keynes forgot that the free market needs different seasons to plant, grow, harvest and renew. It is alive, not a machine.

Keynes admittedly wrote in an earlier age when the work ethic was more deeply entrenched in American and British culture. And as we have documented before, economic analysis shows that Keynesian stimulus can work in relatively primitive societies with closed economies. It mostly fails to be a wise government "investment" in advanced societies, however, where computerized stock exchanges discount it in milliseconds.

Keynesian stimulus is apparently the wrong drug to cure modern economies.

It is prescribed to stimulate. Instead, it induces symptoms that in modern economies resemble those produced by Prozac or tranquilizers. The boom and bust cycle is leveled somewhat, like the highs and lows of someone with bipolar disorder, but the effect is to put an economy's "animal spirits" into a trance-like state that reduces energy, vitality, productivity and innovation.

The Progressive welfare state likely intensifies such effects. This is what happens when those who work skillfully and achieve are hit with a shock wand of higher taxes and regulation that deny people the rewards their work merits.

The modern welfare state and "Too Big To Fail" policies of the Fed and government, on the other hand, protect others from risk. But in the natural world, we ought to invest our lives and fortunes based on a prudent consideration of risk and reward.

By shielding people from risk, our Progressive society encourages both laziness and recklessness. No economy or society can remain healthy, balanced and prosperous for very long by pretending we can take risk out of life's equation. This ultimately cannot be done. Risk is inevitable, whether we accept it or not.

Extortion's Consequences

If Keynesian stimulus and Fed fiddling with the economy are the wrong prescription, what is the right one?

Humans have always faced disruptive challenges – plagues, locusts, drought, invasions – and these have caused economic problems.

Yet as Murray Rothbard observed, the economic cycle of Boom and Bust that Keynes aimed to cure apparently did not exist prior to the widespread use of fractional-reserve banking, a system that amplifies the lesser cycles that manifest as human enthusiasm or dissatisfaction. Former Fed Chair Alan Greenspan's belief that the business cycle is built into our DNA might be mistaken.

Fed stimulus and the redistributionist state were adopted in part as ways to even out the sharp oscillations of the Boom and Bust cycle. Both have created a drug-like dependency, and hence a constituency of voters. And both have caused more harm than good because they are simply the wrong treatment for what ails our economy and society.

Stealth aircraft are said to need a computer to fly them because their odd aerodynamic shapes require adjustments many times each second to keep the airplane flying.

Our economy now operates so far from the self-balancing natural mechanisms of the free marketplace that politicians feel a need to tinker with it constantly to prevent a crash. In the process, they have made our system increasingly unstable.

The problem for Progressives is that good economics are terrible politics, and good (i.e., winning) politics produce terrible economics.

Progressives past and present, of both political parties, gain and hold power by buying votes. These votes may be bought with a welfare card or check paid for with money gouged out of a minority of hard-working taxpayers. They may be bought with special crony favors, preferential hiring and college admissions, student loans, tax breaks, government jobs or government contracts that someone else will pay for.

Progressives aim to make as many people dependent on and beholden to government as they can. Making people dependent on government, and then telling them their welfare check or other special government breaks will be taken away if conservatives win, is not the only way leftist politicians hold onto power.

Progressives by the late 1970s found a way to give away trillions of dollars' worth of goodies and stick America's banks with the bill. This giveaway came at a time when banks had a chance to expand their opportunities in amazing new ways – but only if they had government permission to do so. Progressive politicians put a shockingly high price tag on giving that permission.

The unintended consequences of this political extortion of the banks led to the 2008 near-collapse of our economy and the flattened economy we continue to live with today. It is a story worth retelling from the perspective of homeowners, as well as from the perspective of the banks.

*"In the summer of 1982, large American banks lost close to all their
past earnings (cumulatively), about everything they ever made in
the history of American banking – everything.*

*"They had been lending to South and Central American countries that
all defaulted at the same time....*

*"So it took just one summer to figure out that this was
a sucker's business and that all their earnings came from
a very risky game.*

*"All that while the bankers led everyone, especially themselves, into
believing that they were 'conservative.'*

*"They are not conservative;
just phenomenally skilled at self-deception by burying
the possibility of a large, devastating loss under the rug.
In fact the travesty repeated itself a decade later...*

*"The Federal Reserve bank protected them at our expense:
when 'conservative' bankers make profits, they get the benefits;
when they are hurt, we pay the costs....*

*"Financial institutions have been merging into a smaller number of very
large banks. Almost all banks are now interrelated.
So the financial ecology is swelling into
gigantic, incestuous, bureaucratic banks...
when one falls, they all fall....*

*"We would be far better off if there were a different ecology,
in which financial institutions went bust on occasion
and were rapidly replaced by new ones...."*

-- **Nassim Nicholas Taleb**
The Black Swan

Chapter Five
Banking Left

"It is wholly impossible for a central bank
subject to political control,
or even exposed to serious political pressure,
to regulate the quantity of money in a way
conducive to a smoothly functioning market order.

"A good money, like good law, must operate
without regard to the effect that decisions of the issuer
will have on known groups or individuals.

"A benevolent dictator might conceivably
disregard these effects. No democratic
government dependent on a number of
special interests can possibly do so."

– Friedrich A. Hayek
Nobel laureate economist

The 2008 near-collapse of our economy, the Great Recession, and today's lowest job participation rate in almost 40 years all began because Progressive politicians misused government regulatory power to coerce banks into redistributing home mortgages to groups of people the politicians favored. Today such politicians plan to use regulatory power to squeeze money out of our banks, and your bank account, in even more sinister ways.

"The power to tax involves the power to destroy," wrote Supreme Court Chief Justice John Marshall in his 1819 ruling that the State of Maryland could not legally tax a branch office of the Second Bank of the United States.

Today we should add: "The government's power to tax *and regulate* involves the power to destroy."

America's regulatory agencies are increasingly "weaponized," holding and forcefully using ever-expanding powers that, if politicized, can crush individuals, companies and entire industries at the mere whim of unelected bureaucrats and partisan or ideological politicians.

America's economic near-collapse in 2008, as well as the Great Recession and today's economic malaise, began with an attempt to use regulatory power to tilt our nation's banking system to the left and force banks to fund a Progressive political agenda.

This ideological attempt to redistribute trillions of dollars of wealth from our banks by using extreme regulatory threats and extortion is a shocking story. We have analyzed facets of it before, yet it is worth reexamining from the perspective of the banks that continue to be targeted by government.

President Barack Obama has said repeatedly that because a Republican House of Representatives will not enact his proposed policies, he intends to impose them by himself.

"I've got a pen, and I've got a phone," says the President, meaning that he can issue Executive Orders, rally supporters, and impose via government regulatory agencies what Congress refuses to enact as laws.

By reexamining how regulatory political weapons have been used to beat banks into submission in the past, we can learn what it means that President Obama is now unleashing more heavy regulations and pressure on our banks and other private companies than ever before in American history.

Progressives would have you believe that banks are "under-regulated" and that government should have even more power over them. In fact, banks have long been among the most heavily regulated institutions in America.

Politicians want to regulate banks in order to protect the public, of course, but even more so to be able to tell banks what to do with their money. This chapter looks back at one pattern of banking regulatory abuse and the consequences, intended and unintended, that this power grab continues to cause for all of us.

Irregulation

The economic devastation of the Great Recession has been immense. The shock wave of this bubble bursting circled the world in 2008 and 2009, wiping out $50 Trillion in investor equity – an amount approaching one year's Gross Domestic Product for the entire planet. At least $10 Trillion of that loss was from American equities, as a stock market that had topped 14,000 plummeted to 6,600.

The average home price in America fell by 30 percent or more, a loss to homeowners of more than $5 Trillion in what for most was the biggest investment in their lives, the equity nest egg many had planned to use for retirement or their children's college education.

This Great Unraveling cost more than five million people their homes, lost to foreclosure or fire sales. Millions more lost their life savings, typically spent to hang on in what then-Federal Reserve Chair Ben Bernanke called an "unusually uncertain" wild roller coaster economy.

With roughly 19 percent of Gross Domestic Product connected to housing, the ripple effect of this real estate price plunge continues to be felt in fewer sales and more job layoffs in businesses ranging from construction and appliances to cable TV and gardening supplies.

Few believe this crisis is near its end. Many fear that worse, perhaps much worse, is soon to come. We continue to suffer in a fragile recovery that is taking longer than what followed the Great Depression.

And 65 percent of us, according to one NBC/*Wall Street Journal* poll, now fear that America has gone into decline – and that our children could enjoy less prosperity, opportunity and freedom than we have known.

The liberal media tell us that greedy capitalist "banksters" are the cause of today's crisis. Giant banks certainly share a sizable portion of the blame, but there is a lot to go around.

Homeowners who walked away from their "underwater" house and mortgage hurt not only the lenders who trusted them, but also their former neighbors whose property values fell as a result of these unethical "strategic defaults" next door. These "walkaways" in many cases got their homes through fraud, by claiming on their mortgage application that they earned far more money than was true, yet almost none have been prosecuted.

The biggest villain in this moral lesson is the liberal media's ally, the very government that liberal journalists tell us should be given vastly more power to fix a problem that politicians and their policies caused.

Milking the Banks

Like so much that now threatens and bedevils the United States, the seeds of today's Great Recession were planted by President Jimmy Carter. Mr. Carter won the presidency in 1976 because the political and gold-abandoning economic problems caused by President Richard Nixon weakened his successor Gerald Ford.

In 1977 Mr. Carter signed into law the Community Reinvestment Act (CRA), which would weaken banks and ultimately lead to the housing value meltdown and economic near-collapse of 2008.

Originally sold as only a law to gather data on bank lending to minorities, CRA immediately became a hammer whose data was used to accuse banks of racism and discrimination in their lending policies.

The liberal media accused banks of "redlining," making few loans in certain neighborhoods. The media almost never mentioned that Franklin Delano Roosevelt's very "Progressive" Federal Housing Administration (FHA) is what first imposed "redlining" during the 1930s, mapping and discouraging loans in deteriorating neighborhoods where property values were declining. The FHA pushed banks to adopt this government guideline.

Making loans on the basis of politicized social engineering rather than credit worthiness is never a sound business decision, and it always creates unintended consequences.

Those who took out what came to be called "liar loans" – in which buyers, not required to provide documentation, simply claimed to make far more income than was true – ought to bear more responsibility for what has happened than have the government-coerced banks.

If the government were scrupulous about financial propriety and law, it would now be checking whether borrowers committed fraud by making false income claims. What does it tell us that left-liberal politicians have never lifted a finger to do this?

Bank-Bashing

By the late 1970s the CRA was already being used by both government and radical activists to intimidate banks into lowering their lending standards so that more poor and minority borrowers could qualify for loans.

In 1993 new President Bill Clinton, backed by a Democrat-dominated Congress, greatly expanded this power. Banks were now given a so-called "CRA rating" of their minority lending policies and practices, a measure that involved any of four government bureaucracies.

Banks given a "poor" CRA rating could be refused permission to expand as their competitors did, or to add new branches.

"Banks that got poor reviews were punished," wrote University of Texas economics Professor Stan Liebowitz. "Some saw their merger plans frustrated; others faced direct legal challenges by the Justice Department."

"The pressure to comply with CRA was astounding," recalled former bank manager Noel Sheppard, "especially at Great Western as it was expanding throughout the country. Its ability to acquire other institutions was directly related to its CRA rating."

"When legislation was pending in 1999 during the Clinton Administration to permit banks to diversify into selling investment securities," writes economist Thomas Sowell of Stanford University's Hoover Institution in his 2009 book *The Housing Boom and Bust*, "the White House urged 'that banks given unsatisfactory ratings under the 1977 Community Reinvestment Act be prohibited from enjoying the new diversification privileges' of this legislation." [84]

Either implicitly or explicitly, banks were expected to meet an arbitrary quota for loans to poor and racial minority borrowers to get a CRA rating. At the high point of this policy, one key mortgage institution was directed to have 55 percent of its mortgages helping these minorities.

ARMing Ninjas

What followed, wrote *Investor's Business Daily*'s Terry Jones in 2008, was that "in the name of diversity, banks began making huge numbers of loans that they previously would not have. They opened branches in poor areas to lift their CRA ratings...."

A large percentage of these were what the bankers nicknamed "Ninja" loans, given mostly to minority applicants who had No Income, No Job nor Assets.

In 2010 former Republican Speaker of the House Newt Gingrich described what the Clinton Administration strong-armed bankers into offering: "If you can't afford to buy a house, we'll waive your credit. If you can't afford to buy a house, we'll let you come in without a down payment. If you can't afford to buy a house, we'll let you have three years without paying any principal. If you can't afford to buy a house, we'll give it to you below interest rate. And guess what: None of it worked."

"That's how the contagion began," wrote Jones. "With those changes, the sub-prime market took off. From a mere $35 billion in loans in 1994, it soared to $1 trillion by 2008."

Many of the loans given were ARMs, Adjustable Rate Mortgages, often with low initial teaser rates to qualify a borrower for a home. When the teaser rate ended or loan interest rates adjusted upwards, many borrowers were no longer able, or willing, to keep making the higher mortgage payments.

Imposing Equality

Behind the Clinton Administration policies of housing for the poor was a radical leftist ideal of equality that it was not enough to provide shelter for the poor. The unfortunate poor, Mr. Clinton believed, should be given housing as good as that owned by the rich, the fortunate who are merely "the winners of life's lottery."

In the name of radical egalitarianism, for example, the Clinton Administration used taxpayer money to give poor people homes in San Diego County's wealthiest beachfront California Riviera suburb La Jolla (Spanish for "The Jewel"), a community almost as pricey as Beverly Hills or the movie star beach colony at Malibu.

As part of its new Progressive-Left vision of "mixed-income communities" that include the poor, the Clinton Administration also established halfway houses for felons and drug addicts in homes located in well-to-do neighborhoods, thereby endangering and driving down the property values of those next door who had worked hard to earn their dream homes in what until then had been safe upscale communities.

Fannie and Freddie

To enable this ideology of the redistribution of property wealth to the poor, a Democrat-controlled Congress gave two nominally-private for-profit banks approval to backstop risky bank lending to poor people who, prior to CRA, would never have qualified for a mortgage.

These two banks were empowered by law, wrote Jones, "to finance it all by buying loans from banks, then repackaging and securitizing them for resale on the open market...."

"Wall Street eagerly sold the new mortgage-backed securities. Not only were they pooled investments, mixing good and bad, but they were backed with the implicit guarantee of government."

These two banks quickly "grew to become monsters, accounting for nearly half of all U.S. mortgage loans," reported *Investor's Business Daily* in September 2008. "At the time of their bailouts...they held $5.4 trillion in loans on their books. About $1.4 trillion of those were sub-prime."

These two "monsters" that today hold an even larger percentage of U.S. mortgages are the Federal National Mortgage Association (FNMA), popularly known as Fannie Mae, and the Federal Home Loan Mortgage Corporation (FHLMC), known as Freddie Mac.

Both were GSEs, government-sponsored enterprises, that although nominally "private" (like the U.S. Post Office or Federal Reserve), are deeply intertwined with the government and are endowed with special government-granted resources and powers.

Fannie Mae was founded in 1938, during the Great Depression, to acquire the loans of other banks and thereby free them to make new local loans. It would then "securitize" these mortgages by bundling them into securities for sale. What we now call Fannie Mae is the private stockholder-owned corporation created by Congress in 1968 when it spun off half the original entity, apparently to remove Fannie Mae's activity from the federal budget.

Freddie Mac was created in 1970. Like Fannie Mae, it pools, securitizes and sells mortgages.

Partisan Piggies

The relationship between Fannie Mae and Freddie Mac, the government, and the Democratic Party, has been more than intertwined; it has been incestuous.

Investor's Business Daily has described Fannie Mae and Freddie Mac as a "Democrat Piggy Bank."

Senator Chris Dodd, Democrat of Connecticut and Chairman of the powerful Senate Committee on Banking, Housing and Urban Affairs, is co-author of the giant banking reform bill known as Dodd-Frank. He retired from the Senate in January 2011.

Between 1989 and 2008, however, Dodd pocketed at least $164,900 in campaign contributions from Fannie Mae and Freddie Mac employees and Fannie-Freddie Political Action Committees.

Senator John Kerry, Democrat of Massachusetts and his party's 2004 presidential nominee, received at least $111,000 from Fannie and Freddie. Senator Hillary Clinton, Democrat of New York, fattened her coffers with at least $75,550. Rep. Barney Frank, Democrat of Massachusetts and co-author of the Dodd-Frank law, took more than $40,000.

One of the top two beneficiaries of such Fannie Mae-Freddie Mac political contributions was then-Senator Barack Obama, Democrat of Illinois, who during only two years of service in Congress larded his campaign war chest with at least $120,349 from these mortgage monsters.

Republican lawmakers also received contributions from Fannie and Freddie, although usually in smaller amounts. Most beneficiaries from both parties held seats on committees that could influence these entities.

Senator Dodd and Congressman Frank chaired committees with regulatory authority over Fannie Mae and Freddie Mac, yet took their money with no concern that this might be perceived as a conflict of interest, or even a bribe or kickback.

Political Profiteers

These quasi-public entities have also been used to pour other easy cash into prominent Democrat pockets. Rahm Emanuel, President Obama's White House

Chief of Staff until October 2010 and currently the Mayor of Chicago, was appointed to the board of Freddie Mac by a departing President Clinton in 2000. Emanuel was paid at least $320,000 for the onerous work of attending six board meetings per year on this patronage job.

When scandals arose concerning campaign contributions and accounting irregularities involving Freddie Mac during Emanuel's tenure as a director there, the Clinton Administration stonewalled Freedom of Information Act requests for Freddie Mac documents that critics said might have incriminated Emanuel.

Emanuel resigned from Freddie Mac's board in 2001 to run for Congress. During his brief time as an Illinois Congressman, Emanuel also pocketed more than $51,000 in Fannie and Freddie campaign contributions.

Emanuel is famous for spelling out the chief political tactic of the Obama Administration: "You never want a serious crisis to go to waste. What I mean by that is that it's an opportunity to do things you could not do before."

However the money Emanuel received from Freddie Mac is small compared to how other Democrat political profiteers have done with Fannie and Freddie.

Jamie Gorelick, President Clinton's Deputy Attorney General, was appointed Vice Chair of Freddie Mac and earned a reported $26 Million.

Longtime Democratic insider James Johnson was CEO of Freddie Mac for seven years before serving as head of Senator Obama's Vice-Presidential selection committee. He got a reported $21 Million from Freddie Mac.

Franklin Delano Raines was Assistant Director of President Carter's Domestic Policy Staff from 1977 until 1979. In 1996 he retired as Fannie Mae's Vice Chairman to become President Clinton's Director of the U.S. Office of Management and Budget. In 1999 he returned to Fannie Mae as its CEO, where he resumed his influence on its controversial lending policies.

Raines reportedly walked away from Fannie Mae with $90 Million in salary and bonuses he had maximized by, among other things, pushing this entity to take on large numbers of what proved to be risky loans.

Raines and Johnson both denied that they were "members of Mr. Obama's political circle" as a *Washington Post* editorial claimed. Raines insisted that he had merely "gotten a couple of calls" from the Obama campaign and had given it advice on "general housing, economic issues."

Endless Spending

In September 2008 both Fannie and Freddie were placed under the conservatorship of the Federal Housing Finance Agency (FHFA). Both continue to function.

Rep. Barney Frank, then-Chairman of the House Financial Services Committee, in a 2010 interview on CNBC described the two mortgage giants as a "public policy instrument....a kind of public utility."

While private banks were attacked for paying bonuses to their executives, Fannie and Freddie got little heat in 2009 for their million-dollar retention bonuses for their top executives.

On Christmas Eve 2009, the U.S. Treasury announced a "taxpayer massacre lifting the $400 Billion cap on potential losses for Fannie Mae and Freddie Mac as well as the limits on what the failed companies can borrow," reported the *Wall Street Journal*. "The Treasury is hoping no one notices...."

In 2010 the Obama Administration announced that it was bailing out Fannie and Freddie to the tune of about $150 Billion. But these entities continue to acquire toxic assets from other banks, and to bleed red ink that taxpayers will be bled to replace. Fannie and Freddie have, in effect, been given unlimited spending authority to absorb toxic debts.

Although President Obama signed into law a 2,300-page bill to regulate American financial institutions, that bill contained NO NEW REGULATIONS over Fannie Mae or Freddie Mac, entities that played a huge role in bringing on the Great Recession.

Ironically, one entity eliminated by this financial reform law was the Office of Thrift Supervision, which had played a role in supervising Fannie and Freddie after the crisis began.

It seems grimly funny that the government office charged with overseeing thrift(s) is the one axed by President Obama.

Bank Robbery Obama-Style

The Federal Government's stake in keeping Fannie and Freddie solvent eventually climbed to around $187.5 Billion, alongside many private investors who had been talked into helping fund these struggling banks.

"By early 2012, Fannie and Freddie started to make money. Lots of it," wrote *Wall Street Journal* reporter David Skeel in 2014. "Thanks to a recovering real-estate market and the absence of any real competitors, their profits would eventually be big enough to pay the [required]10% dividend to the government and still have profits left over." [85]

"In August 2012, Treasury did something truly outrageous," wrote Skeel. "It restructured the deal to make sure that Fannie and Freddie's other shareholders could never get a penny of these profits. Under the new arrangement known as the Third Amendment, any profits are subject to a 'net worth sweep.' In short, the 10% dividend due the U.S. Treasury was changed to 100% – forever.... Thanks to astonishingly duplicitous behavior by the federal government, [these private investors] may never get another dime from their investment."

Two government entities, as Skeel explains, simply got together and discussed cutting off the private shareholders' share of profits from the two banks, as revealed in a memo discovered as part of a lawsuit by investors who believe that this was an illegal "taking" of their property.

This is all the more outrageous because Obama Administration officials, after discussing a cutoff of their profits, continued to encourage private investors to sink their money into Fannie and Freddie.

Skeel predicts that the private shareholders will win in court and "fare better than other investors (such as Chrysler's senior lenders) who have been blindsided by the government's growing penchant for picking winners and losers, regardless of the law."

"An Act of Expropriation"

In the Chrysler bankruptcy, President Obama simply shoved aside and threatened the secured bondholders, then gave what centuries of legal precedent should have made their share of the company to his political allies in the United Auto Workers, one of the biggest union contributors to the Democratic Party.

Is it any wonder that investors now think twice about putting their money into American companies while a capitalism-hating Progressive community organizer occupies the White House?

What Obama Administration officials did at Fannie and Freddie was "in essence an act of expropriation," wrote Skeel. "Worse, the new arrangement gives the government a strong incentive to maintain Fannie and Freddie's privileged and dominant position in the mortgage market rather than reforming mortgage finance."

As Karl Marx and Friedrich Engels wrote in 1848 in *The Communist Manifesto*, one of the 10 best ways to destroy capitalism is for government to seize power over all lending and credit. Imposing raw government control over the two banks, Fannie and Freddie, which now own or guarantee roughly 50 percent of new American mortgages, is a huge step towards this Marxist objective. The profits from these two banks now go to enrich and enlarge the government.

Believe it or not, a government program called Affordable Advantage in five states – Idaho, Illinois, Massachusetts, Minnesota and Wisconsin – soon again began providing mortgages to poor people who paid no money down.

State agencies in this program, as the *New York Times* reported in September 2010, "buy the loans from lenders, then sell them as securities to Fannie Mae. Because the government now owns 80 percent of Fannie Mae, taxpayers are on the hook if the loans go bad." [86]

Unless structural changes are made to these GSEs, we can expect more taxpayer losses.

Radical Reinvestment

Democrats have other ways to benefit from the CRA housing policies launched by President Carter and massively enlarged by President Clinton. These policies have become, both directly and indirectly, a rich source of seed money for radical community activists, including young Barack Obama.

Such activists have become the shock troops of the Democratic Party, especially in inner cities. They propagandize poor residents with messages of class warfare, register them to vote (sometimes packing voter rolls with ghost voters as well), and get people to fill out absentee ballots or transport them to the polling place on election day.

The best known of such groups was ACORN, the Association of Community Organizations for Reform Now.

Founded in 1970 by two 1960s New Left activist veterans of Students for a Democratic Society (SDS), ACORN pursued several agendas, the two biggest being voter registration and housing rights.

While a community organizer in Chicago, Barack Obama held seminars to teach radical techniques to ACORN leaders. Mr. Obama also was one of several lawyers representing ACORN in a motor-voter legal case. For nearly two years Mr. Obama was Illinois head of a voter registration organization that was one of almost 100 groups run by ACORN.

Over the years left-liberal local, state and federal politicians and bureaucrats have funneled taxpayer money to ACORN and its many organizations.

When Bill Clinton was near the end of his presidency, the Department of Housing and Urban Development estimated, ACORN in the 2000 budget year received $42 Million taxpayer dollars.

Congress' House Oversight and Government Reform Committee estimated that between 1994 and 2009 ACORN received at least $53 Million in taxpayer dollars.

Squeezing the Banks

Both sides of the aisle in Congress became familiar with ACORN. In 1991 the radical group staged a two-day takeover of the House Banking Committee hearing room to protest attempts to weaken President Carter's CRA, which had already become the most powerful leftist tool for transferring private property to the poor.

Adept in the confrontation tactics of Chicago radical Saul Alinsky – the same community organizer about whom Hillary Clinton wrote her college thesis – ACORN was quick to smear or demean any who stood in the way of what its leaders wanted.

Banking giants "Chase Manhattan and J.P. Morgan donated hundreds of thousands of dollars to ACORN," according to an investigation by Michelle Minton of the Competitive Enterprise Institute, "at about the same time they were to apply for permission to merge and needed to comply with CRA regulations."

Fannie Mae and Freddie Mac donated funds to ACORN and its organizations. These entities also bought bank mortgages of Ninja borrowers if those borrowers had paid to take "mortgage counseling," and ACORN pocketed that loot squeezed from poor borrowers by becoming one of the nation's biggest mortgage counselors.

After his election, President Barack Obama talked for a time as if, despite allegations that ACORN was guilty of widespread voter registration fraud, he would give this radical organization a major role in the 2010 U.S. Census and channel up to $8 Billion of taxpayer money into ACORN coffers.

This sparked loud objections because a dishonest Census count could be used to put more congressional districts in Democrat-dominated places and fewer in Republican-majority places, thereby tilting reapportionment leftward and rigging future Congresses by giving an unfair advantage to Democrats.

ACORN soon became too much of a pariah for President Obama to bankroll. Among the factors discrediting the leftist organization were secretly-made videotapes of ACORN office employees offering ways to break various laws. The brother of ACORN's founder was caught embezzling almost a million dollars from the organization's tax-exempt coffers.

Perhaps the final nail in ACORN's coffin was its firing of employees who attempted to unionize. These employees testified that ACORN bosses expected them to work 54 hours per week for a yearly salary of $22,000.

ACORN sought, but failed to get, an exemption from minimum wage laws. This left-wing organization was recruiting the poor and, despite its sizable cash flow, was keeping these workers poor.

Good news for these radicals is that President Obama's funding for Obamacare bankrolls a huge number of jobs for "navigators" to help people find their way in this confusing, gigantic program. Investigative reporters have found that these new jobs – which pay $45 per hour and give "navigators" access to clients' confidential medical information – are somehow often going to former ACORN operatives.

"Tear Them Down"

Capitalism defeated Communism in the marketplace of the real world. One reason was that a socialist command economy run by a few government planners lacks the sophisticated and complex natural feedback mechanisms of a free marketplace. Without such information, socialist bosses make foolish decisions.

This happens because Progressive government planners presume that they are smarter than the free market and try to impose their will.

This is what has happened with President Obama and his liberal predecessors trying to command American banking and housing.

And compounding their errors have been left-liberal ideology and partisan opportunism.

In the name of social equality, Presidents Carter, Clinton and Obama have showered privilege and favoritism on groups that just happen to vote overwhelmingly for Democratic candidates and in other ways advance the agenda of the Democratic Party.

To a man with a hammer (and sickle), every problem looks like a nail. To the worshipper of Big Government like Barack Obama, the only solution he sees to every problem is more taxes, more regulation, and more power in the hands of government...especially to solve problems that excessive government caused.

The logical corollary to this in Mr. Obama's ideology is that nothing is acceptable that makes government smaller or weaker (unless it shrinks and weakens only the U.S. military). This explains his unwillingness even to consider free market solutions to today's problems.

"The administration made a bet that a rising economy would solve the housing problem and now they are out of chips," a former Clinton Administration housing official, Howard Glaser, told the *New York Times*. "They are deeply worried and don't really know what to do."

What President Obama has turned to is the example of other past and present left-liberals such as President Franklin Delano Roosevelt.

During the Great Depression FDR's solution for poor farmers was a mix of policies that included price supports, subsidies for not growing crops, and the deliberate destruction of excess food supply.

In a world with starving people, millions of gallons of milk were poured down drains so that the milk that remained would fetch higher prices for farmers.

If this seems crazy, then consider the housing deconstruction plans left-liberals are contemplating and already implementing.

Government-Made Ghost Towns

Douglas Duncan, the vice president and chief economist for Fannie Mae, in 2010 proposed that the problem with American home prices is that too big a supply of homes for sale exists, along with a "shadow inventory" of foreclosed homes owned by banks.

Duncan's solution in a chilled economy where many are homeless: "Some of that shadow inventory could have to be torn down," the *Washington Post* quotes him as saying.

"It's un-American to think about tearing down housing," Duncan told a Texas gathering of journalists. "But we have a long history of ghost towns." Yes, the ghosts of what we left behind continue to haunt today's crisis.

The City of Detroit has begun to bulldoze much of its abandoned housing as a way to make what remains more valuable and neighborhoods more livable. We discussed Detroit's situation at length and in depth in our 2013 book *The Great Withdrawal*.

Meanwhile, liberals find ways to feed the vultures of the Great Unraveling.

During the crisis savvy contractors from around the country had been snapping up abandoned homes in Detroit for anywhere from $1 to $2,500.

They then turned to the government and offered to rent these homes to the poor. The government obliged, taking over responsibility for each home while paying the contractors at least $700 per month out of taxpayer money.

In less than four months the contractor owned the property, owed virtually nothing in property taxes because of each house's low purchase price, and thereafter has been pocketing at least $8,400 per year as pure gravy from houses bought for as little as $1.

It helps, of course, to be a favored government insider or crony when seeking such opportunities. But in cases like Detroit's, one persistent idea of modern "Progressive entrepreneurship" in America consists of finding and milking government programs funded by taxpayers.

This is the brave new world that community organizers such as Barack Obama created, a bleak and bankrupt urban rustbelt wasteland in which the government-privileged few pick the pockets of the many working taxpayers.

All Fall Down

Outside of today's ruling elite and their circle of media comrades, saner voices can yet be heard.

"Housing needs to go back to reasonable levels," said Anthony B. Sanders, a real estate finance professor at George Mason University. "If we keep trying to stimulate the market, that's the definition of insanity."

The problem with housing, many free market economists now say, is that President Obama's ill-conceived stimulus and other rescue efforts never let the "housing bubble" fully deflate.

Mr. Obama is spending hundreds of billions of taxpayer dollars to prop up an artificial situation that sooner or later will collapse.

Even the *New York Times* has quoted economists who said "Let it collapse."

"We have had enough artificial support and need to let the free market do its thing," housing analyst Ivy Zelman told the *New York Times*.

The message from such experts is clear: let the free market determine true house values, even if these are lower than today's reduced prices.

Let the free market end today's economic uncertainties by pulling away the government props so homes can be purchased by people who have earned the right to own them.

Recent Progressive housing policies are the biggest cause of the Great Recession and of the financial nightmare of millions of homeowners.

Herded into Home Mortgages

The roots of the Great Recession also reach further back – to President Richard Nixon's final breaking of the U.S. Dollar's link to gold, and even back to 1913, the same year the Federal Reserve Board and Income Tax began.

In 1913 the U.S. Government offered a surprising compensation to citizens for its newborn Fed seizing control of America's money supply and the government imposing an income tax.

The government made interest on loans tax-deductible at the federal level. This deductibility applied to home mortgages as well as other loans, including those that had nothing to do with business.

Until 1986, Americans could deduct the interest on their credit card balances and other borrowing from their taxable income. Government repealed most of this, but it kept the mortgage interest deduction in place.

By ending the level playing field for deducting all interest, politicians created a powerful mortgage incentive that virtually herded people into buying a home instead of other things.

Government and the Federal Reserve Board then put the value of those homes on a roller coaster of easy money and artificial low interest rates while at the same time strong-arming banks into giving millions of mortgages to Ninjas who were unlikely ever to pay back these loans.

People also could sell a house and owe no capital gains tax on their profit so long as within two years of the sale they rolled that profit into the purchase of another home.

This tax law made buying a home "on time" possible for many who otherwise could not afford it. Its rollover provision made homes a good way to save money while moving up.

In a pre-CRA era, buying a home was a serious decision. A buyer seeking a mortgage had to have excellent credit, a proven income, and typically the savings to pony up 20 percent of the home's cost as a down payment.

These rules gave great stability to the housing market. Banks knew that the borrower was a good credit risk. The down payment invested the buyer in a home, making it costly to walk away. Those who stopped making monthly payments would lose the house, including their equity paid into it. The down payment also minimized bank concerns that the house might lose value.

In Canada these tried-and-true old rules still largely apply. Canada did not plunge into huge housing or banking crises, except insofar as America's huge economic problems have spilled across the Canadian border to affect their income and unemployment rate.

American mortgage interest tax deductibility nudged millions of people into buying rather than renting their homes.

This was widely seen as positive. Homeowners tended to be more involved with their communities, in part because of a desire that their property taxes be spent wisely and that public schools remain good. Home ownership was a key to the "Father Knows Best" values of family, faith, friendly neighbors, social cohesion and rootedness.

Governments benefited not only from property taxes but also from citizens holding the bulk of their wealth in a form that could not easily be put in a suitcase and carried out of the country beyond the grasp of American tax collectors. Homeowners who stopped paying property tax would find their homes seized by the local government landlord.

Father Knew Best

The "Leave It to Beaver" world of the 1950s was in many ways astonishingly different from that of today's young people.

In, say, 1954 a typical family paid two percent of what it earned as income tax. The average income was $3,960. A large new car cost $1,700. A new home cost $10,250 and was viewed as a secure, stable investment, not a way to get rich in a hurry.

The U.S. Dollar was tied to gold, which had a steady value of $35 per ounce. Inflation during the 1950s was very low, which is typical of what happens with a gold-backed currency. What cost $1 in 1950 cost only $1.15 in 1960 – which is an annual inflation rate of only 1.5 percent.

Even during the volatile 1960s, with Presidents Johnson and Nixon printing money to fund American forces in Southeast Asia, the gold-backed dollar helped keep inflation in check.

In 1970, just prior to Mr. Nixon's abandonment of the Bretton Woods agreement link between the dollar and gold, it cost consumers only $1.31 to buy what they could have purchased for one dollar in 1960; this measure of inflation during the 1960s grew by only three percent per year during these years of social change.

This meant that a family could live comfortably with one wage earner. Women could choose to stay home and be with their children. Few children were "latchkey kids" who came home from school to an empty house with little adult supervision.

By 2014 much has changed. Today's "real world" price inflation rate is 6-10 percent, as calculated using pre-gimmick accounting by John Williams of *ShadowStats.com*. Today both husband and wife have jobs. The lower-income spouse – the husband in 40 percent of such households – works mostly to pay taxes and rising prices.

With both parents away all workday, their children become "latchkey kids." The bonds of family values are weakened. Children are raised less by their parents and more by peers and teachers in government schools, whose values become more influential.

The weakening dollar caused much of this underlying inflation, but it was masked by several factors. Feminism, for example, persuaded many women that going to work asserted their rights and abilities and made them the equal of wage-earning men.

This both disguised and caused inflation, because the higher family income brought more dollars to the supermarket to buy the same supply of potatoes – and thus the Law of Supply and Demand simply drove up prices. It took more dollars to buy those potatoes.

Running in Place

The two-income family has found that rising prices leave them worse off. They are now trapped with prices that require two incomes instead of the one that during the 1950s had been enough.

In 2009 the average income was $44,000, but bouts of inflation since President Nixon broke the dollar's gold anchor meant that a shopper now needed $7.98 to buy what cost only $1 in 1954. In 2009 an ordinary new car cost $28,400. The average new home nationwide cost $210,000.

Taxes bite hard on middle-class wallets. In California a typical resident can lose 20 percent or more of income to federal income taxes, several percent more in state income tax, plus a sales tax of about 8.75 percent on almost everything purchased.

California cities, in violation of Proposition 13's limit on direct property taxes, typically charge property-related homeowner fees such as street "tree-trimming" charges that used to be covered by the property tax.

This appears to be part of a long-term government approach to pocket the old taxes, then gradually find ways to charge taxpayers a second time with separate fees for each government service. And on top of this come hidden taxes that raise the price of everything.

By one estimate, 37 percent of the cost of a new home in California comes from hidden government taxes and regulations. It is not free, for example, when a community restricts land use because of environmental concerns. This can make every new house smaller in size and much larger in price.

Older Americans grew up thinking of America as a country that cherishes free enterprise. Truth be told, our country has the heaviest business income taxes – 35 percent – of any advanced industrial nation in the world. Add this to the average 5 percent state income tax on business, and companies can lose a crushing 40 percent of their net income to tax collectors.

While President Obama advocates imposing even higher taxes on American companies, other advanced nations have been reducing their business taxes – and seeing their economies improve because of lower taxes.

The heavy U.S. tax burden makes it hard for American companies to succeed internationally against the advantage held by lower-taxed competitors. Our taxes are also hard on American consumers, who pay these soaring taxes that are passed on to them invisibly in the higher price tags of products.

The greedy Progressive politicians who pocket these sky-high business taxes are quick to make class warfare attacks against "greedy" companies that charge such high prices. In truth, businesses have simply been forced to be both taxpayers and tax collectors for the welfare state.

Fading Freedom

In 2009, the year Barack Obama's presidency began, but before his policies had taken full force, the Heritage Foundation/*Wall Street Journal* annual *Index of Economic Freedom* ranked the United States as the sixth most economically free country on Earth – below only Hong Kong, Singapore, Australia, Ireland and New Zealand.

In 2014, the United States has plummeted to Number 12 on this list, surpassed by countries we ranked above in 2009: Canada, Switzerland, Chile, Estonia, Mauritius and even the Scandinavian welfare state Denmark.

We have also fallen from being among the "Fully Free" nations to being "Mostly Free," barely above Number 13, the tiny Persian Gulf Islamic island Kingdom of Bahrain.

"The U.S. is the only country to have recorded a loss of economic freedom each of the past seven years," the *Index* analysts wrote in 2014.

"Substantial expansion in the size and scope of government, including through new and costly regulations in areas like finance and health care, has contributed significantly to the erosion of U.S. economic freedom," they wrote. "The growth of government has been accompanied by increasing cronyism that has undermined the rule of law and perceptions of fairness." [87]

American families may have a big-screen TV, iPods, cell phones and other technological advances. But in many ways we are poorer and have a less bright economic future than we did six decades ago in 1954.

What President Nixon cost America when he severed the dollar's anchor was a U.S. Dollar that was literally as good as gold.

Vladimir Lenin, founder of the Communist Soviet Union, said that the way to destroy the capitalist bourgeoisie was to "grind them down between the wheels of taxation and inflation."

This is precisely what liberal presidents since Richard Nixon have done.

In 1975, however, FDR's ban on gold ownership ended, so people once again are free to protect themselves by creating their own personal gold standard.

Our Squeezed Middle Class

The aim of left-liberals and so-called Progressives, with the 1913 establishment of the Federal Reserve Board and the income tax – and continuing today – apparently has been to create disintegrating paper money....all the better to tax you with.

Economic historian G. Edward Griffin explains this provocative idea in his history of the Federal Reserve Board, *The Creature from Jekyll Island*:

"Inflation has now been institutionalized at a fairly constant 5% per year. This has been determined to be the optimum level for generating the most revenue without causing public alarm. A 5% devaluation applies, not only to the money earned this year, but to all that is left over from previous years. At the end of the first year, a dollar is worth 95 cents. At the end of the second year, the 95 cents is reduced again by 5%, leaving its worth at 90 cents, and so on. By the time a person has worked 20 years, the government will have confiscated 64% of every dollar he saved over those years. By the time he has worked 45 years, the hidden tax will be 90%. The government will take virtually everything a person saves over a lifetime."

Our Nixonian no-longer-gold-anchored paper dollar is losing value every decade to inflation, and this is happening not by accident but by design to those who keep their savings in politician paper promissory fiat dollars.

Government tax and regulatory policies are snatching away our earnings, in part by making almost everything we buy more expensive.

Because of this, the American working class has scarcely increased its real purchasing power in almost 40 years.

And this grand paper dollar con game uses other tools as well. Liberals and Progressives prey on human envy and covetousness. "Let's tax the rich who have more than you do," they say.

Today the successful Middle Class American, whose dollar income (but not purchasing power) has risen mostly because of inflation, now pays a confiscatory tax rate that was originally supposed to rob only the rich.

As a June 2014 *USA Today* study found, it now takes an income of $130,000 per year to live what we used to call the Middle Class "American Dream" of owning a home with a picket fence and sending two kids to college.

Large parts of President Obama's laws include tax and fee increases that are deliberately NOT indexed for inflation. The coming inflation will soon make you "rich," just as the Alternative Minimum Tax (AMT) has done for millions of middle class Americans, and subject you to these government money grabs.

Altitude Sickness

By 2005 the median sales price of a single-family home had risen in less than a decade by 79 percent in New York, by 110 percent in Los Angeles, and by 127 percent in San Diego. This, most did not know, was close to their peak.

Americans briefly felt wealthy as, in places such as Los Angeles, the price of an average decent suburban home began to approach $1 Million.

America briefly may have had new millions of "millionaires," at least on paper.

The trouble was that we never had enough buyers with a million dollars to buy homes at such stratospheric prices.

Those soaring real estate prices got so high so fast that people found themselves owning homes that at their income they could no longer afford to buy.

Many parents in Southern California felt the strange anguish of seeing their adult children move away because young married couples eager to start a family of their own could not afford even a small "starter" house in the communities where they grew up.

People thought that they had become wealthy by a rising tide that lifted all property prices. But when they looked down, they saw that they were high atop an unstable gigantic price wave that was about to crash into the rocky shore of reality.

What will happen when people wake up and realize that - in inflation-adjusted dollars - they are earning little more today than they did three decades ago?

Castles in the Air

Sometime around 2005-2006 a mass hypnotic spell began to break, and when it did the vast bubble of stratospheric property prices popped.

Real estate prices simply could rise no higher into the unbreathable thin air where only the wealthy could afford to buy homes.

As with the stock market mania in 1929, or the 17th Century Dutch tulip mania, people had been paying sky-high prices on margin, mortgage money borrowed with little or nothing down, betting that prices would keep rising, pay off these debts, and make them winners.

Cable television channels such as HGTV launched programs encouraging people to "flip" homes – to buy them with small down payments, then after a few months of cosmetic improvement to resell them for tens or hundreds of thousands more.

This was a get-rich-quick scheme, one of many that flourished around the country, that promised wealth without much work. For those who grew up in a consumer culture and political culture whose propaganda told them wealth was their birthright, this was a seductive come-on they were all too eager to embrace.

Millions were playing musical chairs, expecting to unload their risk onto the next home buyer and pocket huge profits from this speculation. But when the music suddenly stopped, many were caught holding heavily-mortgaged homes they could neither afford to keep nor profitably sell.

Awakening from this mass delusion of wealth was chilling, because many had believed it and spent money as if they were millionaires.

Lending Frenzy

While housing prices skyrocketed until around 2006, televisions were full of ads urging people to take out home equity loans. "You can borrow up to 125 percent of your home's appraised value," the message went. "You can borrow without documenting your income."

"In the 2004-2006 period," writes former president of the Federal Reserve Bank of Cleveland Jerry L. Jordan, "MEWs (mortgage equity withdrawals) reached 9% of disposable income, which....fueled an extraordinary boom in auto sales, furnishings, appliances, consumer imports of all kinds, as well as remittances to other countries."

Remittances? Lending standards for mortgages became so loose that experts estimate as many as five million illegal aliens may have joined the throngs receiving home loans. Banks and the government, of course, refuse to release such information and thereby make the exact number impossible to document.

Plastic Paradise

Riding this rapid rise in home prices and subsequent borrowing boom, banks and credit card companies flooded middle-class mailboxes with offers. At the height of this frenzy, families with average income and a decent credit score might get an offer to borrow $100,000 on their credit card with no fee at Zero percent interest for a year or more.

Many rationalized borrowing such an amount with the belief that they could put it in the bank at five percent interest, and pay it back after a year while pocketing $5,000 in bank interest.

But seductive lenders were betting that such money will "burn a hole in most people's pockets," that borrowers will spend at least part of it, be unable to repay in full, and get stuck with high credit card interest rates.

This hallucinatory "wealth effect" prompted many to spend their home equity loans speculating on future stock increases. Was this what fueled the then-rise to more than 14,000 on the stock market?

The Federal Reserve's dumping of trillions of easily-conjured fiat dollars would likewise push the market above 17,000 by mid-2014, despite lack of positive economic news to explain this Indian-rope-trick stock rise.

Home equity lenders stood to gain a valuable house if their borrowers defaulted, or to earn reasonable interest if they did not.

Many homeowners, of course, fell into the trap of borrowing on one credit card to pay down another. Many had little choice, because real inflation-adjusted Middle Class wages continued decades of decline. For many, this became a downward spiral of debt that devoured or cratered their American Dream.

Progressive Social Engineering

President Jimmy Carter signed a law that gave government the means to strong-arm banks into making billions of dollars of loans to uncreditworthy individuals who were in politically-favored groups. These coerced bank loans, which have been a kind of expropriation from bank shareholders and short-changed, fee-bitten depositors, precipitated the Great Recession whose effects continue to drag down the U.S. economy.

This Community Reinvestment Act (CRA) was a Progressive ideological effort to make banks absorb much of the cost of providing housing for low income Democratic Party voters. It worked so well that today, after the continuing crisis it set in motion, home ownership is at a 30+ year low.

President Obama in 2013 had resumed strong-arming banks to do such lending.... and by mid-2014 banks were, indeed, giving away subprime mortgages again in growing numbers. Government simply has too much power to reward or ruin banks. The President's wish is their command. Welcome to CRA 2.0.

In 2014 Mr. Obama has taken Progressive social engineering to troubling new levels with a Housing and Urban Development (HUD) effort to enforce a policy called an "Affirmatively Furthering Fair Housing" rule.

"The Orwellian-sounding regulation...would force some 1,200 municipalities to redraw zoning maps to racially diversify suburban neighborhoods," wrote *Investor's Business Daily* in June 2014.

"Under the scheme, HUD plans to map every U.S. neighborhood by race and publish 'geospatial data' pinpointing racial imbalances," writes *IBD*. "Areas deemed overly segregated will be forced to change their zoning laws to allow construction of subsidized and other affordable housing to bring more low-income minorities into 'white suburbs.'"

"The crusade has already started in New York's Westchester County, where HUD is withholding millions of dollars in community development block grants until the area relaxes zoning rules and builds 750 affordable housing units," says *IBD*. "Aurora, Ill., is under order to build 100 such units. Suburban counties in California, Texas and Iowa are under similar HUD order. And they're just the tip of the iceberg."

"This has zero to do with housing discrimination, which has been illegal since 1968," opines *Investor's Business Daily*. "This is about redistribution of resources. It's also about political redistricting, a backdoor attempt by Democrats to gerrymander voting districts." [88]

Spreading the Wealth

Progressives, we must never forget, hate the suburbs. America has long been divided into two political values – pro-city like Alexander Hamilton, who saw cities as dynamic productive places, or pro-countryside and anti-city like Thomas Jefferson, who saw cities as places of corruption and immorality.

In America today the biggest cities mostly have Democratic mayors who stay in power by buying support with the goodies of a welfare state. Big cities tend to impose high taxes on local businesses and successful residents to pay for these goodies. Therefore businesses and successful individuals are inclined to flee what many of today's big cities have become.

"Modern cities," said architect Frank Lloyd Wright, "have banks and prostitution and not much else."

The suburbs, beginning after World War II, were where city dwellers moved to escape urban crime and decay. This infuriated Progressives, who saw suburbs as tax havens just beyond the greedy grasp of city tax collectors. Without such taxes, it has been difficult to fund their welfare city-states of many takers and few makers.

President Obama has waged relentless war against a largely-Caucasian suburban America that he and his Progressive party do not control, as journalist Stanley Kurtz explored in his 2012 book *Spreading the Wealth: How Obama is Robbing the Suburbs to Pay for the Cities*. [89]

We should see Mr. Obama's use of HUD to attack the suburban communities around cities as part of this ongoing ideological assault on those who vote with their feet to flee high-tax welfare states, whether national or local. We should also see this motive behind President Obama's encouragement of mass youth migration from Latin America, and his 2014 busing and flying of these tens of thousands of Latinos without warning into targeted towns and suburbs throughout the nation. [90]

Progressives have long felt frustrated because America lacked an essential ingredient in Marxist class warfare – a Proletariat, a working class that felt it had nothing to lose and a world to win by overthrowing the capitalist business class. In socially-mobile America, workers have aspired not to overthrow the rich but to join them.

How can Progressive class warfare activists like Mr. Obama create their desired socialist-Marxist "Dictatorship of the Proletariat" without a Proletariat?

Mr. Obama appears to have found an answer. If such people will not grow naturally in the traditional thriving soil of America, he will import them from Honduras and El Salvador as shock troops in his Progressive class war.

The more than 50,000 Latino youngsters who came flooding into America in mid-2014 are not refugees. They are Mr. Obama's recruits.

Homeland

Ground down by the killing power of high taxes and heavy regulation, many Americans feel they are being driven not only out of their homes but also out of their homeland.

Like their ancestors, who pulled up stakes and came to America seeking freedom and opportunity, millions of Americans have begun looking for a better place in the world to move.

As we explore in the next chapter, our current government is busy cutting off our avenues of escape, at least if you intend to take your savings with you to a bank in another land.

It is shocking to discover how far our government's regulatory and taxing grasp now reaches around the world.

"The belief that the fiscal state
can effectively redistribute income,
and thereby reform society
through taxation and subsidies,
has been decisively disproven.

The least egalitarian countries
are those that have tried hardest
to redistribute income:
the Soviet Union; the United States; Great Britain.

All they accomplished was to give us
the 'pork-barrel state' –
the most dangerous
degenerative disease that the body politic
is suffering from.

So far no one knows how we can get rid of
this legalized looting of the commonwealth."

– Peter F. Drucker
Post-Capitalist Society

Chapter Six
The Wars Against Tax Havens

*"I've achieved the American Dream
by moving most of my assets off shore."*

– **Roy Delgado**
Wall Street Journal cartoon caption

**No one would call a company or family evil for moving from high-tax
California to low-tax Texas. Supporters of welfare-statism, however,
speak ill of those moving from the United States to less taxing countries.
Revenue-greedy politicians have begun putting a worldwide squeeze
on foreign banks and confiscating accounts in tax havens. Their aim
is to prohibit people from "voting with their feet" (as was said of those
fleeing Communism) for more economic freedom by escaping the high
taxation of welfare-state nations.**

On July 1, 2014, the withholding rules of a new American law took effect
throughout much of the world. The law is FATCA, the Foreign Account Tax
Compliance Act, which requires foreign banks and other financial institutions to
notify the U.S. Government of any American accounts holding over $50,000.

Why would a foreign bank hand over confidential information about its American
customers to the U.S.? Because the United States has applied enormous arm-
twisting pressure to foreign governments and banks that have commercial
relationships with the U.S. to let American law impose its will on their banks.
Uncle Sam now commands banks around the world.

"An astonishing 77,000 banks and financial institutions – even some in Russia – have
registered under FATCA," wrote *Forbes* columnist Robert W. Wood in June 2014.
"The fact that 77,000 banks have registered and some 70 countries are providing
government help to the IRS means almost no foreign account is secret." [91]

Obama's FATCA Power Grab

"Hoping to avoid sanctions, threats and crushing compliance costs, institutions around the world are dumping Americans' accounts," writes former U.S. diplomat James George Jatras. Making it harder for overseas Americans and U.S. companies to find welcoming banks and other financial institutions is apparently *not* an unintended consequence of FATCA.

"Enacted in 2010 by an all-Democratic Congress with almost no legislative review and no cost/benefit analysis, FATCA was slipped into an unrelated jobs bill as a minor budgetary pay-for provision," writes Jatras.

"FATCA supposedly is aimed at 'fat cat' American tax cheats with money stashed abroad," he writes, "but [it] includes not a single provision targeting actual tax evasion."

"Instead, FATCA creates an indiscriminate NSA-style information dragnet requiring – under threat of sanctions – all non-U.S. financial institutions (banks, credit unions, insurance companies, investment and pension funds, etc.) in every country in the world to report data on all specified U.S. accounts to the IRS," writes Jatras. "No proof or even suspicion of wrongdoing is required." [92]

Ironically, FATCA itself may be illegal, according to Law Professor Allison Christians of Canada's McGill University. FATCA has been implemented by the Obama Administration using political and economic pressure. It has persuaded foreign governments to sign agreements to enforce FATCA, even where this is contrary to national privacy laws.

At least 40 of these are "Intergovernmental Agreements" (IGAs), which, in effect, are treaties between the U.S. and other countries. The United States Constitution has very specific rules for making treaties, rules that have not been followed in the case of FATCA.

Professor Christians has carefully studied all the provisions of law and regulation that the Treasury Department has invoked in an attempt to legitimize FATCA.

"None of these sources of law contain any authorization to enter into or implement the IGAs," she says. "It is patently clear that no such authorization has been made by Congress." [93]

FATCA, says Jatras, is "another instance where the Administration not only has far exceeded its constitutional and statutory authority but has misrepresented its actions and sought to thwart Congressional inquiry into them....with, literally, incalculable impact on the American and global economy." [94]

Heidi Ho

"If only God would give me some clear sign!" filmmaker Woody Allen joked in his book *Without Feathers*, "Like making a large deposit in my name in a Swiss bank!"

Swiss banks, once famous for keeping accounts secret and hence difficult to tax [95], are now, under FATCA, registered "Foreign Financial Institutions." They are required at their own expense to identify American customers and provide the IRS with these customers' account numbers, balances, names, addresses, and U.S. identification numbers. Any American customers who do not provide such information face 30 percent withholding on their accounts.

Americans with foreign accounts exceeding $10,000 are required to file a Report of Foreign Bank and Financial Accounts (known as FBAR) form. Tax evasion can mean a $250,000 fine and five years in prison, but an FBAR failure can bring fines of up to $500,000 and up to 10 years in prison.

Is the U.S. Government tightening the screws on foreign bank accounts to gain more tax revenue? Presumably, yes.

Billions in tax revenue are said to be at stake. The Tax Justice Network used to say that $11 Trillion is hidden in private overseas accounts worldwide. Today this Progressive organization claims that the world's wealthy have $31 Trillion in accounts that have been beyond the reach of their own nation's tax collectors. This incredible amount would be nearly half the annual Gross Domestic Product of our entire planet.

Oddly, the Association of Certified Financial Crime Specialists (ACFCS) has calculated that FATCA is likely to raise only about $800 Million per year, but its full implementation will cost up to $10 Billion. It might take more than 12 years for FATCA revenues to break even with the new law's cost.

Government-Owned Americans

The United States is the only major nation that taxes citizens' income no matter where in the world they live and earn. Taxation here has been attached to citizenship, not residency, ever since Republican President Abraham Lincoln imposed our first income tax in 1861.

This helps to explain why Americans in 2013 and 2014 have been renouncing U.S. citizenship in record numbers, in part to be free of FATCA.

Many have discovered that giving up your citizenship, however, now might also require paying the Expatriation Tax, a bit like Cubans forced to buy their freedom as government-owned slaves or serfs from Cuba's Communist dictatorship.

This is how rapacious for taxes the U.S. Government has become, and the bigger our government and its dependent population get, the hungrier it gets to devour what citizens have privately saved.

Fee Enterprise

Our government is even more resistant to letting our corporations escape taxation by moving abroad or by "inversions," merging in a way that puts foreign companies on top as the corporate headquarters in a lower-tax jurisdiction.

The United States pretends to favor free enterprise, but what our Progressive rulers now demand is more like "Fee Enterprise." American corporations here pay the highest business taxes of any advanced nation on Earth – a business income tax rate of 35 percent plus an average 5 percent state business tax, which means that government skims up to 40 percent of a company's net profits right off the top.

Add all other business levies to this, and the average American company pays 46.3 percent of its income in taxes, according to the PricewaterhouseCoopers study *Paying Taxes 2014: The Global Picture: A Comparison of Tax Systems in 189 Economies Worldwide*. Ranking nations from the least business-taxed to the most, this survey ranks Canada the 8th lowest business-taxed nation on Earth, the European welfare state Denmark 12th, the United Kingdom 14th, Vladimir Putin's Russian Federation 56th, and the United States 64th with a tax burden that cripples our businesses' worldwide competitiveness. No wonder our companies feel forced to keep at least $2.1 Trillion of their earnings (and potential jobs) overseas. [96]

And to this injury, the Obama Administration adds class warfare insults.

"What we need as a nation is a new sense of economic patriotism, where we all rise or fall together," wrote Treasury Secretary Jack Lew in a July 2014 letter to the Chairman of the Senate Finance Committee Ron Wyden (D.-Oregon).

"We should not be providing support for corporations that seek to shift their profits overseas to avoid paying their fair share of taxes," wrote Lew, giving a wrong picture of what happens in such inversions. [97]

Lew's letter suggested that Congress not only ban such inversions but also make their ban retroactive to May 2014. This would *ex post facto* punish companies that had recently created legal inversions. [98]

In August 2014, Secretary Lew – who previously acknowledged that he and President Obama had no way to halt corporate overseas tax inversions – announced that he was now looking for what a *Wall Street Journal* editorial called "heretofore undiscovered legal ways" to block them. "Where's the law," the *Journal* asked, "that gives Jack Lew the power to raise taxes?" [99]

The Royal Lew

CNBC producer Jake Novak offered a wonderful riposte to Secretary Lew, a commentary in the form of a letter from the British monarch at the time of America's revolution, King George III:

"We send our hearty congratulations to the American Treasury Secretary Jack Lew for his exemplary comments about the importance of paying taxes to the government, regardless of how high and confiscatory they may be...."

"Mr. Lew's invocation of the term 'Economic Patriotism' is precisely the turn of phrase all of us at the Palace and Whitehall have been looking for to remind you colonists of your primary duty to the crown over and above this infernal 'liberty' thing we hear coming out of the mouths of traitors like Samuel Adams, John Hancock, and the colonial terrorist George Washington," says Novak's letter from King George III to Secretary Lew.

"For monarchs like us, the idea that firms or individuals might choose economic liberty over their duty to their sovereign is dangerous. So are the ridiculous notions of religious liberty, freedom of assembly, and something we're hearing about 'the pursuit of happiness'."

"Our colonial subjects, please remember that when the crown taxes your tea, playing cards, candles, raw materials, etc., we do it not for your own good, but for the protection and promotion of the throne."

"Remember that this is not a democracy or a republic. This is a kingdom – an imperial kingdom to be exact – and we will not tolerate anything but total loyalty to our throne." [100]

Novak's King George III offers to honor Secretary Lew with a knighthood for his devotion to those who rule over the people.

Corporate Loyalty Oaths

Treasury Secretary Lew "thinks we are the grapes to be squeezed to make the state's wine...that patriotism is to serve the state, not seek fulfillment for our own lives," said Fox Business News commentator and author Judge Andrew Napolitano.

Progressive journalist Jonathan Alter in August 2014 went even further than Lew's "economic patriotism" by urging President Obama to issue an Executive Order requiring all U.S. companies with government contracts to sign "non-desertion agreements," loyalty oaths pledging not to move out of the United States to avoid taxes.

Alter writes that he would also pressure companies without government contracts to sign such "non-desertion" agreements by threatening them with "public shaming...boycotts, petitions, angry shareholder meetings full of the language of patriotism." [101]

Progressives like President Obama and Mr. Alter are furious that the U.S. Supreme Court has granted corporations a measure of citizenship, including First Amendment rights of political free speech and religious protection.

Progressives want to massively tax businesses while denying them the right to speak and vote. Is this not what America's Founders denounced as "Taxation without Representation?" If corporations are not people, as those on the Left insist, then stop taxing them!

True Economic Patriotism

True patriotism, as we see it, is loyalty and devotion to America's Constitution and founding ideals.

We oppose the crime of tax evasion. We do not necessarily oppose legal and ethical tax avoidance, arranging one's affairs to reduce how much tax is legally owed. As of this writing, it can be legal for U.S. and foreign companies to merge in what is popularly called a tax inversion.

(How free are we if government tax deductions herd you, e.g., into buying an unneeded home because of tax write-offs favoring the real estate industry? Such politicized tax breaks can cause huge malinvestments in the economy.)

We believe it can be patriotic to pay as little tax as the law requires when Progressive regimes like President Obama's use our taxes to expand government, increase dependency by enlarging the welfare state, and wage unrelenting class warfare against Americans who want the same kind of small government and economic freedom as did America's Framers.

Most of our ancestors pulled up roots in their original homelands and came here in search of freedom and the right to earn and own property. American Exceptionalism exists, in part, because we are a self-selected nation whose people carry the genes of brave pioneers who moved here for religious and economic liberty.

As we explored in *The Inflation Deception*, American DNA may disproportionately carry what geneticists call D4-7 dopamine receptor alleles that predispose many of us to migration, risk-taking, novelty-seeking, exuberance, ambition and love of individual liberty and enterprise. [102]

As Progressives turn America into the sort of low-opportunity country our ancestors fled to come here, some may feel terrible, health-endangering stress and a restless impulse in their genes to again seek liberty on distant shores. The same entrepreneurial DNA that built America now drives some to seek a new haven free from oppressive regulation and taxation.

Seizing the Banks

The ancient Greeks believed that their goddess of love and beauty, Aphrodite, first came ashore on the eastern Mediterranean island of Cyprus.

Times have changed, and so has the European spirit of love and beauty. The female figure who, at least symbolically, waded ashore on a Cyprus beach in 2013 was German Chancellor Angela Merkel, a ruler of Prussian discipline.

Cypriots awoke on March 18, 2013 to find their banks closed, local ATMs drained of cash, and their savings and checking accounts inaccessible. Their bewilderment and outrage soon boiled over in angry street protests.

Imagine how you would feel if you were suddenly locked out of your bank and bank accounts. How would you pay your bills or buy food for your family if you had set nothing aside for emergencies? How and why did this happen? These are important questions, because what happened in Cyprus could soon be coming to the banks where you live.

The European Central Bank had implicitly promised to protect Eurozone bank accounts for up to 100,000 Euros – even though the ECB lacks the reserves to make such a guarantee good in a crisis – as a way to make people feel secure and not rush to withdraw their savings.

Those who seized the banks In Cyprus had forgotten this guarantee. They had planned to extract money from all Cypriot accounts, from the biggest to the smallest. Afterwards, all deposits above this "insured" amount took a 45.5 percent "haircut."

This is the latest chapter in a very ancient place. Cyprus, with its rich farmland and balmy Southern California-like climate, has been coveted by conquerors for thousands of years. The valuable metal that ancient Greeks mined there took its name from the island, *aes Cyprium*, later shortened to *Cuprum*, then *copper*.

Prior to Merkel's power play, the most recent occupiers have been Turkish troops who seized the northern third of the island in 1974. They later proclaimed it the Turkish Republic of Northern Cyprus, and remain today as an Islamic 18 percent of the partitioned island's roughly one million people. Most Cypriots are Greek Orthodox Christians.

Until 2013, the 77 percent of Cypriots who are of Greek ancestry naively assumed that what they had earned by the sweat of their brow and saved in local banks was their money. They would soon learn otherwise.

Euro Peons

The Republic of Cyprus in January 2008 joined the Eurozone and accepted the Euro as its currency, just in time for its economy to be pulled down by the Great Recession which later that year hit much of Europe and the U.S.

Like their Eurozone kin in Greece, the Greek Cypriots had a fragile economy but strong credit – because lenders assumed that Germany would bail out any Eurozone nation's debt to protect the Euro. The Cypriots borrowed heavily and invested heavily in Greece. When, with Eurozone encouragement, Greece stopped paying on its bonds, the banks of Cyprus lost billions. By March 2013 the two biggest banks of Cyprus were near bankruptcy.

The Greek Cypriot government and Cyprus' once-respected banks desperately needed a bailout and made a deal to get at least 10 Billion Euros from the "troika" – the European Commission, European Central Bank, and International Monetary Fund (IMF)

Germanic Discipline

The Eurozone was intended to have a disciplined common currency that should give Germany an advantageous trading position with neighboring, Euro-using nations. Some saw it as Germany's third attempt to conquer Europe in the 20th Century, this time with economic power instead of tanks and bayonets. [103]

What German policy miscalculated was that some Eurozone nations, especially the PIIGS – Portugal, Italy, Ireland, Greece and Spain – would be offered large loans by banks that assumed Germany would ultimately pay any such debt to keep Euro nations from defaulting. The PIIGS were intoxicated by the multi-billion-dollar credit cards they were offered as Eurozone members, and they spent like drunken teenagers, running up huge debts that they could not pay when the global economy slid into recession.

From Germany's point of view, the result has been a nightmare of more than $600 Billion worth of bailouts, with never-ending pressure to do more. To get this money, the Cypriot government agreed to ante up another 5.8 Billion Euros itself – to be raised by imposing a progressive "levy" on all island bank accounts...6.75 percent on accounts up to 100,000 Euros, 9.9 percent on accounts above 100,000 Euros, and 15 percent on accounts above 500,000 Euros.

The Eurocrats of the troika blessed this deal to confiscate a hefty chunk of all Republic of Cyprus bank accounts, despite the Cypriot government guarantee against loss of up to 100,000 Euros in all bank accounts – similar to the Federal Deposit Insurance Corporation protection for American bank accounts.

Government's Needs

Like American Progressives, these Eurocrats assumed that governments' needs are always superior to individual rights.

Americans are usually shocked when they read the European Declaration of Rights, because every specified human right ends with a clause saying that it can be ignored whenever government "needs" to do so. American rights, by comparison, are what our Declaration of Independence calls "unalienable" and come from the Creator, not from self-serving governments and politicians. This Cypriot confiscation was exactly what the newly-elected President of Cyprus had explicitly promised only two weeks earlier that he would never do. Imagine, after this promise, learning that a hunk of money equivalent to several years' interest would be seized from your savings.

Furious citizens demanded to know why ordinary people were being robbed to cover the debts to foreign bankers – especially German bankers – that had been incurred by Cypriot politicians and banks.

The troika, it seemed, had invaded Cyprus – like so many other invaders over millennia – and was looting the savings of ordinary citizens, merely because politicians needed the money and therefore felt entitled to take it.

In today's world of debased, inflatable fiat money and debased, rapacious politicians, our savings and retirement bank accounts are not necessarily safe.

You cannot trust government fiat money and insurance promises – whether from the Economic and Monetary Union [EMU] of the European Union or from the United States Government – to secure the value of your savings. [104] You must do that yourself, by using means that have protected individual savings for thousands of years.

Government owns your bank account, according to the European Central Bank, the European Commission and the International Monetary Fund (IMF). For the Mediterranean island of Cyprus, this "troika" affirmed in March 2013 that private bank accounts – originally to have included even mom-and-pop accounts of less than 100,000 Euros that had been guaranteed against loss by the Cypriot government – can be looted through a one-time levy if government decides it needs the money.

The precedent of Cyprus creates uncertainty about the legal status and individual ownership rights of *all* private property in the 17-nation Eurozone, a legal precedent that governments outside of Europe also might soon use because today's politicians as never before are addicted to taxing and spending.

In Cyprus, people could see that today's Santa Claus welfare states come into our lives not only to deliver gifts, but also to loot and steal. As renowned British journalist Ambrose Evans-Pritchard wrote, Cyprus "has finally killed the myth" that Big Government "is benign." [105]

The Cyprus Omen

Like the Black Plague that killed up to 60 percent of Europe's people seven centuries ago, a financial "Green Plague" spreading economic contagion has been unleashed by the account looting in Cyprus.

The Green Plague's first symptom is a loss of trust in government and banking. Its second symptom is a desire to withdraw one's cash and flee....or, at a minimum, not to make additional deposits. In the U.S., the first "immune response" to news of the bank account seizures in Cyprus was a brief triple-digit plummet in the stock market, and a double-digit surge in the price of gold.

This contagion has the potential to plunge Europe into recession or depression, an economic death spiral that, in the interconnected global economy, could quickly drag China and the U.S. down, too.

The precedent Cyprus has set is for government closing banks without warning, and then announcing that it is confiscating depositor money.

Cyprus also set precedents for government imposing controls that restrict how much money an account holder can withdraw or remove from the country. It allowed the government to turn liquid accounts into fixed-term accounts that depositors cannot withdraw for years without paying a substantial penalty.

Under the deal reached on March 25, 2013, Cyprus' second-biggest bank, known as Laiki or the Cyprus Popular Bank, was restructured into two entities, a "good" bank for insured deposits of 100,000 Euros or less, which would remain intact and be moved to the larger Bank of Cyprus, and a "bad" bank for deposits too big to be fully insured. For the "bad" bank's depositors, their "haircut" means a loss of 20 percent, 40 percent or even more of what was in their bank account.

This will not inspire confident Eurozone investing. In other struggling Eurozone economies such as Greece, Spain, Portugal and Italy, the example of Cyprus could prompt millions of local and foreign depositors to take the money out of their bank accounts before money-hungry politicians do. The memory of Cyprus will also deter others from putting new money into European banks. [106]

The Template

Cyprus is causing a deficit of trust, a loss of faith in government and financial institutions likely to last for generations. This deficit of trust could reduce growth and cast a shadow over the optimism and resilience needed to build our economic future.

"We hope people will believe us, believe the collective leadership of the European Union," the Finance Minister of Cyprus Michael Sarris told CNBC on Sunday, March 17, 2013, promising that when his nation's banks re-opened that Tuesday, people would be able to move their money out of the country. [107]

From now on, Sarris said, Cypriots "can be very confident that nothing will happen to their savings....there is [sic] no capital restrictions."

The Cypriot banks never opened on Tuesday, and when they did open on Thursday it was with Draconian capital restrictions limiting daily withdrawals to 300 Euros, prohibiting the cashing of checks, and giving government the power to confiscate any significant amount of money carried by people leaving the country.

Perhaps Mr. Sarris can understand why no sane person any longer believes "the collective leadership of the European Union."

Markets were shaken all over the world when then-head of the Eurogroup of 17 national Finance Ministers, Jeroen Dijsselbloem of the Netherlands, told an interviewer that what happened in Cyprus would be a "template" for future bank bailouts in Europe, i.e., that Eurocrats would again loot savings accounts before using government money to bail out banks on the verge of bankruptcy. [108]

Shaken Trust

No wonder that in an interview with *Der Spiegel*, German economist Peter Bofinger warned that what Eurocrats set out to do in Cyprus "will shake the trust of depositors across the Continent. Europe's citizens now have to fear for their money."

"The Spaniards, Italians and Portuguese may not run to the banks today or tomorrow," Bofinger continued, "but as soon as the crisis intensifies in a euro-zone country, the bank customers will remember Cyprus. They will withdraw their money and, by doing so, intensify the crisis."

Such fearful Great Withdrawals, Bofinger warned, could cause a domino effect, and every economic downturn leaves savers asking if their country is the next Cyprus. The seeds of continental bank runs have been planted. [109]

And in Europe, the media reverberate with advice like that of Member of the European Parliament and leader of the United Kingdom Independent Party (UKIP) Nigel Farage: "Get all your money out of Europe now." [110]

In the 2014 elections for the European Parliament, UKIP and several other populist European parties won roughly 25 percent of total votes, in some cases topping the vote totals of the old welfare state socialist parties and frightening their long-ruling elites.

Cyprus, writes *Time* columnist Rana Foroohar, might "become the economic equivalent of the assassination of Austrian Archduke Ferdinand, which started World War I," by shattering the economic unity and slow recovery of Europe. Today's Europe is roughly 25 percent of the global economy. [111]

"I am chilled by the realization of how similar circumstances in Europe in 2013 are to those of 100 years ago" on the eve of World War I, Luxembourg's Prime Minister Jean-Claude Juncker said in a March 11, 2013 interview with Germany's *Der Spiegel*. Juncker in 2011 said of touchy economic matters in Europe, "When it becomes serious, you have to lie." [112]

American Takings

A major factor in today's sick economy is that governments in both Europe and the United States have turned regulatory power into *de facto* government ownership and politicization of the banks.

The political sin of Cyprus was not that its once-solid banks had faltered after it joined the Eurozone in January 2008, only months before recession hit. Nor was it the near bankruptcy of Cyprus' banks and the need for a bailout of 17 Billion Euros – a relatively small amount to pay by a Eurozone that since May 2010 had spent more than $600 Billion to bail out other member nations such as Greece.

Cypriot banks paid much higher interest rates than mainland European banks, and held tens of billions of Euros of deposits from wealthy Russian oligarchs. German Chancellor Angela Merkel, up for re-election in September 2013, did not want German taxpayers and banks paying to protect the fortunes of Russians.

The heavy levies on large Cypriot accounts, on the other hand, would seem to fall like a "progressive" tax on the 4 percent of depositors who accounted for 60 percent of all the money in its bank deposits – and presumably a large share of these 4 percent are Russians.

As the dust of Cyprus continues to settle, however, evidence is starting to show that the biggest Russian oligarchs tended to use Cypriot banks as transit points, with hot money seldom staying there for long.

During the week the Cypriot government delayed signing an agreement with the troika, reported Reuters, many Euros in nominally-closed banks somehow left the country via still-open Cyprus-owned banks in London and Moscow, and perhaps via corporate jets. [113]

A year later, while President Obama was threatening to seize Russian assets in the U.S. because of Russia's occupation of Crimea in Ukraine, Russians were rapidly removing wealth from American soil. This wealth apparently included $105 Billion worth of Russian-owned U.S. Treasury notes on deposit with the Federal Reserve Bank of New York. [114]

Our banks may prevent ordinary Americans from making withdrawals, as documented in our Introduction. The New York Federal Reserve refuses to let our ally Germany even *see* its own gold deposit there. But Russia was apparently somehow able to withdraw and remove from the U.S. more than a tenth of a trillion dollars, without delay.

One of Russia's most powerful lawmakers, Andrei Klishas, proposed a measure that if Mr. Obama seized Russian assets, Russia could respond by seizing U.S. assets there owned by Ford, General Motors, Exxon Mobil Corp., PepsiCo, and the giant banks CitiGroup and JPMorgan Chase, among other companies.

When the Obama Administration asked by what right Russia might do this, Klishas replied: "The recent events in Cyprus spring to mind, where the confiscation of assets was the main demand made by the European Union in return for economic aid." [115]

This is a precedent that could haunt and hector our world for as long as banks, the dollar, and private property endure....which may be less time than we now know.

*Animal Farm*ers

Who got caught in the Eurozone's giant cash grab of private bank accounts? Russians did, but mostly small and middling businesspeople, not billionaires. So did ordinary families whose mom-and-pop accounts exceeded 100,000 Euros after a lifetime of scrimping, saving and earning interest; they have lost a hefty hunk of their life savings. Those with bank loans and mortgages will still have to pay, except, of course, certain Cypriot politicians whose debts reportedly have been written off by the banks. [116]

Welcome to the Progressive welfare future George Orwell foresaw in *Animal Farm*, where everyone is equal but some animals are more equal than others.

Angela Merkel's government made it a condition of bailing Cyprus out that it could no longer be the kind of "financial center" it has been. Between 25 percent and 30 percent of Cypriots were employed by banks and the financial sector, so this Diktat means that the island's economy will now sink – and the promised Eurozone bailout will be far too little to keep Cyprus from insolvency. [117]

Some at the time feared that this could push Cyprus out of the Eurozone, into the arms of Russia, and back to its previous national currency, the Cypriot Pound. This might mean that if the current Lebanon-ruling Syrian regime allied with Russia falls, we might soon see Cyprus as the new Russian naval base in the Mediterranean. We might also see Gazprom oil rigs tapping the potentially-large oil deposits undersea in Cypriot waters, despite Turkey's objections.

It is true that Cyprus' banks housed accounts worth 716 percent – more than seven times – the small nation's Gross Domestic Product (GDP), a very high ratio, yet far from the highest in Europe. (By comparison, America's proportion of bank assets to GDP is approximately 93 percent.) [118]

Luxembourg's banking sector as a share of GDP is 2,174 percent – and Luxembourg has recently told the Eurozone to keep its hands off its banking sector and accused Germany of "striving for hegemony" in the Eurozone by crushing the banking sector in Cyprus. [119]

Another Mediterranean island nation, Malta, has a banking sector to GDP ratio higher than Cyprus at 792 percent, and Ireland's is also higher at 718 percent.

It is also reportedly true that Russians and other foreigners did money laundering in Cyprus. Oddly, however, Germany says relatively little about even more money laundering being done in Malta, Lichtenstein and London.

The real political sin of Cyprus was that it was a small, vulnerable tax haven in a European Union hungry for more taxes, and that Cyprus' banks may have held tens of billions of Euros in deposits from wealthy Russian oligarchs that looked ripe for the plucking.

Before the seizure of its private bank accounts, Cyprus in 2012 was ranked the 20th freest economy on Earth by the Heritage Foundation/*Wall Street Journal* annual *Index of Economic Freedom.*

In 2014 Cyprus had fallen to 46th, a huge decline that still leaves the island nation ahead of Spain (49th), Poland (50th), Hungary (51st), Portugal (69th), France (70th), Italy (86th) and Greece (119th) in this ranking of global economic freedom. [120]

Seeking Shelter

For centuries people around the world have looked to America as a place they could escape to if the government where they lived became too oppressive. Just knowing that the United States existed gave people hope and, more importantly, was a reminder to rulers that their best and brightest citizens had someplace else to go.

Some look at Cyprus and wonder why they should care. We should care because every tax haven is a place of economic liberty. Every tax haven is a place of escape and shelter.

Every tax haven is a beacon of tax competition that reminds rulers worldwide that their power to tax is not infinite. Even a single tax haven in the world is evidence that human taxes can be lower and less oppressive.

As noted, how ironic it is that the United States, unlike almost every other country, heavily taxes its own citizens even if they live overseas, earn their money overseas, and are no burden on the social services of the United States.

At the same time, the United States has lenient laws for foreign investors and companies that make it a tax haven for citizens of many other nations.

America should be a tax haven for all. The more we cut our taxes, the more wealth will pour in from around the world.

Instead, the U.S. increasingly has joined with the socialist welfare states of Europe to snuff out tiny tax havens such as Cyprus. Their citizens went in search of the economic liberty we used to have, and that foreign investors to a large extent still have in America.

Because we have the highest business income tax rate of any major nation, American companies are not repatriating at least $2.1 Trillion that could be making jobs in the United States.

Oddly, the Progressives' American Dream now appears to be a land with a new Statue of Liberty with her hand out in New York harbor, and a Statue of Equality with her hand out on Alcatraz Island in San Francisco Bay.

Those, like our ancestors who came here seeking a land of free enterprise with no king to pick their pockets or raid their business, increasingly are forced to look for the American Dream by moving their assets out of America.

Progressives talk as if tax havens were pirates that rob noble high-tax welfare states of urgently-needed revenues.

This is nonsense, like the usual "rob the rich, give to the poor" Leftist misinterpretation of England's legendary Robin Hood. The original tale makes clear that Robin Hood took from the government – the Sheriff of Nottingham and a wicked king – and returned to the people the money government had stolen from them.

The real pirates are governments that expropriate more than half of the average citizen's income in federal, state, local and hidden indirect taxes. Tax havens give citizens a way to vote with their feet against being a minority robbed by the discriminatory, unequal Progressive taxes of these pirate governments.

"Of all the many ways of organizing banking,
the worst is the one we have today.
Change is, I believe, inevitable.
The question is only whether
we can think our way through
to a better outcome
before the next generation is
damaged by a future and bigger crisis."

-- **Mervyn King**
Governor, The Bank of England
October 25, 2010 Speech

"It's a safe banking system, a sound banking system.
Our regulators are on top of it.
This is a very manageable situation."

-- **Henry Paulson**
U.S. Secretary of the Treasury
CBS News, July 20, 2008

"You have to eventually nationalize U.S. banks....
In my view, actually most of
the U.S. banking system is insolvent."

-- **Nouriel Roubini**
Financial Analyst
Bloomberg TV, January 29, 2009

Chapter Seven
Political Bank Robbers

*"We still find the greedy hand of government
thrusting itself into every corner and crevice of industry,
and grasping at the spoil of the multitude.
Invention is continually exercised to furnish
new pretenses for revenue and taxation.
It watches prosperity as its prey
and permits none to escape without a tribute."*

– Thomas Paine

**The bigger a Progressive welfare state becomes, the more of other
people's money it needs to devour. Our politicians have targeted banks,
and our accounts in those banks, as pools of wealth they intend to
plunder. The biggest uncertainty today is merely which will loot your
bank accounts first – our own government's possible confiscation of
retirement accounts, or a fast-approaching Global Wealth Tax. Both
will be imposed by surprise, without warning, like a thief in the night.
And the politicians have additional ways to snatch even more money
from your bank and your accounts there.**

A major flaw in Progressivism is its ideological obsession with redistributing
wealth while punishing the successful capitalists who are needed to make more,
to keep producing goods for politicians to expropriate and give away to buy votes
tomorrow and tomorrow and tomorrow.

Even Karl Marx understood that socialism is a system of redistribution, not
production, and that an era of capitalism must come before socialism to produce
enough wealth for socialism to succeed. What Marx apparently never considered in
his "scientific socialism" was that these goods taken from capitalists will eventually
all be consumed – and no efficient capitalist producer will be left to make more.

As the leftist welfare state grows, the once-expanding American economic pie that used to produce enough prosperity for all has begun rapidly shrinking.

With more than half the population now receiving benefits or pay from government, and roughly half of working-age Americans paying no direct income tax, the takers now outnumber the makers. Mistletoe is now taking so much sap from its tree that the parasite is killing its host.

"Socialist governments traditionally do make a financial mess," said British Tory leader and future Prime Minister Margaret Thatcher in 1976. "They always run out of other peoples' money."

The Vampire State

Progressive politicians are now on a desperate search-and-devour mission to expropriate whatever remaining pools of private wealth they can find.

They urgently need ever-larger transfusions of capital, the lifeblood of capitalism, to keep their failing Vampire Progressive governments alive.

When asked why he robbed banks, master criminal Willie Sutton purportedly replied: "Because that's where the money is."

Banks today, more than ever, are where some of the largest pools of private money and capital can be found.

No wonder that leftist politicians are plotting a variety of ways to rob private bank accounts, and to repeatedly stick up and shake down the banks themselves.

Some of this Progressive looting of banks is designed to become routine, just one more predictable cost of doing business. These costs will almost certainly be passed on to bank customers in the forms of more and higher fees, less service, and even lower or "negative" interest paid on savings accounts.

On the other hand, some of what Progressives are planning will come in sudden unexpected raids to penalize banks, seize bank assets, and get greedy politician hands on customer accounts.

Here is a foretaste of some of these Progressive schemes:

The Bank Tax

In January 2010, President Barack Obama announced his plan to impose a "Progressive" tax on 50 or so of Wall Street's biggest firms. [121]

This "bank tax" on firms with assets of $50 Billion or more – officially called the "Financial Crisis Responsibility Fee" – would be designed to bring $90 Billion into government coffers over 10 years to help offset the expected $120 Billion taxpayer loss from TARP, the $789 Billion Troubled Asset Relief Program.

"We oppose this very targeted and punitive tax, especially when it affects firms that have either already repaid, with interest, their TARP funds or never took TARP funds in the first place," said Andrew DeSouza of the Securities Industry & Financial Markets Association.

"We want our money back, and we're going to get it," said President Obama in a White House speech. "If these companies are in good enough shape to afford massive bonuses, they surely are in good enough shape to afford to pay back every penny to taxpayers." [122]

"In general, I am skeptical of narrow-based taxes, as they feed a particularly nasty kind of politics, where the majority gangs up on a minority," said Harvard economics Professor Greg Mankiw. [123]

"And I am turned off by the populist rhetoric coming from the administration, which suggests the issue pits Wall Street fat cats against ordinary citizens," Mankiw continued. "Nonetheless, on the economic merits, there may be a case for the bank tax."

Some legal scholars were concerned that Mr. Obama was, in effect, proposing a Bill of Attainder – a law that declares some person or group guilty of some crime and punishes them without a judicial trial. Bills of Attainder are prohibited by the U.S. Constitution. [124]

Bipartisan Bank Grab

President Obama's measure languished, then suddenly came back to life in early 2014 because House Ways and Means Committee Chairman Dave Camp (R.-Michigan) got behind a small but similar bank tax. [125]

In March, 2014, Goldman Sachs canceled a GOP fundraiser to protest Rep. Camp's proposed tax of 0.035 percent on consolidated assets of banks with more than $500 Billion in assets. [126]

The banks remain determined to keep any such tax from becoming law, both because it would cost them billions today and because what might start as a small tax can with relative ease be raised again and again whenever future politicians want to squeeze more money out of the banks.

JPMorgan Chase has become a "piñata bank," says CNBC host Jim Cramer. Piñatas are Hispanic *Papier-mâché* hangings at children's parties that are whacked and smashed open to get at the pieces of candy inside. [127]

In 2013 and 2014 the Obama Administration shook down JPMorgan for $15 Billion, Bank of America for $16.65 Billion, Citigroup for $7 Billion, Goldman Sachs for $3.15 Billion, and is preparing many more cases to make such bank stickups routine. Former Wells Fargo Chairman and CEO Dick Kovacevich calls this "a pattern of the government extorting the banks."

An adage among modern politicians has been that if you want more campaign contributions, threaten to impose more regulations on banks. Banks have ample money to contribute, and those widely described in the liberal media as "banksters" are unpopular with a wide cross-section of the population.

This unpopularity, as well as their vulnerability to tiny government regulatory changes, make bankers easy targets for political shakedowns. Class warfare against bankers can pay well if you are a Progressive politician.

This is one more indicator of how our social and cultural values have changed. Bankers used to be among the most respected members of traditional American communities....and in small local banks often still are.

"Operation Choke Point"

In early 2013 the Obama Administration launched a chilling new exercise in politically controlling America's banks and those who use them.

The Justice Department "is asking banks to identify customers who may be breaking the law or simply doing something government officials don't like," wrote President and CEO of the American Bankers Association, Frank Keating. [128]

"Banks must then 'choke off' those customers' access to financial services, shutting down their accounts," wrote Keating.

"Operation Choke Point," as this project has been named, is an undertaking of President Obama's Financial Fraud Enforcement Task Force, which includes the Federal Deposit Insurance Corporation, the sinister new Consumer Financial Protection Bureau (CFPB) funded directly by the Federal Reserve instead of Congress, and other agencies.

"Justice's premise is simple," writes Keating. "Fraudsters can't operate without access to banking services, and so the agency is going after the infrastructure that questionable merchants use rather than the merchants themselves. Most of these merchants are legally licensed businesses on a government list of 'risky profiles.' These include payday outfits and other short-term lenders."

"Unfortunately, the strategy is legally dubious," writes Keating, a former FBI agent, U.S. Attorney and Associate Attorney General of the United States.

"Justice is pressuring banks to shut down accounts without pressing charges against a merchant or even establishing that the merchant broke the law," writes Keating.

"It's clear enough that there's fraud to shut down the account, Justice asserts," writes Keating, "but apparently not clear enough for the highest law-enforcement agency in the land to prosecute."

"Banks contribute significantly to the law-enforcement mission and remain committed to helping agencies detect terrorist financing, money laundering and fraud," writes Keating. "Justice shouldn't turn that commitment against them."

You might not be the owner of a "Choke Point"-targeted company, but this exercise of capricious government power nevertheless can harm you. You could be employed by such a company, or sell products or services to it, or rely on it to supply things your company needs. These "Choke Point" targets have not necessarily been convicted of any crime, which is precisely why the government aims to hurt them by arbitrary extra-legal means. "Choke Point" uses regulatory pressure to compel their bank to spy on and injure them at secret government direction.

Gunning for Business

The Federal Government already requires banks to report any transaction of $10,000 or more and expects them to tell the government of "unusual" patterns in customer deposits and withdrawals.

Like Keating, we all would like to see an end to fraudsters, but "Operation Choke Point" expands government power far beyond this objective. Justice now expects banks to divulge even more and more detailed customer information, including everything that bankers might deem odd or questionable financial behavior.

"Operation Choke Point" throws a very wide net. It requires banks to impose government policy in ways that may be ideological, unethical or even illegal against people and legal businesses that have been convicted of no crime whatsoever. The Obama Administration's categories list, first developed for similar purposes in 2011 by the FDIC [129], of businesses it associates with "high-risk" financial activity includes:

Ammunition Sales	Life-Time Memberships
Cable Box De-scramblers	Lottery Sales
Coin Dealers	Mailing Lists/Personal Info
Credit Card Schemes	Money Transfer Networks
Credit Repair Services	On-line Gambling
Dating Services	PayDay Loans
Debt Consolidation Scams	Pharmaceutical Sales
Drug Paraphernalia	Ponzi Schemes
Escort Services	Pornography
Firearms Sales	Pyramid-Type Sales
Fireworks Sales	Racist Materials
Get Rich Products	Surveillance Equipment
Government Grants	Telemarketing
Home-Based Charities	Tobacco Sales
Life-Time Guarantees	Travel Clubs

Note two enterprises on this list: ammunition sales and firearms sales. These are activities in which the Obama Administration has an obsessive ideological interest. The Obama Administration has purchased billions and billions of rounds of ammunition, enough to leave the shelves nearly bare for months at stores selling ammunition, with little explanation as to why Administration agencies needed all these bullets.

The effect among firearms owners has been almost like a "denial of service" computer hack attack that swamps targeted websites and makes them inaccessible because of a never-ending "busy" signal. This was the government denying gun owners ammunition by crowding out others via buying up a huge fraction of the bullet industry's supply of gunpowder, brass and lead.

The Obama Administration has made no secret of its aim to further restrict private gun ownership, a right guaranteed by the Constitution's Second Amendment because America's Framers wanted the ultimate protection against tyranny, an armed citizenry.

Guns and ammunition may be personally hazardous in the wrong hands, but they pose no special financial risk unless those hands belong to a modern Jesse James. Unlike many other things on this list, gun selling is a business already monitored and regulated by the government, with each firearm recorded by serial number and each sale specifically cleared by government via a background check of the buyer.

Yet the Obama Administration is ordering banks to keep a close eye on any customer whose business involves selling firearms or ammunition and to then share their financial information with the government.

Attorney General Eric Holder's Justice Department is pressing banks to shut down these businesses' bank accounts and access to credit, loans, and other financial services at the first hint of any vaguely suspicious activity.

This could easily turn into gun control by the "bank door," and the National Rifle Association has reported that instances already exist of banks severing relationships with customers in the firearms industry. [130]

What would happen to your business if the government suddenly ordered your bank to cut you off from all financial services, including bank lines of credit, even though you had broken no law?

"Operation Choke Point" gives government the power to make your bank do this, not only if you are a criminal, but also if you are merely someone who for ideological reasons President Obama has targeted to put out of business.

Do the words IRS and Tea Party come to mind? The potential abuse of this government power over our banks could prove to be similar.

Banks Under Pressure

Many bad things can happen that could put your money at risk because Progressive politicians over-regulate and control our banks.

It is bad enough that we have fractional-reserve banking, which in a "Too Big To Fail" world means that government sees a frantic need to prevent failure of America's biggest banks at all costs.

When you combine this problem with an endless effort by politicians to use banks as their own ATMs to fund ideological and political wishes, you have recurring disasters such as today's largely-stagnant economy.

"Four of the five biggest problems in our banks and economy are being caused by the Fed," says Michael Cox, director of the O'Neil Center for Global Markets and Freedom at Southern Methodist University. Cox is also a former Senior Vice President and Chief Economist at the Federal Reserve Bank in Dallas, Texas.

According to Dr. Cox, the Fed and the rules of Dodd-Frank, authored by Democratic lawmakers Senator Chris Dodd of Connecticut and Congressman Barney Frank of Massachusetts, have over-regulated banks, making them afraid to lend money to anyone (except government and wealthy companies).

Dodd-Frank became law in 2010, yet by 2014 less than 70 percent of the thousands of pages of detailed rules and regulations it authorizes have been written. This has slowed the economy as businesspeople defer investment and hiring decisions until they can see how onerous its final rules will be.

"Firing Squad On Capitalism"

Many expected Dodd-Frank to curtail or even break up "Too Big To Fail" banks. Instead, it created a new "Financial Stability Oversight Council" (FSOC) of heads of government agencies, including CFPB. FSOC's job includes "identifying systemically important financial institutions (SIFIs)."

In other words, as Heritage Foundation analyst Norbert J. Michel puts it, this council does not intend to eliminate entities "Too Big To Fail," at least initially. It is, on the contrary, "helping to enshrine" them. [131]

The council has identified as "Too Big To Fail" dozens of banks, insurance companies, mutual funds and more. It seems to be throwing its net wider and wider. And every company caught in that net is a target for extra government scrutiny and pressure.

Fellow regulator Michael Piwowar, a commissioner at the Securities and Exchange Commission, sees ominous forces at work in the new FSOC.

Its initials, Piwowar declared in a speech before the American Enterprise Institute, stand for "Firing Squad On Capitalism." The council, he said, is an "Unaccountable Capital Markets Death Panel," a "Vast Left-Wing Conspiracy to Hinder Capital Formation," "The Modern-Day Star Chamber," and "The Dodd-Frank Politburo." His words about this often-secretive, largely left-of-center council are harsh but may prove to be accurate. [132]

Commissioner Piwowar's own Securities and Exchange Commission, however, has its own regulatory quirks. In July 2014 it by a split vote narrowly approved tighter rules for Money Market Mutual Funds.

The new rules will give these institutions permission to delay returning a customer's money for up to 10 days, or to charge a withdrawal fee during times of economic duress, to prevent panicky runs like 2008's that could cause severe problems. [133]

These new SEC rules, as the *New York Times* reported, "give funds the ability to stem investor redemptions during times of stress. Money market funds, in these situations, will be able to impose fees and delays that temporarily prevent investors from taking out their cash." [134]

Money Market Mutual Funds (not to be confused with what some banks call Money Market Funds) have long been perceived as almost risk-free, even though they are not insured in any way by the Federal Deposit Insurance Corporation.

They are "basically mutual funds, though with a share price fixed at $1," Forbes columnist Keith Weiner has written. That share price was widely perceived as a kind of anchor. The new SEC rules replace the $1 par value with a floating "net asset value" (NAV), at least for the "prime" funds. In 2008 a run of frightened customers drained these of $300 Billion in one week after the fall of Lehman Brothers forced associated Reserve Primary Fund shares to drop from $1 to 97 cents. [135]

With the SEC trying to avoid a repeat of the chaos of 2008, this may be a good change, according to portfolio manager at Sag Harbor Advisors James Sanford.

The perception that a manager insures the fund by promising never to "break the buck" was never true, says Sanford. Letting investors know that they are exposed to risk in the money-market portfolio should produce more realism, and reality ought to lead to more stability.

A loss of confidence in these uninsured funds, however, could cause serious economic dislocation. These funds are a $2.6 Trillion industry.

One can view these new rules as prudent and logical, or as one more of many examples where the government is closing the escape exits and locking the doors so people cannot get their money and leave. To us, this seems too close to yet more currency controls that we see hints of in our banks. We have rightly warned of *the Great Withdrawal* happening in many ways around us. We join James Sanford in recommending that people steer clear of these tighter-controlled Money Market Mutual Funds and say "Don't Bank On It!"

By flooding banks with money conjured out of thin air, the Fed has put banks in a liquidity trap.

And by keeping interest rates near zero, the Fed has given near-zero incentive to lenders, including savers who have lent their deposits to banks; this has impaired genuine investment capital formation, hiring and economic growth.

CNBC commentator Rick Santelli once inspired the creation of the modern Tea Party movement with one of his famous passionate tirades. In July 2014 he on air fervently denounced the Federal Reserve's policies of Quantitative Easing and holding interest rates near zero.

"If I'm a bank, why would I lend to some person at a sub risk-reward rate?" asked Santelli. "[Investment] capital will come out if it can get a decent return." [136]

From the Tower of Basel

The head of the Basel, Switzerland-based Bank of International Settlements, the "central bank of central banks," in July 2014 offered a similar voice of sanity. "Overall, it is hard to avoid the sense of a puzzling disconnect between the markets' buoyancy and underlying economic developments globally," said Jaime Caruana. "As [economist John Maynard] Keynes said, markets can stay irrational longer than you can stay solvent."

Caruana is concerned about what appear to be stock markets intoxicated by easy money and interest rates they believe will remain low for a long time. The global economy that he sees does not warrant such optimism or soaring stock markets. It is a bubble economy based on money printing and the expectation that today's borrowing can be paid off with debased currency.

"There is something strange about fighting debt by incentivizing more debt," said Caruana. [137]

We live in a surreal economy in which the Fed lends money at almost no cost to the banks in order to encourage investment, and the banks, because they fear being accused of making bad loans, lend that money back to the Fed or government.

In March 2014, former Deputy Assistant Treasury Secretary David Malpass wrote in the *Wall Street Journal* that "the banking system had lent over 18% of its entire assets to the Fed, $2.6 Trillion of the $14 Trillion in total assets." (138)

Sadly, Americans no longer live in a free marketplace. We are becoming a "Fedocracy" whose investment resources flow not to productive enterprises but to the Federal Reserve itself because banks fear its vast regulatory powers. This grows the already-wildly-obese government even larger.

The Great Withdrawal

So what has come from the Progressive politicizing of our banks, our currency, and our lives?

In America today more than 28 percent of us do not deal much with banks, but we all, voluntarily or involuntarily, deal with government.

Only 101 million Americans now have full-time jobs, and of these only 86 million work in the private sector where their paycheck does not come from other people's taxes.

This is the lowest full-time job participation rate since Jimmy Carter, the president who turned off the lights in the White House and in the American economy.

These full-time workers are the ones who make the goods and pay the majority of personal income taxes, who pull the wagon that everybody else rides in.

As of December 2012, 49.5 percent of Americans live in a household where at least one person receives a government benefit. Such households likely want to keep benefits coming and growing.

Welcome to the "Too Big To Fail" and "Too Obese To Survive" welfare state, where future elections may become little more than bidding wars in which politicians win by promising the most free goodies and by most loudly demonizing those who will be taxed and squeezed to pay for it.

Class Warfare

The Class Warfare game behind this is all too obvious. "See that evil banker over there who refused to give you a home or car loan?" says the Progressive politician. "We're going to force him to give you a loan, or we'll put him out of business."

Evita Peron had her own version of this in 1940s fascist Argentina. She would go on the radio in Buenos Aires and announce that Jose's Appliance Store had offered to give 50 free washing machines to her followers, the *descamisados*, the "shirtless ones."

Jose, of course, did not know he had made this offer. But when a mob of *Peronistas* shows up in front of your store carrying torches and demands the free goodies Evita promised, you dare not call the First Lady a liar or refuse the giveaway.

Very bad things happened to those who crossed Evita, just as under the Community Reinvestment Act (CRA) very bad things have happened to banks that went against Progressive politicians and regulators eager to give away other people's money.

America already has 15 states in which welfare pays more than a minimum wage job, thereby destroying the incentive to take such jobs. In Hawaii, untaxed welfare pays more than one would earn, after taxes, from a $60,000 per year job.

As fewer and fewer Americans work and pay taxes, more and more money must be taxed away from a shrinking group of workers to sustain and expand the welfare state – and the dependent voters who keep its Progressive politicians in office.

Bank Piggy

With an ever-growing need for more revenues, the politicians relentlessly look for new ways to take it from our banks.

President Obama, who refuses to cut deals with a Republican House of Representatives that might rein in his fast-growing welfare state, has begun raising vast revenues he can spend.

He has begun doing this by using the regulatory state to milk huge amounts of money from corporations in general and banks in particular to fund his Executive Branch of the Federal Government.

As an example of what is likely if Democrats keep control of the U.S. Senate in the November 2014 elections, we noted earlier that Obama regulators recently squeezed $16.65 Billion out of Bank of America and $15 Billion out of JPMorgan Chase – more than 1 percent of a Trillion dollars each from individual banks, with billions more in fines from them and other banks coming.

JPMorgan Chase as a result laid off 6,000 workers, adding to the unemployment burden on the economy and welfare state. We suspect that Progressives will see this merely as more recruits for their Big Government, anti-capitalist legion of class warriors.

President Obama's Administration has begun imposing huge *de facto* taxes on America's banks (and other corporations) in the form of penalties and fines, to enrich the government. The leftist carrot-and-stick shakedown to get this money is the implicit offer that those bank executives who give in and transfer billions to the government will not go to jail for their purported financial high crimes.

The money thus extorted by the government's reign of intimidation is not taken solely from bank shareholders. It is also taken from every depositor who is paid less interest on his or her savings.

In January 2014 federal regulators opened a new probe into JPMorgan and three other giant American banks, a probe that will almost certainly result in billions more in fines and penalties. Heaven only knows how many political campaign contributions can be extorted by making examples out of just a few major companies.

Remember, depositors at JPMorgan and at five other of the biggest banks – which, combined, control at least 50% of private American bank accounts – reportedly have had difficulty withdrawing or wire-transferring funds from their accounts. These reports might be early signs of "capital controls" these banks expect very soon to be ordered to impose.

Cyprus, U.S.A.

One vast pool of money in America not yet seized by politicians is comprised of our retirement accounts – 401(k)s, IRAs, pension funds and more – that add up to more than $20 Trillion dollars.

The Obama Administration is acutely aware of what Argentina did in 2008 – how its still-Peronist government struck in the dead of night.

People there woke up the next day to find that the money saved in their bank retirement accounts was gone. In place of their life savings was an equal face value in Argentine government bonds.

Trouble was, the real market value of those bonds was, at best, only about 29 percent of their face value – so in the name of protecting the people, the government in effect stole nearly three-quarters of their retirement savings.

The Obama Administration is considering an even bigger expropriation of retirement accounts here. When an exploitable crisis provides a pretext, do not be surprised if the government suddenly confiscates the money in our accounts – as happened in Cyprus.

The Mutant Agency and Nuclear Option

When President Barack Obama and his party controlled both houses of Congress, Democratic lawmakers created the powerful new regulatory agency, the Consumer Financial Protection Bureau, funded not by Congress but directly by the Federal Reserve.

The CFPB's Obama-appointed director boasted that he is "exploring" ways to control Americans' 401(k)s, IRAs and other retirement plans.

"The runaway, unaccountable regulators at the Consumer Financial Protection Bureau would like to 'protect' the IRAs of U.S. citizens by making them into a $20 Trillion ATM for the government," warned famed financial author George Gilder.

American savers might soon "be forced to buy Federal debt" by having their savings seized and replaced with government bonds," wrote *Forbes* Magazine columnist William Tucker.

This certainly could now happen here, because shortly before Christmas 2013 the Democrat-controlled U.S. Senate suddenly erased a 225-year-old rule allowing filibusters against certain presidential appointees. President Obama immediately used this change to pack the D.C. Circuit Court of Appeals with judges who share his ideology.

This is the second most important court in America, the court that prevents regulators from abusing their power.

This change removed the last barrier preventing President Obama from governing by himself, almost like a king, via regulatory agencies, and from taxing without the Congress by imposing huge regulatory fines and seizing trillions in bank accounts.

It was no exaggeration that experts called this Senate power grab "the Nuclear Option." It just blew much of what was left of our Constitution to smithereens and opened the door to the President confiscating the wealth of savers and banks.

Seizing Your Savings

How will the Progressives seize your retirement savings? The public got a glimpse of one of their plans in 2008 and again in 2010 when the then-Democrat-run House Education and Labor Subcommittee invited Economics Professor Teresa Ghilarducci of the New School for Social Research in New York City to discuss her proposed new "Guaranteed Retirement Account" (GRA).

The GRA she envisions would replace today's 401(k)s and their $80+ Billion in annual tax breaks, as well as your Individual Retirement Accounts (IRAs) that she believes unequally benefit the upper middle class and the rich. [139]

"The government would deposit $600 (inflation indexed) every year into the GRAs," explained American Enterprise Institute economist James Pethokoukis. "Each worker would also have to save 5 percent of pay into the accounts, to which the government would pay a measly 3 percent return." [140]

GRAs would pay less than half the average return of the stock market, but they would be "safe." Or perhaps not, because GRAs would invest worker "contributions," taken from their paychecks just like Social Security taxes, in government debt paper.

This is a good deal for government, because its Treasuries have become a hard sell on world markets. The Federal Reserve has had to step in and buy more than 80 percent of them in recent years. GRAs will compel the purchase of such government debt and its low returns by ordinary working Americans.

So here is what Professor Ghilarducci and her Progressive politician comrades want for you. Government will take the IRA or 401(k) you now own and control, and will convert it into a GRA effectively owned by the government.

The government will pay you a small but reliable annuity based on government debt paper, meaning that your GRA will be a kind of "Social Security 2.0," only smaller. Ms. Ghilarducci's program would, she promises, even be administered by Social Security.

And like Social Security, if you die early your family will not get the money you would have gotten from your IRA or 401(k). The government would likely take at least half of it, maybe more. Social Security takes it all.

Ultimately, as Ghilarducci told Seattle radio host Kirby Wilbur, her plan favors "giving everybody a flat amount so that it's more equal....spreading the wealth." GRA's real aim, in other words, is the redistribution of society's wealth – especially away from private sector capitalists and towards Progressive government.

In 2013 California lawmakers considered their own "Secure Choice Retirement Savings Program" that would require private employers to squeeze 3 percent from every employee paycheck, then send it to be mingled in a state fund with public employee contributions. The purpose: to cover the huge shortfall caused by California not adequately funding public employee retirements....and to become another slush fund politicians can loot. [141]

The Missing Lock-Box

Apparently no "lockbox" protects your involuntary GRA contributions in her plan. "If subsidies for 401(k)-style plans and IRAs can be relocated to Guaranteed Retirement Accounts, why not use this money to shore up and expand Social Security? This is certainly an option," writes Ghilarducci. [142]

In 2014 America passed a milestone. Our Federal Government has now "borrowed" $5 Trillion from what were supposed to be the untouchable trust fund lock-boxes of various government programs. [143]

Our Progressive politicians have looted more than $2.66 Trillion from Social Security's trust fund, $736 Billion from the Medicare trust fund to launch Obamacare, and much, much more.

Our politicians left IOUs in place of the trillions they stole to buy their re-elections, but we, our children and our grandchildren must now be taxed all over again to pay those IOUs.

The Federal Reserve and our government can always conjure magic money from a printing press to cover these shortfalls, but this will further destroy the value of dollars Americans have struggled to save in their bank and retirement accounts.

The Obama Administration is already finessing this by reneging on Social Security Cost-Of-Living Adjustments (COLAs). Mr. Obama allowed zero increases in 2009, 2010, 2011, and only in election year 2012 did he permit a tiny increase for retired seniors on fixed incomes.

Social Insecurity

From a strictly legal point of view, the courts have confirmed that, despite taxing you all your working lifetime, Social Security has no obligation to pay you any particular amount in retirement. It could drop its payments to $1 per year, and you would have no legal recourse to demand more.

Remember that under government bookkeeping, the Federal Budget does not show the $5 Trillion of added unfunded liability Social Security accrues each year.

The politicians barely acknowledge the near-50 percent increase in the number of people receiving Social Security Disability payments. This is happening because President Obama lowered standards so almost anyone willing to claim he hears voices in his head can qualify for its lifetime payments. This is pushing Social Security towards bankruptcy for all the rest of us far sooner than previously expected.

Friends, if you want a secure, reliable retirement, then like the Little Red Hen in the fable you will have to "do it yourself." Our Progressive government, which will do what benefits the politicians and public employees and not you, cannot be trusted. Ultimately you have no guarantee with these "Guaranteed" Retirement Accounts and no security with Social Security.

If politicians need to confiscate your retirement and bank accounts, they will do so. And at this point, no knowledgeable person can doubt that they soon will need your money. They are hopelessly addicted to spending.

Did you know that, prior to the 1980s, Social Security was not taxed as it is now? The tax on your earned benefits is one of the ugliest political "claw-backs" in the history of American politics. It is, in effect, taxing you *again* on what you had already paid as a tax. Unlike welfare recipients, you will be taxed on your Social Security benefits because Progressive politicians have forced many of you to keep working into old age. Average persons now under age 40 will never get back all that they must pay into Social Security.

Plans such as Professor Ghilarducci's are already prepared, waiting for some opportune moment such as an economic breakdown to lock them in place around your neck. This will be easiest for politicians to do if you have left all your savings in a government-regulated bank.

Inflation: Endgame Stealth Tax

In the United States and other major Western nations, easy-money-addicted spendaholic politicians able to print debased money have run up what a December 2013 International Monetary Fund (IMF) Working Paper by two famous Harvard University economists describes as the greatest "debt in 200 years." [144]

The best way to deal with "the endgame" to this "global financial crisis" of stratospheric debt, propose Harvard economists Carmen M. Reinhart and Kenneth Rogoff, is a combination of debt restructuring, deliberate inflation, a "variety of capital controls under the umbrella of macroprudential regulation," and *"an opaque tax on savers"* (emphasis added) using "financial repression" to siphon off the purchasing power from saver bank deposits.

This kind of stealth confiscatory tax, targeting private savings accounts, is in keeping with the theories of late British economist John Maynard Keynes, who wrote of the "paradox of thrift."

Thrift since ancient times had been seen as a virtue, but in the new Progressive Keynesian economics thrift was seen as evil. Keynesians deem it evil because when thrifty people save money, they slow down its velocity through the economy. This, according to Keynes, makes their nation less prosperous.

Inflation is a hidden tax that relentlessly expropriates money from such savers' bank accounts and allows governments to steal its value merely by printing debased fiat money.

Keynes in his 1919 book *The Economic Consequences of the Peace* wrote this:

"Lenin is said to have declared that the best way to destroy the Capitalist System was to debauch the currency. By a continuing process of inflation, governments can confiscate, secretly and unobserved, an important part of the wealth of their citizens...."

"As the inflation proceeds and the real value of the currency fluctuates wildly from month to month," Keynes continued, "all permanent relations between debtors and creditors, which form the ultimate foundation of capitalism, become so utterly disordered as to be almost meaningless; and the process of wealth-getting degenerates into a gamble and a lottery."

"Lenin was certainly right," Keynes concluded. "There is no subtler, no surer means of overturning the existing basis of society than to debauch the currency. The process engages all the hidden forces of economic law on the side of destruction, and does it in a manner which not one man in a million is able to diagnose." [145]

Inflation makes a nation's currency and economy weaker. It also makes that nation's individual citizens weaker, less self-reliant and independent, more insecure, and more willing to surrender their rights to a protective, paternalistic government....the same government that through inflation deliberately stole the value of their money.

Pickpocket Policy

"Inflation is as violent as a mugger, as frightening as an armed robber and as deadly as a hit man," said Ronald Reagan, who understood that government-created "inflation" is just another word for theft.

What is a saver to think, therefore, when newly-appointed Federal Reserve chair Janet Yellen, like her immediate predecessor Ben Bernanke, says that it is the Fed's aim to deliberately create at least two percent inflation?

Even the seemingly-small "official" rate of inflation is enough over the next 15 years to steal a third of the purchasing power of the dollars we struggle to save. And we are not talking about robbing one or two people. This is the taking of the life savings and earnings, by then, of more than 360 million Americans.

Now imagine the impact on citizens if the "real" inflation rate is at least three to four times higher, as ShadowStats.com calculates, than the "official" rate.

Two famed Austrian economists understood this perfectly, as we showed in our 2011 book *The Inflation Deception*.

"Inflation is not an act of God," said Ludwig von Mises. "Inflation is a policy."

"History is largely a history of inflation, usually inflations engineered by governments for the gain of governments," said Nobel laureate economist Friedrich A. Hayek.

Hayek advocated free competition among currencies – letting you freely choose the most reliable and honest currencies or gold with which to buy or sell or save – as one way to deter governments from debasing their own money to make their exports cheaper and to sneakily rob their own citizens.

Remember that when dealing with banks, your money's real value is stored in at least two places – the bank itself, and the "store of value" of the currency in which your bank accounts or other instruments are denominated, usually U.S. Dollars.

The essence of "Financial Repression" is that Fed and federal policymakers are deliberately shrinking the value of dollars via inflation faster than your deposit is permitted to gain value from interest. This is a key reason that you lose money every day that you have money deposited in a bank account, even if in the end you withdraw your money safely.

Government then delivers a final insult, demanding that you pay tax on the interest your bank account earned.

The write-downs of debt that Reinhart and Rogoff propose would likely be done via "monetizing" the debt, printing vast amounts of paper currency out of thin air. This will trigger high inflation and greatly diminish the purchasing power of dollars people have saved. Some will benefit from this, especially the government and those whose savings were in solid things such as gold that historically has risen in value as the dollar falls.

President Obama's Keynesian economic policymakers have targeted American savings accounts not only because this is where most of the last vast pools of private wealth are – but also because their aim is to punish thrift and transfer savers' wealth into the hands of Big Government spenders for redistribution.

Another IMF study published in October 2013, titled *Taxing Times*, calls for a global "'capital levy' – a one-off tax on private wealth." This tax, the study advises, ought to be "implemented before avoidance is possible," apparently by surprise against the assets of the wealthy. The assets easiest for government to locate, lock up and easily confiscate are those in bank accounts. [146]

The $34,000 Question

You might not think of yourself as wealthy, but if you earn more than $34,000 per year you are among the top one percent of income earners on Earth....and the IMF's aim is wealth redistribution on a global scale.

The world's current astronomical debt crisis could be solved, this IMF study predicts, with a "one time" levy "of about 10 percent on households with positive net wealth."

As *Forbes* columnist Bill Frezza noted, this IMF tax will go after everybody with property or bank accounts, "everyone with retirement savings or home equity... would have their assets plundered under the IMF's formulation." [147]

"Financial wealth is mobile," write the IMF experts, who call for "enhanced international cooperation to make it harder for the very well-off to evade taxation by placing funds elsewhere." International tax havens, as the banks of Cyprus were before the regulators and financial controls took them over in 2013, must be ended to achieve "a revenue-maximizing approach to taxing the rich...."

"There is a surprisingly large amount of experience to draw on, as such levies [on the wealthy] were widely adopted in Europe after World War I," write the IMF experts.

"And we all know how well that worked out," retorts Bill Frezza.

Many successful Europeans fled with their wealth, leaving poverty and politicians behind. Germany's Weimar Republic sought prosperity as today's governments have – not through productivity but a printing press churning out endless debased currency that enriched speculators, not producers. The resulting devastation of conservative values such as thrift paved the way to a Great Depression and Adolf Hitler.

The Anti-Progressive Conclusion

If you wish to save what is in your bank accounts, consider withdrawing your money in them now before the perfect storm strikes and depletes or confiscates it. Convert a surviving remnant of your cash into something of proven, solid value that the politicians cannot run off a printing press.

You can already see this perfect storm converging, the flashes of its lightning, and the evidence that its targets include your bank account. It is already siphoning the purchasing power from your accounts because "financial repression" is a deliberate policy holding the interest rate you receive lower than the rate of government-created inflation.

You may have little time to act before this storm strikes your accounts. As soon as an election passes, lame duck politicians assume that they can take unpopular actions with no consequences for another two years. For the rest of us, the best time to free a portion of your money from the politicized traps of paper currency and bank accounts is "as soon as possible." This can make your money much safer.

The government would justify seizing our retirement accounts, of course, as "protecting" them for our own good. The money it takes from us will be replaced with government debt paper, in effect IOUs, as happened in Argentina and as has happened to the $2.66 Trillion our honorable politicians looted from the Social Security Trust Fund.

Americans will then receive an "annuity" each year out of these accounts in bondage. Retirees, however, might never be allowed to cash out their government paper, and when they die the government IOUs might simply vanish, not go to their heirs. Unlike IRAs or 401(k)s, your retirement money could be absorbed by the government or redistributed to others who never saved a penny.

Your retirement savings might, in effect, be turned into Social Security Version 2.0, and employers may soon be forced to fund such accounts for all employees – based on required buying of government debt so government can keep growing bigger.

In his 2014 State of the Union speech, President Obama offered to let working poor people participate in a version of a federal worker retirement program he called "Myra." This program would allow workers to acquire government bonds, the same sort of debt paper that foreign nations are now reluctant to buy from us out of fear its obligation might never be repaid. The bonds Mr. Obama offered the poor were paying a bank-like interest rate of 1.7 percent.

Our Progressive President, in other words, is now recruiting even the working poor to help fund his lavish, oversized government.

For in every country of the world...
the avarice and injustice of princes and sovereign states,
abusing the confidence of their subjects,
have by degrees diminished the real quantity of metal,
which had been originally contained in their coins....
to pay their debts...with a smaller quantity
of silver than would otherwise have been requisite....

"[T]heir creditors were really defrauded
of a part of what was due to them....
Such operations...have always proved favourable
to the debtor, and ruinous to the creditor,
and have sometimes produced a greater and more
universal revolution in the fortunes of private persons
than could have been occasioned
by a very great public calamity."

– **Adam Smith**
The Wealth of Nations (1776)

PART THREE
The Choice

Chapter Eight
The Death of Banking
(As We Know It)

*"Since World War I...the budgeting process
has meant, in effect, saying yes to everything....
[This] new dispensation...assumes that there are
no economic limits to the revenues it can obtain, [so]
government becomes the master of civil society,
able to mold and shape it...in the politician's image.
[U]nder the new dispensation it is only too easy
to see national income as belonging to government,
with individuals entitled only to whatever
government is willing to let them have.
The assumption in earlier days was that
everything belonged to the individual...."*

– Peter F. Drucker
Post-Capitalist Society [148]

Banks have served and shaped our societies for thousands of years. Yet in the near future, banks as we have known them may cease to exist. So might the dollar. If we continue down today's economic path, the future could be frightful.

Americans have a favorite banker. His name is George Bailey, the owner of Bailey Bros. Building & Loan in Bedford Falls, New York. George is the fictional character played by actor Jimmy Stewart in the classic 1946 Frank Capra movie "It's a Wonderful Life."

George Bailey was imaginary, yet created from the ideals that used to make the presidents of neighborhood banks among the most respected figures in most small American towns. The banker knew his neighbors personally as friends, understood what challenges each had overcome, and made compassion, care and mutual respect a part of every deposit and loan.

Our word "mortgage" comes from the Old French root *mort*, "death," and means an obligation that will last until you die. In Bailey's Building and Loan Association, however, mortgages became the path to a better life and to the fulfillment of the American Dream.

"It's deep in the race for a man to want his own roof, walls and fireplace, and we'll be helping him get those things," George's generous-hearted father tells him before dying and leaving the bank to his son, who had wanted to travel the world and become an architect.

Instead, George finds himself owner of a risky fractional-reserve bank, like the one where you have your account today. When rumors spark a bank run, he must spend his hard-saved personal honeymoon money to halt the run and keep the bank from bankruptcy.

"You're thinking of this place all wrong. As if I had the money back in a safe," George tells the fearful edge-of-stampeding crowd.

"The money's not here. Your money's in Joe's house....And in the Kennedy house, and Mrs. Macklin's house, and a hundred others," he explains to them.

"Why, you're lending them the money to build, and then, they're going to pay it back to you as best they can," says George. "Now what are you going to do? Foreclose on them?" [149]

Jimmy Stewart delivers an excellent explanation of how fractional-reserve banking works. The milling crowd of frightened depositors shifts back from their herd instinct and mob psychology into individual human beings, friends and neighbors again. However, this speech reminds us that most people thought their money was safe and available, not invested in a high-risk gamble they could lose.

Later, when $8,000 of the Building & Loan's money vanishes, George becomes so distraught that he is about to commit suicide, until his guardian angel intervenes. The $8,000 was diverted by rapacious, miserly banker and Bailey Building & Loan board member Henry Potter, who knew the money had been accidentally mislaid. This diversion brought the Building & Loan to the brink of ruin and put innocent George at risk of going to prison.

In a variation of what happens to tight-fisted Scrooge in Charles Dickens' "A Christmas Carol," Bailey is reminded of the many good things he and his bank have done, and the difference he has made in people's lives.

George is also shown how grim his community's future would have been had he never lived. In this alternative world, Potter, eager to cut off loans to hard-pressed working-class people, controls the community called Pottersville.

Thus, George Bailey faces a choice: does he kill himself and let a ruthless, hard-hearted bankster take control of the financial lives and future of his town? Or does he choose to live and find a way to restore the trust, mutual support and love of his community?

We, both as individuals and as a society, face a similar choice today between two futures for our intertwined stores of value – our banks and our dollars. We shall explain where our present course leads as one of these alternative futures. In Chapter Nine we shall reveal paths to a brighter, freer, more secure and prosperous future.

Bankroll

Our Age of Progressivism has put banks in a slow, downward death spiral to their doom, at least as we have known them.

The past century of Progressive economics has brought us to this point: a near-stagnant economy in a welfare state where roughly half the population gets some kind of government benefit.

To pay for this, America's central bank – the Federal Reserve – and the government's Treasury Department have been conjuring more than $1 Trillion each year by one or another monetary manipulation.

This new money is no longer backed by gold, nor even printed on paper. It exists simply as electronic digits flickering through vulnerable centralized computer systems....like what Thomas Jefferson called paper, the "ghost of money and not money itself."

To keep this new magic money from vaporizing in a blaze of hyperinflation, and to pursue the ideological agenda of Progressivism, much of this money is snatched back by the Fed and government via rising taxes and regulatory penalties on the shrinking private, productive sector of the economy.

As we have learned, Progressive politicians now view America's banks as their personal ATM machines, as places from which money can be commanded via mandates for ideological objectives or extracted in many other ways to bankroll the government and its hive of bureaucrats, dependents and office-seekers.

(Yes, such shakedown politicians have given the old word "bankroll" a whole new meaning. Politicians with increasing frequency "roll" the banks to enrich themselves and stay in power.)

Unspoken Rules

Politicians impose harsh-but-vague rules on banks, then demand huge fines and penalties for purported violations. Bankers are to submit, as well as pay huge political contributions. Bankers are to avoid any criticism of the ruling elite. Look what befell JPMorgan Chase President Jaime Dimon after raising tiny questions about Obama policies.

Well, maybe not always tiny. Mr. Dimon, a big Democratic contributor, described himself in May 2012, months before a presidential election, on NBC's *Meet The Press* this way: "I would describe myself a 'barely Democrat' at this point.... I've gotten disturbed at some of the Democrats' anti-business behavior, the attacks on work ethic and successful people," Dimon said. "I think it's very counterproductive."

"[I]t doesn't mean I don't have their values. I want jobs. I want a more equitable society. I don't mind paying higher taxes.... I do think we're our brother's keeper....," Dimon continued. "But I think that...attacking that which creates all things is not the right way to go about it." [150]

Progressive politicians now routinely invoke regulatory power to silence or destroy critics and opponents, and use favorable regulation to give an advantage to those cronies who are ideologically aligned with them.

When fined, bankers understand that no matter what violations of law they are accused of committing, none of them will go to jail so long as they pay the millions or billions of dollars the politicians demand. This has become the tradeoff for banker acquiescence, compliance and submission.

"Not Too-Big-To-Jail"

When Attorney General Eric Holder in 2014 huffed and puffed and warned that executives at the largest banks were "not Too-Big-To-Jail," he was just playing at populist politics for the cheers of the peanut gallery.

The heads of the biggest banks trust that, in the long run, this is merely a politicized money-laundering operation. By retaining their legal status, large banks retain the privilege of staying in business and will soon be able to refill what politicians siphon from their coffers.

These bankers have deliberately made their institutions "fragile by design," as Calomiris and Haber put it in their book by that title, so that politicians dare not go too far in taking steps that might crush them. [151]

Increasingly, however, today's radical Progressives want to drain *all* the capital from banks, not only to redistribute their money but also to destroy these institutions of Capitalism, which they hate with fanatical fervor. These Progressives are the heirs of Jesse James.

"The urge to save humanity," wrote H.L. Mencken, "is almost always a false-face for the urge to rule it."

The Bible understood perfectly 2,000 years ago who those we today call Progressives really are, right down to their self-righteous and self-servingly dishonest rhetoric. The Gospel of John 12:3-6 (KJV) tells us:

> *"Then took Mary a pound of ointment of spikenard, very costly, and anointed the feet of Jesus.... Then saith one of the disciples....Why was not this ointment sold for three hundred pence and given to the poor? This he said, not that he cared for the poor, but because he was a thief, and had the bag [of Jesus and the disciples], and bare what was put therein."*

This very Progressive disciple who pretended to care about the poor was Judas Iscariot.

Nationalizing the Banks

It should not surprise us that today's radical Progressives, like Democratic Senator Elizabeth Warren of Massachusetts, want to see today's largest private banks taken over and run by the government. They want these banks nationalized.

And who, then, would have *de facto* ownership of the wealth of the banks, in fulfillment of Karl Marx and Friedrich Engels' guidance in their 1848 *Communist Manifesto* that to destroy the bourgeoisie there should be: "Centralization of credit in the hands of the state, by means of a national bank with state capital and an exclusive monopoly." [152]

Does Senator Warren not understand that the banks are already being nationalized?

The government might not "own" the deed to JPMorgan Chase, as Marxism advocates, but today's collectivists have recognized the superior evil cunning of fascism in confiscating property by regulation.

If the government seizes and runs the banks, it can no longer collect corporate or property taxes from them. Mussolini and Hitler understood how easily government can collect such taxes, but then tell a bank how much interest it must pay, who must be given favored loans, who must be hired, what pay and health care its employees must be given, and so forth.

With enough rules and regulations, government can impose its *de facto* ownership over banks and all other companies, while squeezing them for taxes, bribes, mandated goodies for leftist constituents, and political donations.

In America today, almost no enterprise is more regulated than banking. And every regulation is one more pressure point – choke point, if you will – that can be pressed to extort from banks whatever Progressive politicians desire.

Then, whenever bank policies cause public upset, the same politicians enriched by the banks will mount the nearest soapbox to attack "those greedy bankers" for not paying higher interest rates to savers or giving more subprime mortgages to those who are bad loan risks.

Financial Repression

Banks nowadays find themselves caught between regulation and the need to turn a profit.

The Fed and government, as noted earlier, are now practicing what economists call "financial repression" by deliberately holding interest rates below the rate of inflation.

This means that for seniors and others on fixed incomes, having a savings account at the bank is a losing proposition. Inflation eats up the purchasing power of their savings faster than repressed bank interest can build it.

This creates a powerful incentive for people to withdraw their money from the bank and take the moral hazard of betting it on something that could have higher returns, such as the stock market.

We say "bet" because the most recent Nobel laureates in economics won the prize for showing that in the long run the stock market is a rational investment, but in the short run the volatility of stocks is as uncertain and risky as a casino.

Financial repression, however, is a guaranteed loss of the value of your savings. This is a cynical, calculated policy intended to force savers out of the "safety" they naively sought in banks, and into the stock exchange casino, where many will be sheared and fleeced like sheep.

As government and the Fed drive savers out of banks, where will banks get the money to lend for profit? The answer since the economic near-collapse of 2008 has been – surprise – the Fed and the government, which have made huge loans to banks here and abroad.

Recycling Money

And where has this money gone? Much has been lent by the banks back to the government itself, which pays the banks more in interest on the money than it charges the banks. The margins are small, but from the banks' point of view the risk of lending to the government is zero. The government can always print more money to cover its debt to the banks.

Roughly 18 percent of bank assets are on loan to the government. And roughly 40 percent of America's entire Gross Domestic Product comes from federal, state and local government spending.

As added incentive for the banks to lend to government, the government imposed new tighter lending rules following the subprime lending debacle caused by the Community Reinvestment Act (CRA). The banks face potentially huge penalties and fines if they make "risky" loans, with risk to be defined after the fact by bureaucrats and partisan government lawyers.

Yet by mid-2014, an election year, the banks were rapidly increasing their loans to risky private homeowners and businesses after much forceful persuasion from President Obama.

As we explained in Chapter 6, under the CRA, during the presidencies of Jimmy Carter and Bill Clinton, Progressives nearly twisted off the arms of bankers to force them to make such loans by threatening regulatory retaliation if they refused.

The very politicians who imposed the CRA and its rules, after things soured, condemned banks for making the risky loans to uncreditworthy borrowers that government officials had demanded of them.

By mid-2014 it was obvious that bankers were again having their arms nearly twisted off at the shoulder politically to again increase subprime lending.

Even as they lend long, these banks are bracing for the loss of up to $1 Trillion in deposits as the Federal Reserve reverses its emergency economic policies and raises interest rates. JPMorgan by itself, reported the *Financial Times*, "has estimated that money funds may withdraw $100 Billion in deposits in the second half of [2015] as the Fed uses a new tool to help wind down its asset purchase programme and normalise rates."

"An outflow of deposits would be a reversal of a five-year trend that has seen significant amounts of extra cash pour into banks thanks to the Fed flooding the financial system with liquidity. These deposits, which act as a cheaper source of funding, have helped banks weather the aftermath of the financial crisis," reports the *Financial Times*. [153]

Banks might soon be pressed to offer higher rates on deposits. Banks will also find it harder to keep large institutional deposits because the Fed's new tool to cover its retreat, a "reverse repo facility," reports the *Financial Times*, "effectively allows non-banks such as money funds to have reserve accounts at the Fed."

This convergence of pressures "would drain reserves from banks," an analyst at Autonomous Research, Guy Moszkoweski, told the *Financial Times*. [154]

Ghost Banks

In July 2014, the New York Stock Exchange topped 17,000 for the first time – at least without adjusting for inflation.

This event, coming just before America's Fourth of July birthday, popped a few champagne corks but also stirred apprehension. Veteran traders were bracing for what some called a "huge coming correction" that would send the market plummeting.

Their fear was logical: although frustrated savers continue to flee the banks and other relatively safe havens and bring their money to market, experts know that little has actually improved in the real economy. Those savings were seed corn needed to revive a sick and stagnant economy, yet this precious grain was being scattered not on fertile soil but in a Wall Street gambling casino run by sharpers.

Many of America's big investment banks have made risky bets and left themselves dependent on government and the Fed to bail them out. These megabanks are too deep in potential trouble to be saved in a dire crisis. The Fed, according to the Government Accountability Office, from 2007 through 2010 committed $16.115 Trillion in various loans to rescue banks.

However, today's biggest banks have stratospheric exposure to derivatives that even the Fed would find hard to bail out: reportedly at least $44.19 Trillion for Goldman Sachs, $50.13 Trillion for Bank of America, $52.1 Trillion for Citibank, $70.15 Trillion for JPMorgan Chase, and $72.8 Trillion for Deutsche Bank. Just 9 major banks on which the world economy depends have derivative exposure of more than $290 Trillion in a global $693 Trillion derivatives market! Listen for a moment and you can hear this time bomb -- called by Warren Buffett a "Financial Weapon of Mass Destruction" -- ticking. If this explodes, neither the Fed nor the FDIC could put your bank or deposits back together again. The paper dollar would be ashes to ashes, dust to dust.

Borrowers, meanwhile, increasingly turn to shadow banks, venture capitalists, crowdsourcing, and other less-regulated sources of lending and credit.

The "Fed Paradox"

To understand why our economy is wallowing in a slough of despond, we need to remember that our economy is an elaborate shell game that now offers few ways out of today's problems short of monetizing the debt, simply printing vast amounts of money, which would destroy the two percent that remains of the 1912 purchasing power of the pre-Progressive Era U.S. Dollar.

Let's pause and watch this shell game for a moment. Keep your eye on which shell the pea is under:

Politicians created the Federal Reserve in 1913 to rescue us from the Boom and Bust cycle in the economy. This cycle, however, was largely created by the instability of fractional-reserve banking, which we have done nothing to halt.

Politicians created the Federal Reserve to free our money supply from political influence, but charged the Fed to "furnish an elastic currency" that has given our politicians nearly infinite amounts of money printed out of nothing, backed neither by the gold standard nor actual productivity in the economy.

The Fed's original mandate is to protect the value of the dollar, but the Fed openly pursues money-conjuring policies designed to create two percent or more inflation every year to prevent deflation. In a deflation, the dollar increases in value; during inflation, the dollar decreases in value. Inflation is therefore just another word for theft.

"It is a sobering fact that the prominence of central banks in this century has coincided with a general tendency towards more inflation, not less," wrote former Federal Reserve Chairman Paul Volcker in 1994. "By and large," wrote Volcker, "if the overriding objective is price stability, we did better with the 19th Century gold standard...."

The Power to Destroy

"The truly unique power of a central bank," wrote Volcker, "is the power to create money, and ultimately the power to create is the power to destroy." [155]

The Fed's second mandate, issued under President Jimmy Carter, was to maximize employment in the economy. Under the theories of popular British economist John Maynard Keynes, this has meant stimulation of the economy with government spending on the low side of the Boom and Bust cycle.

What we have learned during the continuing Great Recession, however, is that government stimulus spending frightened businesspeople into cutting back on their spending and hiring. As we predicted, Fed and Obama policies proved to be an "anti-stimulus" that continues to make things worse, not better.

Businesspeople feared that dumping trillions of dollars into the economy would cause severe inflation, which until now has been frozen by money having the slowest velocity through the economy in 50 years. Fed stimulus is supposed to increase money's velocity.

The Fed has used its power to drive interest rates in the economy to near zero. This should be good news for those wishing to borrow money. Alas, the Fed and government have also severely tightened lending requirements, so that mostly only those who already have huge assets, and the government, are able to borrow. As comedian Bob Hope once put it, "A bank is a place that will lend you money if you can prove that you don't need it."

For large companies, these rock-bottom interest rates make it easy to keep trillions of dollars in earnings overseas, beyond the reach of America's absurd average 40 percent federal-plus-state business income tax rate. The Fed has made it cheaper for these companies to keep their revenues untaxed abroad while running the U.S. portion of their enterprises by borrowing tax-free near-zero-interest money. This retards hiring in the U.S. and moves our jobs offshore, where the revenue is. This encourages business flight abroad into multi-billion-dollar "tax inversion" mergers that turn foreign companies in lower-taxed nations into the legal parent or owner of American enterprises.

This almost-free money also keeps the casino of speculation we call the Stock Market soaring, high on cheap cash. But record stock market numbers now have almost nothing to do with our sluggish, indebted economy. If anything, they have an inverse relationship, making the market go up on bad economic news likely to force the Fed to conjure yet more easy money, and down on a good economy that would prompt the Fed to print less stimulus money.

Millennials v. Robots

Cheap borrowed money also helps employers buy robot technologies that can replace U.S. workers with machines that never strike or take sick days. Since most new jobs are now part-time and low-paid, the Millennial Generation faces a terrible struggle to fulfill the American Dream....unless it downgrades or redefines that dream.

Our spendaholic politicians are addicted to easy money. Fed economists know that it is disastrous in the long run to keep interest rates near zero, because this severely punishes savers, the retired, and most investors.

As Progressive politicians take us deeper and deeper into debt – the most indebtedness in 200 years around the world – the Fed is moving slowly to let interest rates rise to natural levels in order to restore a healthy economy.

The danger is that every one percent of interest rate rise could cost the government up to $1 Trillion in coming years in interest costs on the enormous debt already borrowed.

In a normal economy, the usual interest rate is between 5 and 6 percent, which could add as much as $3 Trillion to $6 Trillion in interest charges a year. This would devour all current government spending and require that all taxes go merely to paying the debts for yesterday's spending and political promises.

Because this could obliterate our economy, government would at some point simply monetize the debt by printing untold trillions of dollars out of thin air.

As CNBC's Rick Santelli says, why would a banker lend money if he cannot make a decent return on it? Why have a bank account that pays you nothing and charges you fees on top of that? But if everybody withdraws their bank deposits, then the only source of money might be the government.

Truth be told, many bankers are tired of being conventional bankers. They are tired of taking the deposits of savers who can withdraw their savings in a heartbeat with the click of a mouse. They are tired of then being politically coerced to lend this money to "Ninjas" on a risky 30-year mortgage.

In addition, lawyers are now contemplating a class action suit saying that bankers should have known when a borrower was a poor repayment risk and therefore should not have to repay. This is similar to the laws that punish a bartender for selling a borderline drunk a glass of booze...who might sue the bartender for a civil rights violation if he *refuses* to sell to the drunk.

This, of course, is only the tip of the iceberg of the Fed Paradox.

The Search for Better Money

As if by instinct, millions of us sense that something is wrong with our money, even though few know precisely what has gone wrong. Millions feel that today's Central Banks such as the Fed, along with the government, have turned the fiat currency we work for, and have been taught to crave and depend upon, into a con game.

The dollar, we intuitively sense, is being manipulated to extract the maximum work from us while shrinking in value to pay us the minimum reward needed to keep us running on the hamster wheel.

We are aware that the real, inflation-adjusted income of America's squeezed Middle Class has not increased significantly in almost 40 years.

The impulse to escape the dollar has taken some to the emerging technology of new high-tech digital money such as Bitcoin. Is this a way out – a way to regain both our economic independence and our personal privacy from government's economic surveillance – or is Bitcoin a dead-end road?

Bitcoin was devised in 2009 by a master computer programmer, and in its infancy one Bitcoin could be bought for as little as 25 cents.

In late 2013, speculators pushed the price of a single Bitcoin momentarily to $1,241, close to parity with an ounce of gold.

Many with a get-rich-quick itch were persuaded to embrace Bitcoin as "Gold 2.0" or "Gold for Nerds," and joined the Bitcoin Goldrush.

In 2013 alone, this little-understood investment surged 6,000 percent in value, partly by attracting investor money that in earlier years would have bought gold as traditional diversification insurance to hedge against the risk of inflation.

Eager to ride this skyrocket, Sir Richard Branson gained worldwide publicity by offering to accept bitcoins as payment for $250,000 trips to the edge of Outer Space aboard his soon-to-launch Virgin Galactic service.

Within days of reaching its stratospheric high price, however, Bitcoin plummeted to less than half its peak value when China suddenly restricted its use. Branson reportedly declared that he would still accept bitcoins at their now-much-lower value. (He likely would not keep them as an investment, but would instead convert them immediately into cash.)

Tulip Mania 2.0?

Boston University School of Management Executive-in-Residence Mark T. Williams, a former commodities trader and Federal Reserve bank examiner, predicted that the volatile Bitcoin would crash, returning hard to Earth at only $10, less than one percent of its 2013 peak value.

As of the time of this writing, despite wild price fluctuations and the apparent collapse of its Japanese redemption center, Bitcoin has defied the doubters and survived. On August 27, 2014 its approximate value was $513.13.

Even so, warn critics, Bitcoin is "Fool's Gold." Many compare it to the wild speculation over tulips that gripped the Netherlands in January 1637. This judgment-impairing fever caused frenzied investors to eagerly pay more than the price of a house for a single prized tulip bulb. [156]

When this Tulip Mania speculative bubble burst, prices plunged fast and far, much as they did in autumn 2013 for Bitcoin. Some have suggested renaming Bitcoin "Tulip Mania 2.0."

The Dutch obsession with tulips almost four centuries ago was not entirely wasted. Out of it the Netherlands developed a major flower industry that thrives today.

The Bitcoin fad, by contrast, as of this writing is only five years old, but might be bankrupt and replaced by competitors in as little as a year or two. It might be the Neanderthal, fated for failure and extinction, of a new approach to what we think of as money.

The search for an alternative money comes from a valid sense millions of us share – that today's massively over-printed paper fiat U.S. Dollar is politically manipulated and doomed to crash by fundamental laws of economics. A more secure, trustworthy and reliable store of value, unit of account, and medium of exchange to replace the dollar is urgently needed.

What *Is* Bitcoin?

Widely described as a "peer-to-peer cyber-currency" or "crypto-currency," the word Bitcoin actually has two meanings.

Bitcoin is the name of "an online financial network that people use to send payments from one person to another," writes economics journalist Timothy B. Lee of the *Washington Post*.

Bitcoin is primarily a low-cost alternative to credit cards such as Visa or to PayPal. However, it differs from Visa or PayPal in two ways: Nobody owns or controls this decentralized network, and Bitcoin network transactions are conducted not in dollars, Euros, Yuan or Yen, but in its own monetary unit, an imaginary "virtual currency" also called bitcoin, written with a small "b."

The creator of Bitcoin is "Satoshi Nakamoto," the pseudonym of a computer (but not economics) genius who in 2009 proposed this new medium of exchange. He designed an extremely complex open protocol by which computers solve transactional algorithms to "mine" Bitcoins.

As of early 2014, every 10 minutes a Bitcoin "miner" somewhere on Earth is solving the next mathematical computer problem, having it validated by a network node, and thereby earning 25 Bitcoins' worth, in exchange value, around $12,828. Over years, the payback for such efforts is scheduled to decline.

These problems grow in complexity so that, as with gold mining, more effort over time will be required to "mine" each next Bitcoin. The mysterious Satoshi Nakamoto designed his protocol so that by around year 2035 the last of 21 million possible Bitcoins will be claimed, almost twice as many bitcoins as the 12 million already "mined" as of early 2014.

Government vs. Bitcoin

Bitcoins today are not accepted as "legal tender" by any government or mint as government currencies are, nor do Bitcoins have any guaranteed exchange value. Draft legislation in both California and New York, if passed, reportedly might move Bitcoin closer to legal status as currency.

What Bitcoins do have – if their supporters can be believed – is a guaranteed 21 million limit forever on total supply, on how many can be created. So long as people desire bitcoins and not some other cyber-currency, this supply ceiling could be more reassuring than a Federal Reserve willing to print countless trillions of paper dollars out of thin air.

Because Bitcoins ultimately are mere numbers in a computer, each can be digitally divided down to eight decimal places to instantly create fractional bitcoins.

The dollar's history traces back to Spanish "Pieces of Eight," coins sometimes broken into eight equal pieces of silver called "bits." The U.S. Quarter coin inspired the expression that something cheap was "two bit," worth 25 percent of a dollar. This word for money lives on in the name Bitcoin.

Because bitcoins are merely numbers in a computer, they have been hacked, stolen or accidentally misdirected. Since transactions using bitcoins are anonymous, encrypted and permanent, transactions are difficult to reverse.

Anonymity makes Bitcoin a medium reportedly favored by some online gamblers, drug dealers, circumventors of currency controls in places such as Argentina, money-launderers, tax evaders and other criminals, as well as by honest people who simply want freedom from government surveillance.

The privacy afforded by Bitcoins has drawn attention from many governments that are eager to monitor citizen activities, to tax as barter Bitcoin transactions, and to collect not only income and sales taxes but also the hidden tax politicians collect by deliberately inflating their nation's currency.

Unlike today's dollar, Bitcoins can cause deflation – an increase in value over time as owners hoard it. Our book *The Inflation Deception* explains why today's governments want inflation, not deflation.

Governments will harass Bitcoin until this crypto-currency's operators agree to let politicians track, tax and target its users. With the National Security Agency (NSA) preparing to use quantum supercomputers, Bitcoin encryption may be unable to protect user privacy much longer, anyway. But any agreement to surrender user information would limit the appeal of Bitcoin for many suspicious-of-government supporters.

Dawn of Cyber-Currency

Nevertheless, Bitcoin is the first widely-recognized brand name in what could be a very lucrative future wealth transfer technology. Up to 20,000 online merchants and local stores reportedly may be willing to accept bitcoins as payment, including giant *Overstock.com*.

Customer payment via credit card can cost a merchant 3-5%; this is why many cards now offer cash back of 1-2% to encourage card use by customers who do not know that stores have marked up their prices to cover credit card fees. Fees for accepting Bitcoins can be far lower, a potential boon to merchants.

Others see Bitcoin as an inevitable step towards economist Friedrich A. Hayek's dream of a world where people end government money monopolies and freely choose among competing currencies. The libertarian community Galt's Gulch Chile bases its economy on Bitcoin.

Governments also see opportunity in any cyber-currency willing to bend its knee to politicians. Politicians are eager to move from hard-to-track physical money to a "cashless society" in which all future transactions are merely electronic impulses passing through – and being taxed automatically by – government-monitored computers. A politically-submissive Bitcoin-like currency would be a huge step towards "cashless" control.

For today's investors, Bitcoin already has dozens of digital imitators and would-be competitors. Even banking and investment giant Goldman Sachs, with its influential political connections, has reportedly begun laying the legal groundwork for its own Bitcoin-like currency.

Since Bitcoins have no intrinsic value, their price has swung wildly – even falling by several hundred dollars within hours. His own analysis led the conservative *London Telegraph*'s business tech reporter James Titcomb to warn that "Bitcoin has been hijacked by speculators" and that it may be "a Ponzi scheme" whose sharp fluctuations lure get-rich-quick investors but will prevent Bitcoin from being accepted as a reliable alternative currency. Competitors, Titcomb predicts, will overtake and extinguish Bitcoin.

Whatever ultimately happens, the hope many feel for Bitcoin and its digital money rivals suggests that people are losing their once-solid faith in the future of the government and its manipulated monopoly currency.

More and more people are starting to doubt the future of the U.S. Dollar, and because it is now a faith-based currency backed by and convertible to nothing, a loss of belief in the once-almighty dollar could at some point soon bring its collapse and end.

"It's a Wonderful Life"

One theme of the 1946 Frank Capra movie "It's a Wonderful Life" was Bailey being shown what his community would have been like if he and his little bank had never existed.

We are now beginning to see that alternative future in our own world, and what it portends is not pretty.

As our banks become mere middlemen for government money, how long will it be until government simply eliminates these middlemen and itself becomes America's bank?

This could resemble how the Obama Administration expropriated 90 percent of America's student loans, then offered help to those students who still hold the remaining 10 percent to change loan terms to reduce private bank profits.

Student loans have become profitable for government, which has offered to forgive loans for those who take what Progressives see as "politically correct" jobs in the public sector or as activists. Student loans have thus been politicized to a shocking degree.

As we plunge into the "cashless society," banks as we have known them will begin to vanish.

At first we will see more entities such as Ally Bank – formerly known as General Motors Acceptance Corporation (GMAC), the car loan-funding arm of General Motors – boasting that you can now bank via telephone or computer with no need for a local branch office or a safe. [157]

As of January 2012, our government had sunk $12 Billion into Ally Financial, the bank's corporate parent. Ally in March 2012 reportedly failed a Federal Reserve "stress test" for capital adequacy. Its auto loans are profitable, but its spun-off ResCap mortgage subsidiary in 2009, 2010 and 2011 wrote off $22 Billion in bad mortgages, many of them subprime. On May 15, 2012, ResCap went into Chapter 11 bankruptcy. Our government owns approximately 74 percent of Ally shares.

Soon your cell phone or tablet will be your bank, holding your electronic wallet – and behind this, whether heavily publicized or not, will be the government whose Federal Deposit Insurance Corporation (FDIC) already says it insures your accounts.

Public banks in the legal sense cannot operate without government approval, and government approval hinges on political subservience....so for all intents and purposes, your bank already *IS* the government.

The day private banking dies will probably not even be noticed. The transition to government officially becoming your bank will be seamless.

The All-Seeing Eye

Anyone who questions the disappearance of old-fashioned banks will be reminded how much cleaner and safer the cashless society is. No Jesse James will ever be able to rob you again.

Soon, however, you will notice that when you transfer $100 to your son as a gift on graduating high school, the government deletes $20 as tax on this transaction. You then discover that government is taking 20 percent from nearly every transaction.

The news then announces that all transactions in the new society *must* be done via this system that has replaced your bank. The story calls it good news that no criminal will be able to buy or sell anything if the government shuts off his identity in the system.

However, if a criminal or rebel is being hunted, his digital identity may be left intact so that government can track his exact location. Or his identity may be left so that government can compare his lifestyle with his official earnings, so that any discrepancy can be used to prosecute him for the crime of barter off the government's tax books.

Death of Banking and the Dollar

A few days later, the government announces that the cashless accounting unit being exchanged will no longer be called dollars. Henceforth they will be called "credits."

From that moment, nobody actually has spendable dollars anymore, the news reports. Dollars must be exchanged within 30 days on a one-for-one basis for the new "credits." It is now illegal to exchange dollars in any other way.

Days later the government announces – and notifies everyone via their cell phone – that, in the name of Progressive egalitarianism, all old-fashioned accounts containing "money" have been redistributed so we all have an equal share of America's wealth.

The government is extending equal credits to all, including a guaranteed annuity called New Social Security to which everyone will be entitled until death.

(Apart from this, however, nothing may be saved or passed on as an inheritance.)

With roughly half of Americans already receiving one or another kind of social welfare benefit, the majority applauds and supports the new dispensation – the Great Redistribution as it comes to be called.

Second-Hand Life

This will not bring a life of luxury, except for the ruling elite and its cronies. The typical family will be able to afford a 300-square-foot apartment, and it will be furnished with an amazing flat screen television and sound system that draws them into living a vicarious life of second-hand experiences, instead of first-hand material accomplishments.

The average couple will live to age 90, but for some mysterious reason fewer and fewer will be able to have children.

The national population will go into a nosedive. The middle class will disintegrate as society separates into lower classes and those living in gated communities, a ruling elite.

Welfare beneficiaries will be less happy in a few short years when the United Nations imposes its own version of income leveling worldwide.

Few Americans realized that earning or receiving in benefits as little as $34,000 a year puts one in the top one percent of income worldwide – a level of "wealth" that Progressives have targeted for destruction with their global class warfare.

Their wealth will now be redistributed planet-wide, and what remains here in the U.S. will be much, much less.

Henceforth, Americans will no longer be able to afford a slacker welfare state.

Henceforth, Americans will be required to work – mostly for what they grew up thinking of as Third World wages.

Did they not understand that the first flood of poor children from Central America in 2014 was the Progressive importation of a Marxist Proletariat to help wage class warfare in the United States?

Did they not understand that the mass movement of populations to alter and control societies has been used by every empire from ancient Babylon until today?

The *Other* Path

We could choose a different path.

We could restore honest money, currency and tax competition among nations.

What kind of world could await us at the end of this very different rainbow, where you might even discover how to become your own banker?

> *"No bank should be allowed to become so big*
> *that it can blackmail governments."*
> -- **Angela Merkel**
> German Chancellor
> *Financial Times*, August 31, 2009

Former Federal Reserve Chairman Alan Greenspan

QUESTIONER: "How specifically should we address the issue of financial institutions that are too big to fail?"

ALAN GREENSPAN: "If they're too big to fail, they're too big....

"The critical problem...which we've got to resolve, is the too-big-to-fail issue...[I]f we do not confront it, we are going to be in terrible shape....

"At a minimum, you've got to take care of the competitive advantage they have, because of the implicit subsidy, which makes them competitively capable of beating out their smaller competitors, who don't get the subsidy [backing by government bailouts].

"...[I]f you don't neutralize that, you're going to get a moribund group of obsolescent institutions, which will be a big drain on the savings of this society.

"I don't have a simple solution, but...something has to be done.... and I don't think merely raising the fees or capital on large institutions or taxing them is enough. I think...they'll absorb that; they'll work with it; and they will still be inefficient....

"So I mean, radical things, as you – you know, break them up.... In 1911, we broke up Standard Oil. So what happened? The individual parts became more valuable than the whole. Maybe that's what we need."

– October 15, 2009 Speech to the
Council on Foreign Relations

Chapter Nine
A Future You *Could* Bank On

"What is robbing a bank
compared with founding a bank?"

– Bertolt Brecht
The Threepenny Opera

We can choose a different path to safeguard our dollars that combines the best of old-fashioned banking and honest money with new technologies. Each of us has the power to help decide banking's future for ourselves – and even to become our own banker and convert a portion of our bank accounts into our own gold standard.

"You're the richest man in town," George Bailey's brother proclaims after friends and grateful customers chip in to rescue the nearly-bankrupt Bailey Building and Loan in the movie "It's A Wonderful Life."

Can we save the best qualities of banking and the store of value the U.S. Dollar used to be? The good news is that we can, possibly throughout America, and certainly in our personal lives, if we take the right fundamental steps:

Step One: Return to More Honest, Competitive Money

Step Two: Restore the Classic Gold Standard Dollar

Step Three: End the Federal Reserve System

Step Four: Re-create Full-Reserve Banking

Step Five: Replace the Income Tax with Consumption Taxes

Step Six: End all taxation on Americans outside the country

Step Seven: Save Your Money in Non-digital Ways

Step Eight: Become Your Own Banker

As we have learned, the government and Federal Reserve have a magician's trick. It lets them steal the value from your savings, *even* if your money remains securely locked in a bank safe.

The security of your bank or accounts may make no difference, therefore, if the purchasing power of your money itself can be stolen from thousands of miles away. Our money and banking are intertwined, so we must make our money's value theft-proof before we can securely bank on it.

This magician's trick works *only* if your savings are held in the form of the magical paper dollars the Fed has conjured digitally or by printing press out of thin air.

The trick works because America's paper fiat money, our national currency, exists in invisible balance with all the goods and services money can buy. When the Fed and government print more dollars than the increase in the supply of those goods and services, a natural economic law comes into play. The Law of Supply and Demand is just as real as the Law of Gravity, and neither can be repealed by politicians.

(We, of course, wish Congress *could* ease the Law of Gravity a bit so we would have no need to lose weight...but they cannot, and would almost certainly make a mess of the universe if they could....just as they continue to distort the marketplace by thinking they can repeal the laws of economics – and tax, spend and borrow our way back to prosperity. The universe does not work this way.)

Double Your Money

When the Fed and government double the number of dollars people have for shopping at the supermarket, the result is that people can afford more food for a brief time, just as you can defy gravity briefly by jumping up in the air.

The Law of Supply and Demand then quickly balances the bigger supply of money with the same old quantity of cantaloupes. After this rebalancing, these melons cost twice as many dollars and cents as before.

In an earlier, thriftier era, it was said that the best way to "double your money" was to fold it over once and put it back in your pocket. In our era of deliberate inflation, however, your money is not safe in your pocket or in a bank vault. It is melting, which gives savers an incentive to "use it or lose it," to spend now rather than save for tomorrow.

Despite our Fed and government conjuring an additional $1 Trillion per year in recent years to stimulate a stagnant economy and produce deliberate inflation, the rest of the world also operates on such debased paper currencies and with some reluctance continues to accept dollars as the world's reserve currency....although China and Russia, among others, increasingly use their own currencies in global transactions.

The U.S. Dollar's status as our world's "global reserve currency" – what the French Finance Minister under President Charles de Gaulle, Valery Giscard d'Estaing, called America's "exorbitant privilege" – means that we control the supply of the world's official exchange medium for oil and other key commodities. When Japan buys a barrel of oil from Saudi Arabia, the price is set and payment is made in U.S. Dollars. [158]

Without this special status, the United States would have to pay a premium price to buy whatever other currency is used to price and purchase oil. Today other nations must buy our dollars to purchase oil, which gives us a significant advantage in global credit and trade.

This, of course, gives others gas pains when the U.S. Government and Federal Reserve inflate our currency by running trillions off the printing press – thereby exporting our inflation to them, and thereby in effect taxing them to enrich ourselves.

The Dollar Trap

As Eswar Presad, a former International Monetary Fund analyst now at Cornell University and with the Brookings Institution in Washington, D.C., points out in his 2014 book *The Dollar Trap: How the U.S. Tightened Its Grip on Global*

Finance, the very crisis that American politicians and our banks precipitated in 2008 caused frightened foreign governments and international investors into acquiring more dollars for safety. By weakening the global economy, the United States ironically profits and gains financial – and therefore political – power. [159]

"There could be no more effective check against the abuse of money by the government than if people were free to refuse any money they distrusted and to prefer money in which they had confidence," wrote Nobel laureate economist Friedrich A. Hayek.

"Nor could there be a stronger inducement to governments to ensure the stability of their money than the knowledge that, so long as they kept the supply below the demand for it, that demand would tend to grow."

"Therefore," wrote Hayek, "let us deprive governments (or their monetary authorities) of all power to protect their money against competition: if they can no longer conceal that their money is becoming bad, they will have to restrict the issue." [160]

Or we could pass laws that end the U.S. Dollar monopoly as "legal tender" in America – a monopoly that requires dollar payment of taxes and goods priced in dollars. Change the "legal tender" laws so that no one is forced to accept any currency or commodity as payment for debts, public or private, except as a contract specifies – the way pre-1933 American contracts had "gold clauses" giving the creditor the choice of being paid in dollars or in units of gold.

Separation of Money and State

Hayek laid out his argument for the separation of money and state in the 1990 Third Edition of his brilliant book *Denationalisation of Money: The Argument Refined: An Analysis of the Theory and Practice of Concurrent Currencies.*

In earlier times, he argued, governments claimed that their monopoly over a nation's money provided a convenient, consistent currency for its citizens.

Today, wrote Hayek, national (and nationalized) money "has the defects of all monopolies: one must use their product even if it is unsatisfactory, and above all, it prevents the discovery of better methods of satisfying a need for which the monopolist has no incentive."

"If the public understood what price in periodic inflation and instability it pays for the convenience of having to deal with only one kind of money in ordinary transactions...," wrote Hayek, "it would probably find it very excessive." [161]

Hayek envisioned a society in which people could choose to make transactions in many kinds of currency, as well as in silver and gold.

Older citizens will remember when each community had only one telephone company that, being a monopoly, charged high rates for often-poor service and even charged customers for connecting their telephone to their own answering machine.

Hayek wanted people to have choice in the currencies they can use. We see the remarkable innovations, benefits and savings that breaking the telephone monopoly and introducing a little free market competition have produced. How do you like your latest cell phone?

(Or imagine having banks freely compete, without government or the Fed giving a few privileged ones guaranteed survival by being designated "Too Big To Fail.")

Imagine what a country of many currencies, each competing for customers, might produce as a store of value and other qualities. In a natural free market, the cream always rises to the top.

The government could also allow private currency. In some ways we already do.

The store coupon that is worth $1 if used to buy a particular product on or before a particular date is, arguably, a kind of currency. Some cities and localities issue their own local or regional scrip "money," just as many did during the Great Depression. [162]

The *Other* Global Money

The world has another universally-recognized money...unchanged for the past 5,000 years. That money is gold, stored in reserve by all the world's Central Banks including the Federal Reserve.

Politicians hate gold because it is money they cannot run off a printing press in never-ending amounts. When the United States was on a classic gold standard prior to the Progressive takeover of our government in 1913, our dollar was the envy of the world.

Because gold is a universal currency, our dollar then was also a universal currency because of its convertibility to gold and hence to all other gold standard national currencies. This gave enormous stability to the world monetary system and encouraged peaceful trade among nations.

Could our dollar transition back to a classic gold standard? In practical terms, yes, it could, by setting its fixed value somewhere between 1/1,500th and 1/5,000th of an ounce of gold. Many analysts say that the U.S. possesses enough gold in reserve to do this.

Restoring America's Golden Age

In political terms, the very reason Progressives terminated the gold standard with extreme prejudice was so they could take political control of the nation's money supply. Their aim was simply to print enough magical dollars to expand the size of, and public dependency upon, the government to a point of no return.

We are now at the tipping point between our original society of independent, self-reliant individuals and a welfare-state future in which the votes of a majority can be bought and paid for with government freebies. The takers are overtaking the makers, and already did so long ago in many big cities.

Gold is more than money. With it comes the independence of not depending on paper currency manipulated by politicians.

"Gold is money. Everything else is credit," the financier J.P. Morgan told Congress in 1912.

What Morgan meant is that credit, when used, becomes debt, a literal "mortgage" on you, your children's and your grandchildren's future. Our nation now faces unmanageable debt – the flip side of credit – and the bitter fruit of allowing Progressives to replace America's gold standard with fiat paper, promissory notes backed only by politician promises.

The root meaning of our word "credit" is the Latin word *credo*, "I believe." Our modern "credit" money system is, in reality, faith-based, much like our paper dollars backed by nothing. Instead of placing our faith in God and following our Founders' mandate to use nothing but the Biblical standard of gold and silver as money, most have misplaced their faith in government, which is a false god.

Sadly, this false or "fiat" money is what most Americans have been misled into accepting in exchange for their lifetime of labor.

Endogenous Money

Today's alchemy of paper fiat money, fractional-reserve banking and digital credit is hazardous because not only the Fed but also your neighborhood bank is able to conjure money out of thin air.

"Whenever a bank makes a loan, it simultaneously creates a matching deposit in the borrower's bank account, thereby creating new money," at long last acknowledged Michael McLeay, Amar Radia and Ryland Thomas of the Bank of England's Monetary Analysis Directorate in a 2014 study titled *Money Creation in the Modern Economy.*

Post-Keynesian theorists call this "endogenous money," meaning that it comes from within the very nature of every participant in the economy. Not only banks but also each of us influences investment, wages and productivity in the economy by how we choose to earn, save and spend money. A stable economy requires a strong, anchored money whose value cannot easily be manipulated by endogenous forces, business cycles, panics or fads. [163]

Farewell to the Fed

Gold is virtually the definition of self-regulating money, a stand-alone standard of value all by itself. As such, no Federal Reserve would be needed to manipulate interest rates or other factors to give gold its value. Gold *is* the universal yardstick of value.

The dawn of a new classic gold standard would be sunset for the Fed.

Even in transition, as Nobel laureate economist Milton Friedman once said, the Federal Reserve could be replaced by a computer.

This Fed computer would have initial human algorithms and data programmed into it, but thereafter it could juggle monetary factors more-or-less objectively and impartially. We would no longer have a presidentially-appointed Fed Chairman claiming to make his decisions free from political influence.

This computer should be kept offline, however, to minimize any risks from hackers or cyber warriors.

Welcome to Full-Reserve Banking

The Federal Reserve was officially created to reduce the economic shocks of Boom and Bust cycles.

The more logical way to do this would be to remove a major cause of these cycles – fractional-reserve banking, which amplifies every problem and thereby increases the amplitude of these waves in the economy.

An obvious old-fashioned alternative exists: Full-reserve banking, in which the bank merely acts as guardian of your deposit and never puts it at risk by lending it out to earn interest.

Since we are entering an era in which banks plan to charge you a fee rather than pay you interest for having an account, you have nothing to lose and a world of safety to gain.

Remember, however, that government armed with a warrant can seize a bank safe deposit box as easily as it can your accounts.

The safest account would be *physical* gold, not paper fiat money, in a place only you know.

The income tax is a Progressive weapon of class warfare and an outrageous violation of citizen privacy that spies and keeps dossiers on all of us. The IRS is also now being used as a direct political weapon for partisan purposes. The IRS and Income Tax should be replaced with a national consumption tax.

"Stress Testing"

American Banks have been forced to buy state or Federal Government bonds as part of their required reserve since the early 1800s. The cost of doing this has always been passed on to you in the form of lower rates of interest on your savings.

This is why banks that have the inherent risk of being fractional-reserve banks are required to pass "stress tests" to demonstrate their financial soundness and survivability under various economic pressures.

Medium-sized banks have needed to have on reserve as little as $3 for every $100 they have in deposits; the reserve requirement for large banks has recently increased to approximately $10 for every $100 of loans it issues.

In 1929, just before the stock market breakdown behind the Great Depression, inexperienced investors who expected to be the next overnight market millionaires were buying into the market on margin by paying only 10 percent or less of the price for "sure thing" stocks. When stock prices shifted, the margin calls on these equities broke the market.

In the stress tests announced in March 2014, the national media reported that 29 of 30 American banks "passed" with flying colors. New York University analysts found, however, that with even tiny adjustments to test standards, 5 of the 6 biggest banks would have failed.

These banks are living on margin, assuming that their bets will be backed up by their FDIC insurance on deposits and by the Fed if a souring economy triggers bank runs.

One economist notes that, even with its power to print money out of thin air, and despite having approximately $4.3 Trillion in federal paper and other investments it has purchased, the Federal Reserve would fail its own "stress test" standards.

A Professor's Great Withdrawal

In January 2014, when former Harvard University Economics Professor Terry Burnham looked closely at the risk in today's banks, he decided to withdraw nearly $1 Million from his own accounts at one of our nation's biggest banks, the Bank of America. [164]

Dr. Burnham no longer trusts our biggest banks to return his money, nor the Fed to make sound policy. His own Great Withdrawal came hours before Janet Yellen became Chair of the Federal Reserve.

Dr. Burnham, we should add, earned a Ph.D. in Business Economics from Harvard and a Master's Degree from the MIT Sloan School with a concentration in finance. He also has worked for Goldman Sachs & Co.

He understands what is now happening better than most do, and in 2014 he pulled his savings out of one of America's largest banks.

When interviewed in February 2014 by Neil Cavuto on the Fox Business Network, Dr. Burnham expressed what we have been saying for years – that the risk of putting your life savings in a bank account is now far greater than the near-zero reward.

It simply no longer makes logical sense to put your nest egg at such risk for little or no interest.

"Eventually, the absurd effort to create wealth through monetary policy will unravel in the U.S. as it has every other time it has been tried," writes Burnham, "from Weimar Germany to Robert Mugabe's Zimbabwe."

"Ever since Alan Greenspan intervened to save the stock market on October 20, 1987, the Fed has sought to cushion every financial blow by adding liquidity," writes Burnham. "The trouble with trying to make the world safe for stupidity is that it creates fragility."

"We don't need a maestro conducting monetary policy," writes Burnham. "We need a system that promotes stability and allows people (not printing presses) to make us richer."

"But if Bank of America is not safe, where can you and I put our money? No path is without risk," writes Burnham.

Among his suggested options: keep some cash at home, even though this has its own risks; pay off debts; pre-pay taxes and other obligations; and try to find a safer bank....or several, to reduce immediate risk to your deposits via diversification.

Ideally, you should keep at least a portion of your life savings – call it a "saving remnant" -- out of conventional banks and out of all digital media, even if for convenience you maintain a modest bank checking account.

Bank to the Future

"Someone should start a bank...that charges (rather than pays) interest and does not make loans," writes Burnham. "Such a bank would be a good example of how the Fed actions create unintended outcomes that defeat their goals. The Fed wants to stimulate lending, but an anti-lending bank could be quite successful. I would be a customer."

In *The Wealth of Nations*, Adam Smith wrote of such a bank, "another B of A" notes Burnham, the Bank of Amsterdam founded in 1609. It promised depositors that it would not make loans, but eventually it succumbed to the temptation of secret high-risk loans that went bad and sank it.

As hyperinflation began destroying the money in Weimar, Germany, after World War I, people turned to an escape used successfully for thousands of years. Economist Ludwig von Mises remembered what wise German investors called it – *Flucht in die Sachwerte*, "flight into investment in goods."

A safe haven for preserving the value of the fruits of our labor today means something that cannot be magically conjured with a government printing press, nor something that can be digitally stolen by computer hackers half a world away.

The ultimate such haven, of course, is gold. Gold continues as it has for thousands of years – as a reliable store of value with its own global intrinsic worth that acts as prudent insurance against the declines of conjured, politicized fiat money, both paper and digital. Gold, the once and future money, has outlasted all fads, bubbles and competitors.

If you keep a saving remnant of your nest egg in what has been the world's universal money since Biblical times, gold, you have taken a giant step towards financial diversification and security.

For you and your family, a collapse of the stock market would then no longer necessarily bring a collapse of your personal economy.

A collapse of the fractional-reserve and Federal Reserve banks would not necessarily overwhelm you.

A collapse of the dollar would potentially make your hard money store of gold (or of the "poor man's gold," silver) *more* valuable.

The world's universal reserve money, gold, can keep you afloat, even if a flood of inflation sweeps through the U.S. and world economy.

Bottom Line: Don't bank on it until you have become your own banker – and have created your own family gold standard. After you have, it's a wonderful life.

"It is well enough that people of the nation do not understand our banking and monetary system, for if they did, I believe there would be a revolution before tomorrow morning."

-- Henry Ford

Epilogue
The Gamble

*"The fundamental problem with banks
is what it's always been:
they're in the business of banking,
and banking, whether plain vanilla
or incredibly sophisticated,
is inherently risky."*

– James Surowiecki
Financial Journalist

When you open a bank account you are taking a risk. You are making an investment, gambling with the fruits of your labor.

The risk you take by trusting your money to a bank, as this book has shown, is far greater than most people realize -- and that risk is rapidly increasing.

Investors should make their decisions based on a prudent understanding and calculation of risk and potential reward.

This takes us to a fundamental question: how much interest is your bank paying you? The answer that most savers give today is "almost nothing."

The correct answer, alas, is even worse. Because of a deliberate policy that economists call "financial repression" imposed on your bank by the Federal Reserve, your bank deposit is receiving a rate of interest *below* the real rate of cost inflation, which our research calculates in 2014 has been somewhere between 7 and 11 percent.

This means that you are literally *losing* purchasing power every day your money remains in that bank account....while government, to add insult to injury, may require you to pay income tax on the tiny pittance of interest your bank pays.

You are actually being paid – to use an economist term you will soon be hearing frequently – "negative interest," when adjusted to factor in real world inflation.

American banks might soon follow the 2014 policy announced by the European Central Bank – that instead of banks paying depositors interest, depositors may very soon be charged a fee for merely *having* any bank account, even though the bank lends out their money for the bank's profit, thereby putting depositor money at risk.

Would you invest your savings in a stock if you knew it would return zero reward while subjecting you to serious risk of losing all or a substantial part of your investment?

Your bank account is worse than this....a high-risk investment that, when real world inflation is figured in, will at best return less purchasing power than you deposit.

Bank accounts have become a lose-lose investment in which you either lose a little, a lot, or everything. And unlike a casino, your bank gives you zero hope or chance of winning big. The longer you keep your money in the bank, the more you stand to lose.

You would be wise to diversify in ways that protect the safety and value of your money, including some investments that could increase in value whether the economy rises or falls.

In this book we have explained 20 major risks that threaten your bank account.

Because your bank account is already losing value, any *one* of these 20 risks is a sufficient reason to find a better haven to store your life savings.

With your bank account now facing *all 20* of these risks at once, you urgently need a safer, diversified way to protect your nest egg.

You can sleep better after escaping these risks.

The alternative, if even one of these dangers hits your money, could be restless sleep for the rest of your life, regretting that you were warned but hesitated a moment too long to safeguard your money.

Imagine how you would feel if you take this gamble and lose....lose your money, your retirement, your children's or grandchildren's brighter future.

You can win this gamble right now, however, simply by moving a portion of your money out of these 20 risky targeted zones, including your bank.

Here, for your convenience, is a shorthand list of these 20 hazards to your accounts to consider and remember when deciding how best to invest what you have worked so hard to earn:

1. Identity Thieves can potentially access bank accounts by acquiring surprisingly little key information about you.

2. Computer hackers can target your financial life and accounts.

Most are freelance or associated with criminal organizations, but some have foreign government backing and technology to help them.

3. In the dawning age of cyber warfare, banks and the individual accounts in banks will be prime targets for looting, disruption and erasure.

Most cyber warriors have the backing of foreign governments or well-financed movements. This is rapidly becoming a major mode of warfare. Such attacks could also shut down our national power grid and its slow-to-replace power transformers.

4. Cyber terrorism, including Cyber Jihad, aims to weaken and bring down the U.S. economy, which makes our banks and our bank accounts targets of choice for theft and disruption.

This also could disrupt power, water and other vital public resources.

5. Even without a deliberate attack, because our accounts exist as digital signals inside complex computer systems, we may be susceptible to scrambling or erasure by system problems.

These potential problems include a "flash crash" or natural factors such as a "Carrington Event," which could impact our national computer systems much like the coast-to-coast computer-frying effects of a single large H-bomb's Electromagnetic Pulse (EMP) burst at high altitude above America's heartland.

6. With governments running out of real money, politicians are eager to siphon off the wealth held in banks, which, as robber Willie Sutton purportedly said, is "where the money is."

Both Democrats and Republicans have proposed additional taxes on banks, which could make your banking less remunerative, more costly and more risky.

7. Banks are being targeted for regulatory fines and penalties, which is one more way governments can confiscate bank assets.

Banks have responded to such losses by lowering the rate of interest they pay depositors, and by charging higher overdraft and other fees to their customers.

8. Laws and rules are being changed to make government confiscation of bank deposits as "unsecured assets" easier via what governments now call "bail-ins."

Under today's law, you no longer necessarily "own" your bank account. Your bank does.

9. State Governments have stepped up their confiscation of "inactive" private bank accounts.

Georgia now seizes such accounts after as little as one year without any deposits or withdrawals, and puts what it takes into its state treasury for politicians to spend.

10. Banks could fail because of a run of depositors, because of the inherent instability and risk of our fractional-reserve banking system.

11. If bank runs closed our "Too Big To Fail" banks, the Federal Deposit Insurance Corporation from its current reserves and agreements would only be able to reimburse as little as $1 out of every $14 dollars of the $7+ Trillion in accounts that FDIC insures.

In a crisis the Fed and government could print vast amounts of new money to cover depositor losses, but this could take months and the inflation caused by printing many trillions out of thin air would make the reimbursed dollars worth far less than what the depositors lost.

12. Increased regulations make banks hesitant to lend to individuals and companies.

This also makes banks eager to lend to the U.S. Government, which pays far less interest to banks than would other kinds of loans. This limits how much banks are able to pay as interest to depositors, who include many on fixed incomes who had counted on their savings to provide more income.

13. "Financial Repression" by the Federal Reserve makes banks pay depositors a rate of interest lower than the rate of inflation, which means that savers lose purchasing power every day they have a bank account.

This puts pressure on savers to face the "moral hazard" of moving their savings into even riskier investments such as stocks in the Wall Street casino. It is one of the ways Progressives herd people like cattle.

14. European banks – with American banks soon to follow – have begun formally charging savers a fee for their account while paying them zero interest, a policy now formally called "negative interest."

American savers could in the near future be charged a bank fee for the honor of putting their money at risk by being lent out for bank profit.

15. Regulatory power is used to pressure banks to make higher-risk subprime loans to politically-favored groups of people.

This is the same policy that led to the near-collapse of the financial system in 2008, the Great Recession, and an array of continuing problems for bank depositors and our economy today.

16. Strict use of tighter regulatory power is driving small private banks out of business at the same time the government considers giving rural post offices the power to function as banks.

This will bring millions of depositors under more nearly direct government control.

17. Private banks are now being nationalized *de facto* through ever-increasing government regulatory control, taxes and fines.

Banks, as you have known them, will largely cease to exist by the year 2030, except perhaps as crony organizations that depend on the government, not depositors, for their funds...and that make donations to politicians and parties. Your bank account is an at-risk investment in the bank where you save.

In the already-emerging cashless society, you will need no bank to safeguard your digital money, and government will determine how much available credit you will have. In this new society you might be taxed 20% on every cashless transaction, including your final private bank withdrawal.

18. Obama Administration agencies have been developing plans to seize the last vast untapped pools of money in America, the $20+ Trillion in mostly-bank-held IRAs, 401(k)s and other retirement accounts.

Several international legal precedents exist for such seizures, which would be described to savers as "safeguarding your retirement money" by replacing it with an annuity backed by government bonds. Such annuities would also be provided to millions without significant retirement savings; much of the money to pay for this will be taken from those deemed not to need as much as they had saved in their own retirement accounts.

19. International Monetary Fund (IMF) economists and others are devising a new global tax on the "rich" to fund world wealth redistribution.

Such a tax would need to arrive like a thief in the night, begun with a surprise seizure of bank accounts around the world. If you make $34,000 or more per year, you are wealthy by world standards, being in the top 1 percent of global income earners.

Either, or both, of the surprise bank account seizures in points #18 and #19 above would most likely happen just after an off-year election, like the one in November 2014. It would happen after Thanksgiving, close to Christmas, near the start of the final two years of a Progressive ideological President's time in office when he and his party have little or nothing to lose by imposing massive income redistribution.

20. Banks increasingly are resisting and refusing depositor requests for large withdrawals, much as would happen under government "capital controls."

To most Americans, it seems incredible that your bank would refuse to let you withdraw your own money. That is what many have told us.

We challenged them, as we challenge you right now....test this. Go to your bank where the tellers are always friendly and say you want to withdraw $5,000, $10,000 or $15,000 from your account in cash.

What others we challenged have told us, in astonishment, is that their bank refused while asking why they wanted the money. In many banks the tellers and assistant managers appear to have been trained in techniques of putting such customers on the defensive by insisting that they justify such a withdrawal. Stay calm as you remind the banker that this is *your* money and they have no need to know why you want to withdraw it.

If you refuse to withdraw your Withdrawal Slip, the bank will either continue its refusal or offer to give you a check. No, you should insist, you want actual money – not a check, a bank promissory note on which they can stop payment.

As you watch them push back against your request to withdraw your *own* money, remember that this is your bank's response under what today passes for "normal" conditions.

Now imagine asking these bankers for your money at a time of crisis and uncertainty – for example, on the day a major act of terrorism panics our country, or an international crisis cuts off America's oil or electrical grid.

With many other customers crowding the teller windows and demanding their money, what chance on that day of a modern bank run do you think you will have to withdraw your money?

How good would it feel on such a day to have a sizable portion of your savings already under your direct control, not the bank's?

Do not take our word for what will happen when you want a large withdrawal in cash. TEST THIS YOURSELF. If you are like most of the people we have challenged, you will be surprised and shocked by what happens.

Are banks refusing such withdrawals because they have very little actual cash on hand as reserves needed for fractional-reserve lending? Or is it because they dislike doing government paperwork?

You need to be aware that banks are now required to report any withdrawal of $10,000 or more to the government – and not only banks but also many other kinds of companies are expected to report "unusual" or "suspicious" financial activity by any customer to the feds.

Simply withdrawing your own money in cash might therefore flag you for potential government surveillance. How do you think Thomas Jefferson or George Washington would respond to this?

Speaking of politics, if President Barack Obama's party loses control of the U.S. Senate in the 2014 election, then in lame duck session it can continue to function until early in the New Year by approving controversial presidential appointments and otherwise supporting whatever the President has done.

If, on the other hand, the election swings left and the President's party wins control of the House of Representatives, the next Chair of the House Banking Committee will be the extremely-Progressive Rep. Maxine Waters (D.-California). Such a power shift would accelerate many of the fundamental transformations we have discussed.

If you plan to diversify your savings to reduce your risk of such bank seizures and other dangers we have described, remember that some banks have delayed large withdrawals by their depositors.

A wise old saying goes: Five birds are sitting on a wire. Four decide to fly away to escape the danger of an approaching hawk. How many remain on the wire? Answer: Five, because *deciding* to do something is not the same as actually *doing* it.

To minimize these 20 risks, you need to make a decision. Then you need to act decisively and immediately to safeguard your money.

Footnotes

[1] Bob Howard, "HSBC Imposes Limitations on Large Cash Withdrawals," BBC News, January 24, 2014. URL: http://www.bbc.com/news/business-25861717

[2] Tyler Durden, "Creeping Capital Controls at JPMorgan Chase?" *ZeroHedge*, October 16, 2013. URL: http://www.zerohedge.com/news/2013-10-16/creeping-capital-controls-jpmorgan-chase

[3] Jose Berrospide, "Bank Liquidity Hoarding and the Financial Crisis: An Empirical Evaluation" (Monograph). Washington, D.C.: Federal Reserve Board / Finance and Economics Discussion Series (FEDS), March 2013. URL: http://www.federalreserve.gov/pubs/feds/2013/201303/201303pap.pdf; see also Jonathan Sibun, "Credit Markets Frozen as Banks Hoard Cash," *London Telegraph*, September 30, 2008; Larry Elliott, "Three Myths that Sustain the Economic Crisis: Five Years Ago the Banks Stopped Lending to Each Other," *London Guardian*, August 5, 2012.

[4] Tyler Durden, "Germany Gives Up On Trying To Repatriate Its Gold, Will Leave It In The Fed's "Safe Hands," *ZeroHedge*, June 23, 2014. URL: http://www.zerohedge.com/news/2014-06-23/germany-gives-trying-repatriate-its-gold-will-leave-it-feds-safe-hands

[5] Sven Boll and Anne Seith, "Why Germany Wants to See Its US Gold," *Der Spiegel*, October 30, 2012. URL: http://www.spiegel.de/international/germany/german-politicians-demand-to-see-gold-in-us-federal-reserve-a-864068.html

[6] Tyler Durden, "Germany Gives Up On Trying To Repatriate Its Gold, Will Leave It In The Fed's "Safe Hands," *ZeroHedge*, June 23, 2014. URL: http://www.zerohedge.com/news/2014-06-23/germany-gives-trying-repatriate-its-gold-will-leave-it-feds-safe-hands

[7] Birgit Jennen, "German Gold Stays in New York in Rebuff to Euro Doubters," Bloomberg, June 23, 2014. URL: http://www.bloomberg.com/news/2014-06-23/german-gold-stays-in-new-york-in-rebuff-to-euro-doubters.html

[8] Johnny D. Boggs, "The Great Northfield Raid Revisited," *TrueWest* Magazine, August 6, 2012. URL: http://www.truewestmagazine.com/jcontent/history/history/history-features/4714-the-great-northfield-raid-revisited; see also Mark Lee Gardner, *Shot All to Hell: Jesse James, the Northfield Raid, and the Wild West's Greatest Escape*. New York: William Morrow, 2013.

[9] Wallace Henley, "Sweden's Cashless Economy and a Potemkin World," *Christian Post*, March 21, 2012.

[10] Ibid.

[11] Jim Kouri, "$1 Trillion Lost Annually to Cyber Crime, Say U.S. Senators," *Examiner.com*, May 24, 2011. URL: http://www.examiner.com/public-safety-in-national/1-trillion-lost-annually-to-cyber-crime-say-u-s-senators

[12] Lev Grossman, "The Code War: The Internet Is a Battlefield, the Prize Is Your Information, and Bugs Are the Weapons," *Time* Magazine (cover story "World War Zero"), July 21, 2014.

[13] Ibid.

[14] Ibid.

[15] Simone Foxman, "Recent Cyberattacks Could Be Part of a Chinese Military Strategy Started Nearly 20 Years Ago," *QZ.com / The Atlantic*, March 14, 2013. URL: http://qz.com/62434/recent-cyberattacks-could-be-part-of-a-chinese-military-strategy-started-nearly-20-years-ago/; see also Jordan Robertson, "Chinese Hackers Show Humans Are Weakest Security Link," *Bloomberg*, May 19, 2014. URL: http://www.bloomberg.com/news/2014-05-20/chinese-hackers-show-humans-are-weakest-security-link.html; see also Qiao Liang and Wang Xiangsui, *Unrestricted Warfare*.

Panama City, Panama: Pan American Publishing Company, 2002.

[16] Ibid.

[17] Jeremy Rifkin, *The Zero Marginal Cost Society: The Internet of Things, the Collaborative Commons, and the Eclipse of Capitalism*. New York: Palgrave Macmillan, 2014; see also Lily Hay Newman, "The Internet of Things Needs Anti-Virus Protection," *Slate.com*, March 10, 2014. URL: http://www.slate.com/blogs/future_tense/2014/03/10/red_balloon_symbiote_anti_virus_security_software_protects_embedded_devices.html
; Bruce Upbin, "Red Button Flaw Exposes Major Vulnerability In Millions of Smart TVs," *Forbes*, June 6, 2014. URL: http://www.forbes.com/sites/bruceupbin/2014/06/06/red-button-flaw-exposes-major-vulnerability-in-millions-of-smart-tvs/
; Adrienne LaFrance, "New Study: 'Cloud of Things' Could Make Customer-Service Better, Humanity Worse," *The Atlantic*, May 14, 2014. URL: http://www.theatlantic.com/technology/archive/2014/05/new-study-cloud-of-things-could-make-customer-service-better-humanity-worse/370852/

[18] Julia Lovell, *The Great Wall: China Against the World, 1000 BC-AD 2000*. New York: Grove Press, 2007.

[19] Ruth Sherlock, "Al-Qaeda Chief Calls for Attacks on U.S. in 9/11 Speech to Followers," *London Daily Telegraph*, September 13, 2013. URL: http://www.telegraph.co.uk/news/worldnews/al-qaeda/10306755/Al-Qaeda-chief-calls-for-attacks-on-US-in-911-speech-to-followers.html

[20] Peter Bergen and Tim Maurer, "Cyberwar Hits Ukraine," *CNN*, March 7, 2014; Jim Kouri, "Suspected Saboteurs Striking Ukraine's Government Cyber Systems," *Examiner.com*, March 8, 2014.

[21] Lev Grossman, "The Code War: The Internet Is a Battlefield, the Prize Is Your Information, and Bugs Are the Weapons," *Time* Magazine (cover story "World War Zero"), July 21, 2014.

[22] Kevin D. Freeman, *Economic Warfare: Risks and Responses: Analysis of Twenty-First Century Risks in Light of the Recent Market Collapse* (Monograph). Cross Consulting and Services, 2009.

[23] Kevin D. Freeman, *Game Plan: How to Protect Yourself from the Coming Cyber-Economic Attack*. Washington, D.C.: Regnery, 2014. Freeman is also author of *Secret Weapon: How Economic Terrorism Brought Down the U.S. Stock Market and Why It Can Happen Again*. Washington, D.C.: Regnery, 2012.

[24] Robert Preston, "Russia 'Planned Wall Street Bear Raid,'" *BBC News*, March 17, 2014. URL: http://www.bbc.com/news/business-26609548?print=true

[25] Rachel Ehrenfeld and Alyssa A. Lappen, "The Fifth Generation Warfare," *FrontPageMagazine.com*, June 20, 2008.

[26] Eamon Javers, "Pentagon Preps for Economic Warfare," *Politico*, April 9, 2009. URL: http://www.politico.com/news/stories/0409/21053.html

[27] Jonathon M. Seidl, "Pentagon Has Been 'War Gaming' for Economic Disaster Since Early '09," *TheBlaze.com*, December 7, 2010. URL: http://www.theblaze.com/stories/pentagon-has-been-war-gaming-for-economic-disaster-since-early-09/

[28] James Rickards, *The Death of Money: The Coming Collapse of the International Monetary System*. New York: Portfolio/Penguin, 2014. Pages 27-28.

[29] Jim Kouri, "$1 Trillion Lost Annually to Cyber Crime, Say U.S. Senators," *Examiner.com*, May 24, 2011. URL: http://www.examiner.com/public-safety-in-national/1-trillion-lost-annually-to-cyber-crime-say-u-s-senators

[30] Olga Belogolova, "Mullen Addresses Debt, New National Security Team," *National Journal*, April 28, 2011. URL: http://www.nationaljournal.com/nationalsecurity/mullen-addresses-debt-new-national-security-team-20110428

[31] Michael MacKenzie and Telis Demos, "Fears Linger of a New 'Flash Crash,'" *Financial Times*, May 5, 2011. See also John Melloy, "Year After May 6 'Flash Crash,' Rumblings of a Stock Correction," *CNBC.com*, May 4, 2011. URL: http://www.cnbc.com/id/42899594/Year_After_May_6_Flash_Crash_Rumblings_of_a_Stock_Correction ; "2010 Flash Crash," *Wikipedia*. URL: http://en.wikipedia.org/wiki/2010_Flash_Crash

[32] Michael Lewis, *Flash Boys: A Wall Street Revolt*. New York: W.W. Norton, 2014.

[33] Sam Ro, "ART CASHIN: WE May Have Just Witnessed The Presence Of Artificial Intelligence In The Stock Market," *Business Insider*, March 1, 2012. URL: http://www.businessinsider.com/art-cashin-artificial-intelligence-stock-market-2012-3

[34] Ibid.

[35] Cris Sheridan, "Markets, Murmurations, and Machines," *FinancialSense.com*, February 3, 2012. URL: http://www.financialsense.com/contributors/cris-sheridan/markets-murmurations-machines

[36] Ibid.

[37] Cris Sheridan, "Is Artificial Intelligence Taking Over the Stock Market?" *FinancialSense.com*, March 2, 2012. URL: http://www.financialsense.com/contributors/cris-sheridan/is-artificial-intelligence-taking-over-the-stock-market

[38] Kris Devasabai, "Quants Turn to AI for Market Insights," *Hedge Funds Review*, December 20, 2013. URL: http://www.risk.net/hedge-funds-review/feature/2307119/quants-turn-to-ai-for-market-insights ; see also Tom Steinert-Threlkeid, *Securities Technology Monitor*, November 17, 2011. URL: http://www.securitiestechnologymonitor.com/news/machine-readable-tweet-streams-algo-trading-gnip-29578-1.html?ET=securitiesindustry:e3039:180629a:&st=email&utm_source=editorial&utm_medium=email&utm_campaign=STM_BNA_08302010_111711# ; Christopher Mims, "AI That Picks Stocks Better Than the Pros: A Computer Science Professor Uses Textual Analysis of Articles to Beat the Market," *MIT Technology Review*, June 10, 2010. URL: http://www.technologyreview.com/view/419341/ai-that-picks-stocks-better-than-the-pros/

[39] "AI Potentially 'More Dangerous than Nukes," *CNBC*, August 4, 2014. URL: http://www.cnbc.com/id/101892104 ; Allen Wastier, "Elon Musk, Stephen Hawking and Fearing the Machine," CNBC, June 21, 2014. URL: http://www.cnbc.com/id/101774267 ; Stephen Hawking, Stuart Russell, Max Tegmark and Frank Wilczek, "Stephen Hawking: 'Transcendence Looks At the Implications of Artificial Intelligence – But Are We Taking AI Seriously Enough? *The Independent* (UK), May 1, 2014. URL: http://www.independent.co.uk/news/science/stephen-hawking-transcendence-looks-at-the-implications-of-artificial-intelligence--but-are-we-taking-ai-seriously-enough-9313474.html ; Nick Bostrom, *Superintelligence: Paths, Dangers, Strategies*. Oxford: Oxford University Press, 2014.

[40] Stephen Hawking, Stuart Russell, Max Tegmark and Frank Wilczek, "Stephen Hawking: 'Transcendence Looks At the Implications of Artificial Intelligence – But Are We Taking AI Seriously Enough? *The Independent* (UK), May 1, 2014. URL: http://www.independent.co.uk/news/science/stephen-hawking-transcendence-looks-at-the-implications-of-artificial-intelligence--but-are-we-taking-ai-seriously-enough-9313474.html

[31] Harald Malmgren and Mark Stys,"The Marginalizing of the Individual Investor: The Inside Story of Flash Crashes, Systemic Risk, and the Demise of Value Investing," *The International Economy*, Summer 2010. URL: http://www.international-economy.com/TIE_Su10_MalmgrenStys.

pdf; Cris Sheridan, "Is Artificial Intelligence Taking Over the Stock Market?" *FinancialSense. com*, March 2, 2012. URL: http://www.financialsense.com/contributors/cris-sheridan/is-artificial-intelligence-taking-over-the-stock-market; Cris Sheridan, "Is the Entire Market Rigged?" *FinancialSense.com*, March 31, 2014. URL: http://www.financialsense.com/contributors/cris-sheridan/is-the-entire-market-rigged; Jeff Christian, "It's Not Just Gold – Computerized Trading Used to Manipulate All Markets," FinancialSense.com, March 17, 2014. URL: http://www. financialsense.com/contributors/jeff-christian/gold-manipulated-computerized-trading; Paul Saffo, "New Era, New God, Says Paul Saffo," *The Economist*, November 22, 2010. URL: http://www. economist.com/node/17509358; Cris Sheridan, "A.I.: The New God of Economics, Banking and Finance," *FinancialSense.com*, July 5, 2012. URL: http://www.financialsense.com/contributors/ cris-sheridan/artificial-intelligence-the-new-god-of-economics; Cris Sheridan, ;The HFT Revolution: 6 Reasons Why High Speed Trading Is Taking Over the Markets, *FinancialSense.com*, March 21, 2012. URL: http://www.financialsense.com/contributors/cris-sheridan/hft-revolution-six-reasons-why-its-taking-over-markets; Sean Sposito, "Banks Deploy Artificial Intelligence to Deepen Understanding of Customers," *American Banker*, July 23, 2012. URL: http://www. americanbanker.com/issues/177_141/banks-deploy-artificial-intelligence-to-understand-consumers-1051132-1.html

[42] Lowell Ponte, "Terrorism Central?" *FrontPageMagazine.com*, August 18, 2003. URL: http:// archive.frontpagemag.com/readArticle.aspx?ARTID=16740

[43] Michael Riley, "How Russian Hackers Stole the Nasdaq," *Bloomberg Businessweek*, July 17, 2014. URL: http://www.businessweek.com/articles/2014-07-17/how-russian-hackers-stole-the-nasdaq

[44] Chris Strohm and Jordan Robertson, "Russian Hackers' Challenge Is Finding Any Value in 1.2 Billion Passwords," *Bloomberg*, August 6, 2014. URL: http://www.bloomberg.com/news/2014-08-06/russian-hackers-said-to-loot-1-2-billion-internet-records.html

[45] Alexis C. Madrigal, "The Great Pager Blackout of 1998," *The Atlantic,* March 25, 2011. URL: http://www.theatlantic.com/technology/archive/2011/03/the-great-pager-blackout-of-1998/73042/; David Usborne, "Satellite Failure Leaves Millions Speechless in US," *The Independent* (U.K.), May 21, 1998. URL: http://www.independent.co.uk/news/satellites-failure-leaves-millions-speechless-in-us-1157828.html; Volker Bothmer and Ioannis A. Daglis, *Space Weather: Physics and Effects*. Berlin: Springer, 2010; Laurence Zuckerman, "Satellite Failure Is Rare, And Therefore Unsettling," *New York Times*, May 21, 1998. URL: http://www.nytimes.com/1998/05/21/business/ satellite-failure-is-rare-and-therefore-unsettling.html; D.N. Baker, J.H. Allen, S.G. Kanekai and G.D. Reeves, "Disturbed Space Environment May Have Been Related to Pager Satellite Failure," *EOS* / Transactions, American Geophysical Union, Vol. 79 Number 40 (October 6, 1998).

[46] Nassim Nicholas Taleb, *The Black Swan: Second Edition: The Impact of the Highly Improbable: With a New Section: "On Robustness and Fragility."* New York: Random House, 2010.

[47] Christopher Klein, "A Perfect Solar Superstorm: The 1859 Carrington Event," History.com / The History Channel, March 14, 2012. URL: http://www.history.com/news/a-perfect-solar-superstorm-the-1859-carrington-event.

[48] Richard A Lovett, "What If the Biggest Solar Storm on Record Happened Today?" *National Geographic Daily News*, March 2, 2011. URL: http://news.nationalgeographic.com/ news/2011/03/110302-solar-flares-sun-storms-earth-danger-carrington-event-science/; Jennifer O'Mahony, "Solar Storm Could Leave Britain Without Power 'For Months'," *London Telegraph*, June 7, 2013. URL: http://www.telegraph.co.uk/technology/news/10103492/Solar-storm-could-leave-Britain-without-power-for-months.html; see also Jason Samenow, "How A Solar Storm Two Years Ago Nearly Caused A Catastrophe on Earth," *Washington Post*, July 23, 2014. URL: http:// www.washingtonpost.com/blogs/capital-weather-gang/wp/2014/07/23/how-a-solar-storm-nearly-destroyed-life-as-we-know-it-two-years-ago/

[49] James A. Marusek, *Solar Storm Threat Analysis* (Monograph). Bloomfield, Indiana: Impact, 2007. URL: http://www.breadandbutterscience.com/SSTA.pdf.

[50] "Carrington-Class CME Narrowly Misses Earth," National Aeronautics and Space Administration / *NasaCasts*, April 28, 2014. URL: https://www.youtube.com/watch?v=7ukQhycKOFw

[51] Amy Thompson and Cornelius Rahn, "Russian Hackers Threaten Power Companies, Researchers Say," *Bloomberg*, July 1, 2014. URL: http://www.bloomberg.com/news/print/2014-06-30/symantec-warns-energetic-bear-hackers-threaten-energy-firms.html; see also F. Michael Maloof, "'Dragonfly' Virus Strikes U.S. Power Plants," WND.com, July 6, 2014. URL: http://www.wnd.com/2014/07/dragonfly-virus-strikes-u-s-power-plants/print/

[52] Kevin D. Freeman, *Game Plan: How to Protect Yourself from the Coming Cyber-Economic Attack*. Washington, D.C.: Regnery, 2014. Freeman is also author of *Secret Weapon: How Economic Terrorism Brought Down the U.S. Stock Market and Why It Can Happen Again*. Washington, D.C.: Regnery, 2012.

[53] Psalm 137:1-5 (KJV).

[54] James D. Purvis, "Exile and Return: From the Babylonian Destruction to the Reconstruction of the Jewish State." Biblical Archeology Society / BAS Ancient Israel, 2002. URL: http://www.cojs.org/pdf/exile_return.pdf ; Albert T. Clay, "Business Documents of Murashu Sons of Nippur...." in H.V. Hilprecht (Editor), *The Babylonian Expedition of the University of Pennsylvania, Series A: Cuneiform Texts, Volume X*. Philadelphia: Department of Archeology and Paleontology of the University of Pennsylvania, 1904. URL: http://archive.org/stream/cu31924026432488#page/n7/mode/2up; Murashu family in Wikipedia. URL: http://en.wikipedia.org/wiki/Murashu_family; House of Egibi in Wikipedia. URL: http://en.wikipedia.org/wiki/House_of_Egibi; see also Gwendolyn Leick (Editor), *The Babylonian World*. London: Routledge, 2009 -- chapter "The Egibi Family" by Cornelia Wunsch; see also Karen Rhea Nemet-Nejat, *Daily Life in Ancient Mesopotamia*. Ada, Michigan: Baker Academic Publishing, 2001.

[55] Manfred R. Lehmann, "The History of Jewish Banking" (Monograph). New York: Manfred and Anne Lehmann Foundation, 2010. URL: http://www.manfredlehmann.com/news/news_detail.cgi/173/0
; see also Murashu family in Wikipedia. URL: http://en.wikipedia.org/wiki/Murashu_family; House of Egibi in Wikipedia. URL: http://en.wikipedia.org/wiki/House_of_Egibi; see also Gwendolyn Leick (Editor), *The Babylonian World*. London: Routledge, 2009 - chapter "The Egibi Family" by Cornelia Wunsch.

[56] Murray N. Rothbard, *What Has Government Done to Our Money?* Auburn, Alabama: Ludwig von Mises Institute, 2008. Page 74. This book can be downloaded from the Internet at no cost from http://mises.org/Books/Whathasgovernmentdone.pdf

[57] Murray N. Rothbard, "Taking Money Back," *Mises Daily*, June 14, 2008. URL: http://mises.org/daily/2882

[58] Robert L. Schuettinger and Eamonn F. Butler, *Forty Centuries of Wage and Price Controls: How NOT to Fight Inflation*. Washington, D.C.: Heritage Foundation, 1979. This can be downloaded from the Internet at no cost from http://mises.org/books/fortycenturies.pdf

[59] Naphtali Lewis and Meyer Reinhold (Editors), *Roman Civilization: Sourcebook II: The Empire*. New York: Harper Torchbooks, 1966. Page 398.

[60] Ibid., pages 440-445.

[61] Ibid. Pages 463-473; see also Robert L. Schuettinger and Eamonn F. Butler, *Forty Centuries of Wage and Price Controls: How NOT to Fight Inflation*. Washington, D.C.: Heritage Foundation, 1979. Pages 20-27.

[62] James Rickards, *The Death of Money: The Coming Collapse of the International Monetary System*. New York: Portfolio / Penguin, 2014; see also James Rickards, "The Death of Money,"

The American / American Enterprise Institute, April 9, 2014. URL: http://www.american.com/ archive/2014/april/the-death-of-money; "Special Drawing Rights (SDRs)" (IMF Fact Sheet). Washington, D.C.: International Monetary Fund, March 25, 2014. URL: https://www.imf.org/ external/np/exr/facts/sdr.HTM

[63] URL: http://www.merriam-webster.com/dictionary/soldier

[64] Jonathan Williams (Editor), *Money: A History*. New York: St. Martin's Press, 1997. Page 155.

[65] Jack Weatherford, *The History of Money: From Sandstone to Cyberspace*. New York: Crown Publishers, 1997. Pages 126-127.

[66] Murray N. Rothbard, *For a New Liberty: The Libertarian Manifesto* (Revised Edition). New York: Collier Books / Macmillan Publishing, 1978. Page 183.

[67] "The Mystery of the New Fashioned Goldsmiths or Bankers. Their Rise, Growth, State and Decay. Discovered in a Merchant's Letter to a Country Gent Who Desired to Bind His Son Apprentice to a Goldsmith," (Letter circa 1676) published as Apprendix 3 in the *Quarterly Journal of Economics*, Vol. 2 (January 1888), Pages 251-262; see also "Seizure of the Mint (England)" in *Encyclopedia of Money*, October 2011. URL: http://encyclopedia-of-money.blogspot.com/2011/10/ seizure-of-mint-england.html

[68] Stuart I. Greenbaum and Anjam V. Thakor, *Contemporary Financial Intermediation* (Second Edition). Burlington, Massachusetts: Elsevier, 2007. Page 95; see also George Selgin, "Those Dishonest Goldsmiths" (monograph), March 30, 2010. URL: http://ssrn.com/abstract=1589709

[69] George J. Benston, "Regulating Financial Markets: A Critique and Some Proposals." Washington, D.C.: American Enterprise Institute, 1999.

[70] Murray N. Rothbard, *The Mystery of Banking*. New York: E.P. Dutton, 1983; see also "Fractional Reserve Banking," *The Freeman*, October 1995.

[71] Adam Smith, *The Wealth of Nations. Book II:Chapter 2:41. URL:* http://www.econlib.org/ library/Smith/smWN7.html#B.II,%20Ch.2,%20Of%20Money%20Considered%20as%20a%20 particular%20Branch%20of%20the%20General%20Stock%20of%20the%20Society

[72] Charles W. Calomiris and Stephen H. Haber, *Fragile by Design: The Political Origins of Banking Crises and Scarce Credit*. Princeton, N.J.: Princeton University Press, 2014.

[73] "The World's Strongest Banks," *Bloomberg Markets*, May 1, 2013. URL: http://www. bloomberg.com/slideshow/2013-05-01/the-world-s-strongest-banks.html

[74] "'Dixie' Originated from Name 'Dix,' An Old Currency," Louisiana Works Progress Administration Collection, Vol. 2 No. 150 Page 3 Col. 1. Document dated May 29, 1916. URL: http://louisdl.louislibraries.org/cdm/ref/collection/LWP/id/1384

[75] Ben S. Bernanke, "What the Fed Did and Why: Supporting the Recovery and Sustain Price Stability," *Washington Post*, November 4, 2010. URL: http://www.washingtonpost.com/wp-dyn/ content/article/2010/11/03/AR2010110307372_pf.html

[76] Nelson D. Schwartz, "Winners and Losers From Stimulus," *New York Times*, November 13, 2013. URL: http://economix.blogs.nytimes.com/2013/11/13/winners-and-losers-from-stimulus/?_ php=true&_type=blogs&_r=0

[77] Charles Biderman, "How The Fed Is Helping To Rig The Stock Market," *Forbes*, January 30, 2013. URL: http://www.forbes.com/sites/investor/2013/01/30/how-the-fed-is-helping-to-rig-the-stock-market/

[78] Richard W. Fisher, "The Danger of Too Loose, Too Long," *Wall Street Journal*, July 27, 2014. URL: http://online.wsj.com/articles/richard-fisher-the-danger-of-too-loose-too-long-1406499266

[79] Sheila Bair, "The Federal Reserve's Risky Reverse Repurchase Scheme," *Wall Street Journal*, July 24, 2014. URL: http://online.wsj.com/news/articles/SB200014240527023049074045800350119 93737740

[80] Mike Cosgrove, "Why Is Fed Considering Paying Banks Not To Lend To Main Street?" *Investor's Business Daily*, July 18, 2014. URL: http://news.investors.com/ibd-editorials-on-the-right/071814-709531-central-banks-policy-makes-no-sense-for-average-americans.htm?ven=rss

[81] Peter J. Wallison, "Five Myths About Glass-Steagall," *The American* / American Enterprise Institute, August 16, 2012. URL: http://www.american.com/archive/2012/august/five-myths-about-glass-steagall

[82] Ibid.

[83] Thomas Piketty, *Capital in the Twenty-First Century*. Cambridge, Massachusetts: Harvard University Press, 2014; see also Lowell Ponte, "French Economist Advocates Hefty Taxes," *Newsmax*, April 29, 2014. URL: http://www.newsmax.com/LowellPonte/piketty-taxes-distribution/2014/04/29/id/568320/

[84] Thomas Sowell, *The Housing Boom and Bust*. Revised Edition. New York: Basic Books, 2010.

[85] David Skeel, "Now Uncle Sam Is Ripping Off Fannie and Freddie," *MarketWatch* / *Wall Street Journal*, February 27, 2014. URL: http://www.marketwatch.com/story/david-skeel-now-uncle-sam-is-ripping-off-fannie-and-freddie-2014-02-27-184495326 ; see also Gretchen Morgenson, "The Untouchable Profits of Fannie Mae and Freddie Mac," *New York Times*, February 15, 2014; Ruth Mantell, "Legal Hopes Give New Lift to Fannie, Freddie Stock," *MarketWatch* / *Wall Street Journal, July 18, 2014;* Kingkarn Amiaroch, "A Purchase of Fannie Mae and Freddie Mac's Common Stock Is Speculation, Not Investing," *The Motley Fool*, July 21, 2014; Matthew Frankel, "Will The New Bill To End Fannie Mae and Freddie Mac Be Good News For Investors?" *The Motley Fool*, July 17, 2014.

[86] John Leland, "New Program for Buyers, With No Money Down," *New York Times,* September 5, 2010. URL: http://www.nytimes.com/2010/09/05/us/05mortgage.html?pagewanted=all; see also "Affordable Advantage Mortgage," Chicago: Illinois Housing Development Authority. Undated. URL: http://www.ihda.org/developer/affordableplusperm.htm

[87] Terry Miller, Anthony B. Kim and Kim R. Holmes, *2014 Index of Economic Freedom*. Washington, D.C.: Heritage Foundation / *Wall Street Journal*, 2014. URL for free download: http://www.heritage.org/index/download

[88] "Senate Republicans Must Defund Obama's Racial Housing Quotas (Editorial)," *Investor's Business Daily*, June 20, 2014. URL: http://news.investors.com/ibd-editorials/062014-705688-senate-republicans-must-defund-hud-racial-housing-quotas.htm; "Westchester USA: A Case of Racial Engineering that Obama Wants to Take Nationwide," *Wall Street Journal* (Editorial), July 7, 2014. URL: http://online.wsj.com/articles/westchester-usa-1404771358 ; see also Paul Sperry, "Obama OK's Subprime Borrowers for Prime Loans," *Investor's Business Daily*, January 14, 2013. URL: http://www.amren.com/news/2013/01/obama-oks-subprime-borrowers-for-prime-loans/

[89] Stanley Kurtz, *Spreading the Wealth: How Obama Is Robbing the Suburbs to Pay for the Cities*. New York: Sentinel / Penguin, 2012.

[90] Jim Geraghty, "'We're All Becoming Border States Now,'" *National Review,* July 15, 2014. URL: http://www.nationalreview.com/node/382748/print

[91] Robert W. Wood, "IRS Nets Offshore Data From 77,000 Banks, 70 Countries In FATCA Push," *Forbes*, June 3, 2014. URL: http://www.forbes.com/sites/robertwood/2014/06/03/irs-nets-offshore-data-from-77000-banks-70-countries-in-fatca-push/

[92] James George Jatras, "Unauthorized FATCA 'Intergovernmental Agreement' Are Part of Obama's Executive Overreach," *Forbes*, July 28, 2014. URL: http://www.forbes.com/sites/realspin/2014/07/28/unauthorized-fatca-intergovernmental-agreements-are-part-of-obamas-executive-overreach/

[93] Ibid.

[94] Ibid.

[95] Doreen Carvajal, "Swiss Banks' Tradition of Secrecy Clashes With Quests Abroad for Disclosure," *New York Times*, July 8, 2014. URL: http://www.nytimes.com/2014/07/09/world/europe/swiss-banks-tradition-of-secrecy-clashes-with-quests-abroad-for-disclosure.html

[96] *Paying Taxes 2014: The Global Picture: A Comparison of Tax Systems in 189 Economies Worldwide* (Monograph). London: PricewaterhouseCoopers, 2014. URL: http://www.pwc.com/gx/en/paying-taxes/assets/pwc-paying-taxes-2014.pdf

[97] Tim Worstall, "Obama Administration Doesn't Seem To Understand Tax Inversions As It Tries To Stop Them," *Forbes*, July 16, 2014. URL: http://www.forbes.com/sites/timworstall/2014/07/16/obama-administration-doesnt-seem-to-understand-tax-inversions-as-it-tries-to-stop-them/

[98] J.D. Tuccille, "Moving Your Company Overseas Is So Evil, Jack Lew Would Ban It in the Past!" *Reason* Magazine, July 16, 2014. URL: http://reason.com/blog/2014/07/16/moving-your-company-overseas-is-so-evil/print

[99]"Obama's Tax Law Rewrite: Where's the Law that Gives Jack Lew the Power to Raise Taxes?" (Editorial), *Wall Street Journal*, August 6, 2014. URL: http://online.wsj.com/articles/obamas-tax-law-rewrite-1407368237

[100] Jake Novak, "King George III Applauds Jack Lew's Tax Remarks," *CNBC*, July 16, 2014. URL: http://www.cnbc.com/id/101841706

[101] Jonathan Alter, "The United States Needs Corporate 'Loyalty Oaths'," *The Daily Beast*, August 4, 2014. URL: http://www.thedailybeast.com/articles/2014/08/04/the-united-states-needs-corporate-loyalty-oaths.html
; see also J.D. Tuccille, "With Loyalty Oath Demand, Crusade Against Corporate Inversion Gets Even Creepier," *Reason* Magazine, August 4, 2014. URL: http://reason.com/blog/2014/08/04/with-loyalty-oath-demand-crusade-against/print

[102] Craig R. Smith and Lowell Ponte, *The Inflation Deception: Six Ways Government Tricks Us...And Seven Ways to Stop It!* Phoenix: Idea Factory Press, 2011. Pages 131-136; see also Steve Benen, "Political Animal," *Washington Monthly*, April 5, 2009. URL: http://www.washingtonmonthly.com/archives/individual/2009_04/0176 14.php; Emily Bazelon, "Hypomanic American, The," *New York Times Magazine*, December 11, 2005. URL: http://www.nytimes.com/2005/12/11/magazine/11ideas_section2-7.html; Peter C. Whybrow, *American Mania: When More Is Not Enough*. New York: W.W. Norton, 2005; John D. Gartner, *The Hypomanic Edge: The Link Between (A Little) Craziness and (A Lot of) Success in America*. New York: Simon & Schuster, 2005; Lowell Ponte, "Protect the Overprivileged," *Wall Street Journal*, November 14, 1997.

[103] Charles Moore, "Southern Europe Lies Prostrate Before the German Imperium," *London Daily Telegraph*, March 22, 2013 URL: http://www.telegraph.co.uk/news/worldnews/europe/cyprus/9948545/Southern-Europe-lies-prostrate-before-the-German-imperium.html; Mike Shedlock, "Merkel's Vision: 'United States of Germany,'" *Townhall.com*, March 26, 2013.

[104] Clifford F. Thies and Daniel A. Gerlowski, "Deposit Insurance: A History of Failure," *Cato Journal*, Vol 8 No. 3 (Winter 1989). URL: http://www.cato.org/sites/cato.org/files/serials/files/cato-journal/1989/1/cj8n3-8.pdf; Kam Hon Chu, "Deposit Insurance and Banking Stability," *Cato Journal*, Vol. 31 No. 1 (Winter 2011). URL: http://www.cato.org/sites/cato.org/files/serials/files/

catojournal/2011/1/cj31n1-7.pdf; Ambrose Evans-Pritchard, "Cyprus Has Finally Killed Myth that EMU is Benign," *London Daily Telegraph*, March 27, 2013. URL: http://www.telegraph.co.uk/ finance/comment/ambroseevans_pritchard/9957999/Cyprus-has-finally-killed-myth-that-EMU-is-benign.html

[105] Ambrose Evans-Pritchard, "Cyprus Has Finally Killed Myth that EMU is Benign," *London Daily Telegraph*, March 27, 2013. URL: http://www.telegraph.co.uk/finance/comment/ ambroseevans_pritchard/9957999/Cyprus-has-finally-killed-myth-that-EMU-is-benign.html

[106] Wolfgang Munchau, "Europe Is Risking a Bank Run," *Financial Times*, March 17, 2013 URL: http://www.ft.com/intl/cms/s/0/b501c302-8cea-11e2-aed2-00144feabdc0. html#axzz2OcZ4q0n2; George Friedman, "Europe's Disturbing Precedent in the Cyprus Bailout," *Stratfor Geopolitical Weekly*, March 26, 2013. URL: http://www.stratfor.com/weekly/europes-disturbing-precedent-cyprus-bailout

[107] Deepanshu Bagchee, "Cyprus Finance Minister: We Hope People Will Believe Us," *CNBC*, March 17, 2013. URL: Http://www.cnbc.com/100560892

[108] "Cyprus Bailout: Dijsselbleom Remarks Alarm Markets," *BBC News*, March 25, 2013. URL: http://www.bbc.co.uk/news/business-21920574?print=true; William L. Watts and Sarah Turner, "Markets Drop on Fear Cyprus Deal Is New Blueprint," *MarketWatch/Wall Street Journal*, March 25, 2013; Luke Baker, "Cyprus to Shape Future Euro Bank Rescues: Eurogroup Head," *Reuters*, March 25, 2013; Helena Smith and others, "Cyprus Bailout: Savings Raid 'Could Happen Elsewhere,'" *The Guardian*, March 25, 2013; Bruno Waterfield, "Cyprus Bail-Out: Savers Will Be Raided to Save Euro in Future Crises, Says Eurozone," *London Daily Telegraph*, March 25, 2013; Rob Williams, "Cyprus Deal Is Model for Future Bailouts Says Top European Official as Banks are Told to Open," *The Independent*, March 25, 2013; Steve Goldstein, "Dijsselbleom Shocker Is U.S.'s Template, Too," *MarketWatch/Wall Street Journal*, March 25, 2013. URL: http://articles.marketwatch.com/20130325/commentary/37999129_1_insurance-fund-uninsured-depositors-nova-ban

[109] "German Economist: 'Europe's Citizens Now Have to Fear for Their Money" (interview with economist Peter Bofinger), *Der Spiegel/SpiegelOnline*, March 18, 2013. URL: http://www.spiegel. de/international/europe/interview-with-german-economist-peter-bofinger-on-perils-of-cyprus-bailout-a-889594.html

[110] Karl Whelan, "It's Official: The Eurozone Is In Recession," *Forbes* Magazine, November 15, 2012; Marco Gioannangeli and Tracey, "Get All Your Money Out of Europe Now," *London Daily Express*, March 24, 2013. URL: http://www.express.co.uk/news/uk/386559/Get-all-your-money-out-of-Europe-now; Robert Watts, "Ukip Urges Brits to Withdraw Their Money From Spanish Banks," *London Daily Telegraph*, March 23, 2012; Armin Mahler, "Savers Be Warned – Your Money's Not Safe," *Der Spiegel/ SpiegelOnline*, March 25, 2013; Simon Kennedy, "Saving Cyprus Means Nobody Safe As Europe Breaks More Taboos," *Bloomberg*, March 25, 2013.

[111] Rana Foroohar, "Continental Commitment Issues," *Time*, April 1, 2013. URL: http://www. time.com/time/magazine/article/0,9171,2139173,00.html

[112] Jean-Claude Juncker Interview "The Demons Haven't Been Banished," *Der Spiegel/ SpiegelOnline*, March 11, 2013. URL: http://www.spiegel.de/international/europe/spiegel-interview-with-luxembourg-Footnotes235prime-minister-juncker-a-888021.html; Charles Forelle, "Luxembourg Lies on Secret Meeting," *Wall Street Journal*, May 9, 2011. URL: http://blogs.wsj. com/brussels/2011/05/09/luxembourg-lies-on-secret-meeting/

[113] Annika Breidthardt and others, "Insight: Money Fled Cyprus As President Fumbled Bailout," *Reuters*, March 25, 2013 URL: http://www.reuters.com/article/2013/03/25/us-eurozone-cyprus-muddle-insight-idUSBRE92O0TM20130325; Rick Moran, "How Much Cash Fled Cyprus Prior to Bailout Deal?" *American Thinker*, March 26, 2013. URL: http://www.americanthinker.com/ blog/2013/03/how_much_cash_fled_cyprus_prior_to_bailout_deal.html; Tyler Durden, "Have the Russians Already Quietly Withdrawn All Their Cash From Cyprus?" *ZeroHedge.com*, March 25, 2013. URL: http://www.zerohedge.com/print/471901; Tyler Durden, "Cyprus – The Answer Is

Uniastrum," *ZeroHedge.com*, March 28, 2013. URL: http://www.zerohedge.com/print/472062

[114] Min Zeng, "Did Russia Just Move Its Treasury Holdings Offshore?" *Wall Street Journal*, March 14, 2014. URL: http://blogs.wsj.com/moneybeat/2014/03/14/did-russia-just-dump-its-treasury-holdings/?mod=ST1; Michael Mackenzie, "Plunge in Treasury Holdings at Fed Triggers Speculation of Russia Switch," *Financial Times*, March 14, 2014. URL: http://www.ft.com/intl/cms/s/0/51c55c1a-ab8c-11e3-aad9-00144feab7de.html#axzz2w4lhZOPr; Richard Leong, "Eyes Turn to Russia on Record Drop in U.S. Bond Holdings," *Reuters*, March 14, 2014. URL: http://www.reuters.com/article/2014/03/14/us-usa-fed-russia-idUSBREA2D1JW20140314; Susanne Walker, "Fed Custody Holdings Record Decline Fuels Russia Speculation," *Bloomberg*, March 14, 2014. URL: http://www.bloomberg.com/news/2014-03-14/fed-custody-holdings-record-decline-fuels-russia-speculation.html; Patti Domm, "Was that Russia Transferring Dollar Holdings Offshore?" *CNBC*, March 14, 2014. URL: http://www.cnbc.com/id/101495837; Peter Coy, "Is Russia Pulling Money Out of U.S. for Safekeeping?" *Businessweek/Bloomberg*, March 14, 2014. URL: http://www.businessweek.com/articles/2014-03-14/is-russia-pulling-money-out-of-u-dot-s-dot-for-safekeeping; Patrick Jenkins and Daniel Schafer, "Russian Companies Withdraw Billions from West, Say Moscow Bankers," *Financial Times*, March 14, 2014. URL: http://www.ft.com/intl/cms/s/0/ffea2660-ab9e-11e3-aad9-00144feab7de.html#axzz2w4lhZOPr

[115] Tyler Durden, "Russia Proposes Confiscating US, European Assets if Sanctions Adopted," *ZeroHedge*, March 5, 2014. URL: http://www.zerohedge.com/news/2014-03-05/russia-proposes-confiscating-us-european-assets-if-sanctions-adopted; "Hit Us with Sanctions? We'll Seize West's Assets, Russia Warns," *CNBC/Reuters*, March 5, 2014. URL: http://www.cnbc.com/id/101468195; "Can Russia Take My Pepsi? Consumer Brands at Risk," *CNBC*, March 5, 2014. URL: http://www.cnbc.com/id/101469148; "Which Major U.S. Firms Are at Risk With High Exposure to Russia?" *MarketWatch/Wall Street Journal*, March 3, 2014. URL: http://www.marketwatch.com/story/which-major-us-firms-are-at-risk-with-high-exposure-to-russia-2014-03-03

[116] Margarita Papantoniou, "Cypriot Politicians' Loans Written Off," GreekReporter.com, March 29, 2013. URL: http://greece.greekreporter.com/2013/03/29/cypriot-politicians-loans-written-off/

[117] Carsten Volkery, "Last Minute Deal: The End of the Cypriot Banking Sector," *Der Spiegel/SpiegelOnline*, March 25, 2013. URL: http://www.spiegel.de/international/europe/cyprus-to-shrink-bank-sector-under-last-minute-bailout-deal-a-890731.html

[118] Jason Ma, "Eurozone Signals Deposit Grab In Future Bank Bailouts," *Investor's Business Daily*, March 25, 2013. URL: http://news.investors.com/economy/032513-649274-cyprus-template-bank-depositors-bondholders-losses.htm; Moran Zhang, "Cyprus Crisis 2013: Are US Depositors' Money Safe With the Bank?" *International Business Times*, March 31, 2013. URL: http://www.ibtimes.com/cyprus-crisis-2013-are-us-depositors-money-safe-bank-1161807

[119] "Hands Off Our Banking Sector, Luxembourg Tells Euro Zone," *Reuters*, March 27, 2013. URL: http://www.cnbc.com/100596002

[120] Terry Miller, Anthony B. Kim and Kim R. Holmes, *2014 Index of Economic Freedom*. Washington, D.C.: Heritage Foundation / *Wall Street Journal*, 2014. URL for free download: http://www.heritage.org/index/download

[121] Matthew Jaffe, "Obama Bank Tax: Wall St. Mulls Court Challenge," *ABC News*, January 18, 2010.

[122] Jim Puzzanghera, "Obama Proposes to Tax Largest Financial Firms," *Los Angeles Times*, January 15, 2010.

[123] Greg Mankiw, "*The Bank Tax*," Greg Mankiw's Blog, January 15, 2010. URL: http://gregmankiw.blogspot.com/2010/01/bank-tax.html

[124] John Carney, "The Bank Tax And The Constitutional Ban on Bills of Attainder," *Business Insider*, January 21, 2010; Eric Dash, "Wall St. Weighs a Challenge to a Proposed Tax," *New York*

Times, January 18, 2010.

[125] Felix Salmon, "The Bank Tax Rises from the Dead," *Reuters*, February 26, 2014; Stephanie Armour and Ryan Tracy, "Wall Street Trains Fire on Idea of a Bank Tax," *Wall Street Journal*, March 17, 2014.

[126] Michael Ide, "Goldman Sachs Cancels GOP Fundraiser To Protest Proposed Bank Tax," *ValueWalk*, March 18, 2014; Richard Rubin, "Biggest Banks Said to Face Asset Tax in Republican Plan," *Bloomberg*, February 25, 2014; Jake Sherman, MJ Lee and Kate Davidson, "Republicans Take On Wall Street," *Politico*, February 26, 2014.

[127] Paul Toscano, "Has JPMorgan Become a 'Pinata bank'?" CNBC, August 28, 2013.

[128] Frank Keating, "Justice Puts Banks in a Choke Hold," *Wall Street Journal*, April 24, 2014. URL: http://online.wsj.com/news/articles/SB10001424052702304810904579511911684102106

[129] "Managing Risks in Third-Party Payment Processor Relationships," *Supervisory Insights* – Summer 2011. Washington, D.C.: Federal Deposit Insurance Corporation (FDIC), 2011. URL: http://www.fdic.gov/regulations/examinations/supervisory/insights/sisum11/managing.html

[130] "'Operation Choke Point' Raises Alarms," NRA-ILA / Institute for Legislative Action, May 2, 2014. URL: http://www.nraila.org/legislation/federal-legislation/2014/5/operation-choke-point-raises-alarms.aspx

[131] Norbert J. Michel, *The Financial Stability Oversight Council: Helping to Enshrine "Too Big to Fail."* Washington, D.C.: The Heritage Foundation / Backgrounder No. 2900, April 1, 2014. URL: http://thf_media.s3.amazonaws.com/2014/pdf/BG2900.pdf

[132] Michael S. Piwowar, "Remarks at AEI Conference on Financial Stability" (Monograph). Washington, D.C.: Securities and Exchange Commission, July 15, 2014. URL: http://www.sec.gov/News/Speech/Detail/Speech/1370542309109#.U9j8zSgVr8s

[133] Andrew Ackerman and Kirsten Grind, "SEC Approves Tighter Money-Fund Rules," *Wall Street Journal*, July 23, 2014. URL: http://online.wsj.com/articles/sec-to-vote-on-final-money-market-mutual-fund-rules-1406124323 ; James Sanford, "After SEC Rules, My Advice: Stay Out of Money-Market Funds!" *CNBC.com*, July 24, 2014, URL: http://www.cnbc.com/id/101864125; "SEC poised to end $1 a Share for Some Money Funds," *CNBC*, July 23, 2014. URL: http://www.cnbc.com/id/101859233; Keith Weiner, "Will New Money Market Rules Break Money Markets?" *Forbes*, July 26, 2014. URL: http://www.forbes.com/sites/keithweiner/2014/07/26/will-new-money-market-rules-break-money-markets/

[134] William Alden, "After Split Vote, S.E.C. Approves Rules on Money Market Funds," *New York Times*, July 23, 2014. URL: http://dealbook.nytimes.com/2014/07/23/s-e-c-approves-rules-on-money-market-funds/?_php=true&_type=blogs&_r=0

[135] Andrew Ackerman and Kirsten Grind, "SEC Approves Tighter Money-Fund Rules," *Wall Street Journal*, July 23, 2014. URL: http://online.wsj.com/articles/sec-to-vote-on-final-money-market-mutual-fund-rules-1406124323 ; James Sanford, "After SEC Rules, My Advice: Stay Out of Money-Market Funds!" *CNBC.com*, July 24, 2014, URL: http://www.cnbc.com/id/101864125; "SEC poised to end $1 a Share for Some Money Funds," *CNBC*, July 23, 2014. URL: http://www.cnbc.com/id/101859233; Keith Weiner, "Will New Money Market Rules Break Money Markets?" *Forbes*, July 26, 2014. URL: http://www.forbes.com/sites/keithweiner/2014/07/26/will-new-money-market-rules-break-money-markets/

[136] Brian Maloney, "The Mega-Rick Rant Returns!" *MediaEqualizer.com*, July 14, 2014. URL: http://mediaequalizer.com/2014/07/the-mega-rick-rant-returns/

[137] Ambrose Evans-Pritchard, "BIS Chief Fears Fresh Lehman From Worldwide Debt Surge," *London Telegraph*, July 13, 2014. URL: http://www.telegraph.co.uk/finance/markets/10965052/Bank-for-International-Settlements-fears-fresh-Lehman-crisis-from-worldwide-debt-surge.html

[138] David Malpass,"The Fed's Taper Is Already Paying Off," *Wall Street Journal*, March 13, 2014.

[139] Teresa Ghilarducci, *Guaranteed Retirement Accounts: Toward Retirement Income Security* (Briefing Paper). Washington, D.C.: Economic Policy Institute, November 20, 2007. URL: http://www.gpn.org/bp204/bp204.pdf

[140] James Pethokoukis, "Would Obama, Dems Kill 401(k) Plans? Fears About the Stock Market May Prompt Rash Government Action." *U.S. News & World Report*, October 23, 2008. URL: http://money.usnews.com/money/blogs/capital-commerce/2008/10/23/would-obama-dems-kill-401k-plans

[141] Nancy Thorner, "Beward: Guaranteed Retiremen Accounts (GRAs) Rise Again – Could Illinois Be Next?" *Madison-St. Clair Record*, August 8, 2013. URL: http://madisonrecord.com/arguments/258085-beware-guaranteed-retirement-accounts-gras-rise-again-could-illinois-be-next

[142] Teresa Ghilarducci, *Guaranteed Retirement Accounts: Toward Retirement Income Security* (Briefing Paper). Washington, D.C.: Economic Policy Institute, November 20, 2007. Page 12. URL: http://www.gpn.org/bp204/bp204.pdf

[143] Antony Davies and James R. Harrigan, "Government Owes Social Security $5 Tril, But You Have To Pay It Back," *Investor's Business Daily*, July 16, 2014. URL: http://news.investors.com/ibd-editorials-perspective/071614-709061-social-security-goes-bust-in-2020-leaving-half-a-trillion-in-annual-deficit.htm?ven=rss

[144] Carmen M. Reinhart and Kenneth S. Rogoff, *Financial and Sovereign Debt Crises: Some Lessons Learned and Those Forgotten*. IMF Working Paper WP/13/266. Washington, D.C.: International Monetary Fund, December 2013. URL: http://www.imf.org/external/pubs/ft/wp/2013/wp13266.pdf; Ambrose Evans-Pritchard, "IMF Paper Warns of 'Savings Tax' and Mass Write-Offs as West's Debt Hits 200-Year High," *London Telegraph*, January 2, 2014. URL: http://www.telegraph.co.uk/finance/financialcrisis/10548104/IMF-paper-warns-of-savings-tax-and-mass-write-offs-as-Wests-debt-hits-200-year-high.html

[145] John Maynard Keynes, *Essays in Persuasion*. New York: W.W. Norton, 1963. Pages 86-87.

[146] *Taxing Times, Fiscal Monitor/World Economic and Financial Survey*. Washington, D.C.: International Monetary Fund, October 2013. See page 49. URL: http://www.imf.org/external/pubs/ft/fm/2013/02/pdf/fm1302.pdf

[147] Bill Frezza, "The International Monetary Fund Lays The Groundwork For Global Wealth Confiscation," *Forbes*, October 15, 2013. URL: http://www.forbes.com/sites/billfrezza/2013/10/15/the-international-monetary-fund-lays-the-groundwork-for-global-wealth-confiscation/

[148] Peter F. Drucker, *Post-Capitalist Society*. New York: Harper Business, 1993. Pages 126-127.

[149] Frances Goodrich, Albert Hackett, Frank Capra and Jo Swerling, "It's A Wonderful Life" (movie script), page 59. URL: http://www.imsdb.com/scripts/It's-a-Wonderful-Life.html

[150] Juana Summers, "Dimon: I'm 'barely a Democrat'," *Politico*, May 13, 2012. URL: http://www.politico.com/blogs/politico-live/2012/05/dimon-im-barely-a-democrat-123290.html

[151] Charles W. Calomiris and Stephen H. Haber, *Fragile by Design: The Political Origins of Banking Crises and Scarce Credit*. Princeton, N.J.: Princeton University Press, 2014.

[152] Craig R. Smith and Lowell Ponte, *The Great Withdrawal: How the Progressives' 100-Year Debasement of America and the Dollar Ends*. Phoenix: Idea Factory Press, 2013. Page 44.

[153] Tracy Alloway and Camilla Hall, "US Banks Braced for Large Deposit Outflows," *Financial Times*, July 30, 2014. URL: http://www.ft.com/intl/cms/s/0/58848270-1729-11e4-8617-

00144feabdc0.html#axzz39PZv8vp5

[154] Ibid.

[155] Volcker is quoted in Ralph Benko, "The Global Importance of Paul Volcker's Call For A 'New Bretton Woods'," *Forbes*, June 16, 2014. URL: http://www.forbes.com/sites/ ralphbenko/2014/06/16/the-global-importance-of-paul-volckers-call-for-a-new-bretton-woods/

[156] Mike Dash, *Tulipomania: The Story of the World's Most Coveted Flower & The Extraordinary Passions It Aroused*. Waterville, Maine: G.K. Hall & Company, Publishers, 2001.

[157] Aparajita Saha-Bubna, "GMAC Will Change the Name of Its Bank," *Wall Street Journal*, May 15, 2009. URL: http://online.wsj.com/news/articles/SB124234797467422011; Colin Barr, "Treasury Aims to Exit Ally Bailout," *Fortune*, December 30, 2010. URL: http://fortune. com/2010/12/30/treasury-aims-to-exit-ally-bailout/ ; Ben Hallman, "Ally Bank's Aggressive Campaign To Avoid Paying For Housing Crisis," *Huffington Post*, April 11, 2013. URL: http://www.huffingtonpost.com/2013/04/11/foreclosure-settlement-borrowers_n_3054829.html

[158] Eduardo Porter, "Imagining the Dollar Without Its Privilege," *New York Times*, October 15, 2013. URL: http://www.nytimes.com/2013/10/16/business/imagining-the-dollar-without-its-privilege.html?pagewanted=all&_r=0 ; Spencer Kimball, "US Dollar's 'Exorbitant Privilege' At Risk," *Deutsche Welle*, October 17, 2013. URL: http://www.dw.de/us-dollars-exorbitant-privilege-at-risk/a-17156068; see also Barry Eichengreen, *Exorbitant Privilege: The Rise and Fall of the Dollar and the Future of the International Monetary System*. Oxford: Oxford University Press, 2011.

[159] Eswar S. Prasad, *The Dollar Trap: How the U.S. Dollar Tightened Its Grip on Global Finance*. Princeton, New Jersey: Princeton University Press, 2014.

[160] F.A. Hayek, *Choice in Currency: A Way to Stop Inflation* (Monograph). London: Institute of Economic Affairs, 1976. URL: http://www.iea.org.uk/sites/default/files/publications/files/ upldbook409.pdf

[161] Friedrich A. Hayek, *Denationalisation of Money: The Argument Refined: An Analysis of the Theory and Practice of Concurrent Currencies*. Third Edition. London: Institute of Economic Affairs, 1990. Pages 27-28. This can be downloaded from the Internet at no cost from http://mises. org/books/denationalisation.pdf

[162] Clifford F. Thies,"The Economics of Depression Scrip," *Mises Daily*, June30, 2010. URL: http://mises.org/daily/4521

[163] Michael McLeay, Amar Radia and Ryland Thomas, "Money Creation in the Modern Economy" [Monograph]. London: *Quarterly Bulletin* / Bank of England, First Quarter 2014. URL: http://www.bankofengland.co.uk/publications/Documents/quarterlybulletin/2014/ qb14q1prereleasemoneycreation.pdf ; see also Philip Pilkington, "Bank of England Endorses Post-Keynesian Endogenous Money Theory," *FixingtheEconomists*, March 12, 2014. URL: http://fixingtheeconomists.wordpress. com/2014/03/12/bank-of-england-endorses-post-keynesian-endogenous-money-theory/ ; "Endogenous Money," *Wikipedia*, URL: http://en.wikipedia.org/wiki/Endogenous_money ; Frances Coppola, "Martin Wolf Proposes the Death of Banking," Pieria, April 25, 2014. URL: http://www.pieria.co.uk/articles/martin_wolf_proposes_the_death_of_banking

[164] Terry Burnham, "Is Your Money Safe at The Bank? An Economist Says 'No' and Withdraws His," *The PBS NewsHour*, January 30, 2014. URL: http://www.pbs.org/newshour/making-sense/ is-your-money-safe-at-the-bank-an-economist-says-no-and-withdraws-his/; Tyler Durden, "Why This Harvard Economist Is Pulling All His Money From Bank of America," *ZeroHedge*, February 1, 2014. URL: http://www.zerohedge.com/news/2014-01-31/why-harvard-economist-pulling-all-his-money-bank-america; Neil Cavuto, "Is Your Money at Risk at Big Banks?" (video of interview with Professor Terry Burnham), February 5, 2014. URL: http://www.foxbusiness.com/on-air/ cavuto/index.html#/v/3158502520001

Sources

Anat R. Admati and Martin Hellwig, *The Bankers' New Clothes: What's Wrong With Banking and What to Do About It*. Princeton, New Jersey: Princeton University Press, 2013.

Liaquat Ahamed, *Lords of Finance: The Bankers Who Broke the World*. New York: Penguin Books, 2009.

George A. Akerlof and Robert J. Schiller, *Animal Spirits: How Human Psychology Drives the Economy, and Why It Matters for Global Capitalism*.
Princeton, New Jersey: Princeton University Press, 2009.

Daniel Alpert, *The Age of Oversupply: Overcoming the Greatest Challenge to the Global Economy*. New York: Portfolio / Penguin, 2014.

Morris Altman, *Behavioral Economics For Dummies*. Hoboken, New Jersey: For Dummies/John Wiley & Sons, 2012.

John Anthers, *The Fearful Rise of Markets: Global Bubbles, Synchronized Meltdowns, and How to Prevent Them In The Future*. London: FT Press / Financial Times, 2010.

David Archibald, *Twilight of Abundance: Why Life in the 21st Century Will Be Nasty, Brutish, and Short*. Washington, D.C.: Regnery Publishing, 2014.

Tyler Atkinson, David Luttrell and Harvey Rosenblum, *How Bad Was It? The Costs and Consequences of the 2007-2009 Financial Crisis* (Staff Paper No. 20). Dallas, Texas: Federal Reserve Bank of Dallas, July 2013.

Bill Bamber and Andrew Spencer, *Bear Trap: The Fall of Bear Stearns and the Panic of 2008*. New York: Ibooks, Inc., 2008.

James R. Barth, Gerard Caprio Jr., and Ross Levine, *Guardians of Finance: Making Regulators Work for Us*. Cambridge, Massachusetts: The MIT Press, 2012.

William W. Beach and others, *Obama Tax Hikes: The Economic and Fiscal Effects* (Monograph). Washington, D.C.: Heritage Foundation, 2010.

Thorsten Beck (Editor), *The Future of Banking*. Centre for Economic Policy Research, 2011.

David Beckworth (Editor), *Boom and Bust Banking: The Causes and Cures of the Great Recession*. Oakland, California: Independent Institute, 2012.

Noah Berlatsky (Ed.), *Inflation*. Detroit: Greenhaven Press/Opposing Viewpoints Series, 2013.

Ben S. Bernanke and others, *Inflation Targeting: Lessons from the International Experience*. Princeton, New Jersey: Princeton University Press, 1999.

Peter Bernholz, *Monetary Regimes and Inflation: History, Economic and Political Relationships*. Williston, Vermont: Edward Elgar Publishing, 2006.

Peter L. Bernstein, *Against the Gods: The Remarkable Story of Risk*. Hoboken, New Jersey: John Wiley & Sons, 1998.

Mark Blyth, *Austerity: The History of a Dangerous Idea*. Oxford: Oxford University Press, 2013.

Haim Bodek, *The Problems of HFT – Collected Writings on High Frequency Trading & Stock Market*

Structure. Seattle, Washington: CreateSpace / Amazon, 2013.

William Bonner and Addison Wiggin, *Financial Reckoning Day: Surviving the Soft Depression of the 21ˢᵗ Century*. Hoboken, New Jersey: John Wiley & Sons, 2004.

_____, *The New Empire of Debt: The Rise and Fall of an Epic Financial Bubble* (Second Edition). Hoboken, New Jersey: John Wiley & Sons, 2009.

Neal Boortz and John Linder, *The FairTax Book: Saying Goodbye to the Income Tax and the IRS....* New York: Regan Books / HarperCollins, 2005.

Neal Boortz, John Linder and Rob Woodall, *FairTax: The Truth: Answering the Critics*. New York: Harper, 2008.

Nick Bostrom, *Superintelligence: Paths, Dangers, Strategies*. Oxford: Oxford University Press, 2014.

Volker Bothmer and Ioannis A. Daglis, *Space Weather: Physics and Effects*. Berlin: Springer, 2010.

Donald J. Boudreaux, James Scott, Timothy B. Lee and J. Bradford DeLong, *Seeing Like a State: A Conversation with James C. Scott*. Washington, D.C.: Cato Institute / Cato Unbound, 2010.

Richard X. Bove, *Guardians of Prosperity: Why America Needs Big Banks*. New York: Portfolio/ Penguin, 2013.

Jerry Bowyer, *The Free Market Capitalist's Survival Guide: How to Invest and Thrive in an Era of Rampant Socialism*. New York: Broad Side / Harper Collins, 2011.

H.W. Brands, *The Age of Gold: The California Gold Rush and the New American Dream*. New York: Doubleday / Random House, 2002.

_____, *American Colossus: The Triumph of Capitalism 1865-1900*. New York: Anchor Books / Doubleday / Random House, 2010.

_____, *The Money Men: Capitalism, Democracy, and the Hundred Years' War Over the American Dollar*. New York: W.W. Norton, 2010.

Arthur C. Brooks, *The Battle: How the Fight Between Free Enterprise and Big Government Will Shape America's Future*. New York: Basic Books/Perseus Books, 2010.

_____, *Gross National Happiness: Why Happiness Matters for America – and How We Can Get More of It*. New York: Basic Books, 2008.

_____, *The Road to Freedom: How to Win the Fight for Free Enterprise*. New York: Basic Books/Perseus Books, 2012.

Brendan Brown, *Euro Crash: How Asset Price Inflation Destroys the Wealth of Nations (Third Revised Edition)*. London: Palgrave Macmillan, 2014.

Ellen Hodgson Brown, *The Public Bank Solution: From Austerity to Prosperity*. Baton Rouge, Louisiana: Third Millennium Press, 2013.

_____, *Web of Debt: The Shocking Truth About Our Money System and How We Can Break Free (Fourth Edition)*. Baton Rouge, Louisiana: Third Millennium Press, 2011.

Robert Bryce, *Smaller Faster Lighter Denser Cheaper: How Innovation Keeps Proving the Catastrophists Wrong*. New York: PublicAffairs/Perseus Books Group, 2014.

Dedria Bryfonski (Ed.), *The Banking Crisis*. Detroit: Greenhaven Press/Opposing Viewpoints Series, 2010.

James M. Buchanan and Richard E. Wagner, *Democracy in Deficit: The Political Legacy of Lord Keynes*. Indianapolis: Liberty Fund, 1999.

Todd G. Buchholz, *New Ideas from Dead Economists: An Introduction to Modern Economic Thought*. New York: New American Library/Penguin Books, 1989.

John Butler, *The Golden Revolution: How to Prepare for the Coming Global Gold Standard*. New York: John Wiley & Sons, 2012.

Bruce Caldwell (Editor), *The Collected Works of F.A. Hayek, Volume 2: The Road to Serfdom: Texts and Documents: The Definitive Edition*. Chicago: University of Chicago Press, 2007.

Charles W. Calomiris and Stephen H. Haber, *Fragile by Design: The Political Origins of Banking Crises and Scarce Credit*. Princeton, N.J.: Princeton University Press, 2014.

Stephen G. Cecchetti and others, *The Real Effects of Debt*. BIS Working Papers No 352. Basel, Switzerland: Bank for International Settlements, September 2011. URL: http://www.bis.org/publ/work352.pdf

Edward Chancellor, *Devil Take the Hindmost: A History of Financial Speculation*. New York: Plume (Reissue Edition), 2000.

Marc Chandler, *Making Sense of the Dollar: Exposing Dangerous Myths about Trade and Foreign Exchange*. New York: Bloomberg Press, 2009.

Ron Chernow, *The House of Morgan: An American Banking Dynasty and the Rise of Modern Finance*. New York: Grove Press, 2010.

Moorad Choudhry, *An Introduction to Banking: Liquidity Risk and Asset-Liability Management*. Hoboken, New Jersey: John Wiley & Sons, 2011.

Harold Van B. Cleveland, Charles P. Kindleberger, David P. Calleo and Lewis E. Lehrman, *Money and the Coming World Order*, Second Edition. Greenwich, Connecticut: Lehrman Institute, 2012.

Tom A. Coburn, *The Debt Bomb: A Bold Plan to Stop Washington from Bankrupting America*. Nashville: Thomas Nelson, 2012.

Congressional Budget Office, *The Budget and Economic Outlook: Fiscal Years 2011 to 2021*. Washington, D.C.: Congressional Budget Office, January 2011. URL: http://www.cbo.gov/ftpdocs/120xx/doc12039/01-26_FY2011Outlook.pdf

Arnold Cornez, *The Offshore Money Book: How to Move Assets Offshore for Privacy, Protection, and Tax Advantage*. New York: McGraw-Hill, 2000.

Jerome R. Corsi, *America for Sale: Fighting the New World Order, Surviving a Global Depression, and Preserving U.S.A. Sovereignty*. New York: Threshold Editions / Simon & Schuster, 2009.

Diane Coyle, *GDP: A Brief but Affectionate History*. Princeton, New Jersey: Princeton University Press, 2014.

Crews, Clyde Wayne, Jr., *Ten Thousand Commandments: An Annual Snapshot of the Federal Regulatory State*. 2014 Edition. (Monograph). Washington, D.C.: Competitive Enterprise Institute, 2014.

Mike Dash, *Tulipomania: The Story of the World's Most Coveted Flower & The Extraordinary Passions It Aroused*. Waterville, Maine: G.K. Hall & Company, Publishers, 2001.

Glyn Davies, *A History of Money: From Ancient Times to the Present Day*. Third Edition. Cardiff: University of Wales Press, 2002.

Glyn Davies and Roy Davies, *A Comparative Chronology of Money: Monetary History from Ancient Times to the Present Day*. (Monograph based on Glyn Davies and Roy Davies, above.) (2006) URL: http://projects.exeter.ac.uk/RDavies/arian/amser/chrono.html

Hernando de Soto, *The Mystery of Capital: Why Capitalism Triumphs in the West and Fails Everywhere Else*. New York: Basic Books / Perseus Books Group, 2000.

Jesus Huerta de Soto, *Money, Bank Credit, and Economic Cycles, Third Edition*. Auburn, Alabama: Ludwig von Mises Institute, 2012.

Peter H. Diamandis and Steven Kotler, *Abundance: The Future Is Better Than You Think*. New York: Free Press, 2012.

Jared Diamond, *Collapse: How Societies Choose to Fail or Succeed*. New York: Viking Press, 2005.

Peter F. Drucker, *Post-Capitalist Society*. New York: Harper Business, 1993.

Dinesh D'Souza, *America: Imagine a World Without Her*. Washington, D.C.: Regnery, 2014.

_____, *Obama's America: Unmaking the American Dream*. Washington, D.C.: Regnery, 2012.

_____, *The Roots of Obama's Rage*. Washington, D.C.: Regnery, 2010.

_____, *The Virtue of Prosperity: Finding Values in an Age of Techno-Affluence*. New York: Free Press / Simon & Schuster, 2000.

Richard Duncan, *The Dollar Crisis: Causes, Consequences, Cures*. Singapore: John Wiley & Sons (Asia), 2003.

_____, *The New Depression: The Breakdown of the Paper Money Economy*. New York: John Wiley & Sons, 2012.

Gregg Easterbrook, *The Progress Paradox: How Life Gets Better While People Feel Worse*. New York: Random House, 2003.

Mary Eberstadt, *How the West Really Lost God: A New Theory of Secularization*. West Conshohocken, Pennsylvania: Templeton Press, 2013.

Nicholas Eberstadt, *A Nation of Takers: America's Entitlement Epidemic*. West Conshohocken, Pennsylvania: Templeton Press, 2012.

Gauti B. Eggertsson, *What Fiscal Policy Is Effective at Zero Interest Rate?* Staff Report No. 402 (Monograph). New York: Federal Reserve Bank of New York, November 2009. URL: http://www.newyorkfed.org/research/staff_reports/sr402.pdf

Barry Eichengreen, *Exorbitant Privilege: The Rise and Fall of the Dollar and the Future of the International Monetary System*. Oxford: Oxford University Press, 2011.

_____, *Global Imbalances and the Lessons of Bretton Woods* (Cairoli Lectures). Cambridge, Massachusetts: MIT Press, 2010.

_____, *Globalizing Capital: A History of the International Monetary System* (Second Edition).

_____, *Golden Fetters: The Gold Standard and the Great Depression, 1919-1939* (NBER Series on Long-Term Factors in Economic Development). Oxford: Oxford University Press, 1996.

Barry Eichengreen and Marc Flandreau, *Gold Standard In Theory & History*. London: Routledge, 1997.

Kathleen C. Engel and Patricia A. McCoy, *The Subprime Virus: Reckless Credit, Regulatory Failure, and Next Steps*. New York: Oxford University Press USA, 2011.

Richard A. Epstein, *How Progressives Rewrote the Constitution*. Washington, D.C.: Cato Institute, 2006.

_____, *Takings: Private Property and the Power of Eminent* Domain. Cambridge, Massachusetts: Harvard University Press, 1985.

Federal Reserve System, Board of Governors of, *Consumers and Mobile Financial Services 2013* (Monograph). Washington, D.C.: Federal Reserve Board Division of Consumer and Community Affairs, March 2013. URL: http://www.federalreserve.gov/econresdata/consumers-and-mobile-financial-services-report-201303.pdf

Carl Feisenfeld and David Glass, *Banking Regulation in the United States, 3rd Edition*. Huntington, N.Y.: Juris Publishing, 2011.

Niall Ferguson, *The Ascent of Money: A Financial History of the World*. New York: Penguin Press, 2008.

_____, *The Cash Nexus: Money and Power in the Modern World, 1700-2000.* New York: Basic Books, 2002.

_____, *Civilization: The West and the Rest*. New York: Penguin Books, 2011.

_____, *Colossus: The Price of America's Empire*. New York: Penguin Press, 2004.

_____, *The House of Rothschild: Volume 1: Money's Prophets: 1798-1848*. New York: Penguin Books, 1999.

_____, *The House of Rothschild: Volume 2: The World's Banker: 1849-1999*. New York: Penguin Books, 2000.

_____, *The Great Degeneration: How Institutions Decay and Economies Die*. New York: Penguin Books, 2013.

Peter Ferrara, *America's Ticking Bankruptcy Bomb: How the Looming Debt Crisis Threatens the American Dream – and How We Can Turn the Tide Before It's Too Late*. New York: Broadside Books, 2011.

William Fleckenstein and Frederick Sheehan, *Greenspan's Bubbles: The Age of Ignorance at the Federal Reserve*. New York: McGraw-Hill, 2008.

Steve Forbes and Elizabeth Ames, *Money: How the Destruction of the Dollar Threatens the Global Economy – and What We Can Do About It*. New York: McGraw-Hill, 2014.

Ralph T. Foster, *Fiat Paper Money: The History and Evolution of Our Currency*. Second Edition. Shenzhen, China: Shenzhen Jinhao Publishing / Alibaba.com, 2010.

Justin Fox, *The Myth of the Rational Market: A History of Risk, Reward, and Delusion on Wall Street*. New York: Harper Business, 2009.

Kevin D. Freeman, *Economic Warfare: Risks and Responses: Analysis of Twenty-First Century Risks in Light of the Recent Market Collapse* (Monograph). Cross Consulting and Services, 2009. This can be downloaded from the Internet at no cost from http://av.r.ftdata.co.uk/files/2011/03/49755779-Economic-Warfare-Risks-and-Responses-by-Kevin-D-Freeman.pdf or at no cost from http://www.freemanglobal.com/uploads/Economic_Warfare_Risks_and_Responses.pdf

_____, *Game Plan: How to Protect Yourself from the Coming Cyber-Economic Attack*. Washington, D.C.: Regnery Publishing, 2014.

_____, *Secret Weapon: How Economic Terrorism Brought Down the U.S. Stock Market and Why It Can Happen Again*. Washington, D.C.: Regnery, 2012.

George Friedman, *The Next Decade: Where We've Been...And Where We're Going*. New York: Doubleday, 2011.

Milton Friedman, *An Economist's Protest*. Second Edition. Glen Ridge, New Jersey: Thomas Horton and Daughters, 1975. Also published as *There's No Such Thing As A Free Lunch*. La Salle, Illinois: Open Court Publishing, 1975.

_____, *Capitalism & Freedom: A Leading Economist's View of the Proper Role of Competitive Capitalism*. Chicago: University of Chicago Press, 1962.

_____, *Dollars and Deficits: Inflation, Monetary Policy and the Balance of Payments*. Englewood Cliffs, New Jersey: Prentice-Hall, 1968.

_____, *Money Mischief: Episodes in Monetary History*. New York: Harcourt Brace, 1992.

_____, *On Economics: Selected Papers*. Chicago: University of Chicago Press, 2007.

_____, *Why Government Is the Problem (Essays in Public Policy)*. Stanford, California: Hoover Institution Press, 1993.

Milton & Rose Friedman, *Free to Choose: A Personal Statement*. New York: Harcourt Brace Jovanovich, 1980.

_____, *Tyranny of the Status Quo*. San Diego, California: Harcourt Brace Jovanovich, 1984.

Milton Friedman & Anna Jacobson Schwartz, *A Monetary History of the United States, 1867-1960*. A Study by the National Bureau of Economic Research, New York. Princeton, New Jersey: Princeton University Press, 1963.

Francis Fukuyama, *The End of History and The Last Man*. New York: Free Press, 1992.

_____, *Trust: The Social Virtues and The Creation of Prosperity*. New York: Free Press, 1996.

John Fund and Hans von Spakovsky, *Obama's Enforcer: Eric Holder's Justice Department*. New York: Broadside Books, 2014.

Joseph Gagnon, Matthew Raskin, Juliew Remache and Brian Sack, *Large-Scale Asset Purchases by the Federal Reserve: Did They Work?* New York: Federal Reserve Bank of New York / *Economic Policy Review*, May 2011. URL: http://newyorkfed.org/research/epr/11v17n1/1105gagn.pdf

Joseph E. Gagnon and Brian Sack, *Monetary Policy with Abundant Liquidity: A New Operating Framework for the Federal Reserve*. Document PB 14-4 / Policy Brief. Washington, D.C.: Peterson Institute for International Economics, January 2014. URL: http://www.piie.com/publications/pb/pb14-4.pdf

James K. Galbraith, *The Predator State: How Conservatives Abandoned the Free Market and Why Liberals Should Too*. New York: Free Press, 2008.

Mark Lee Gardner, *Shot All to Hell: Jesse James, the Northfield Raid, and the Wild West's Greatest Escape*. New York: William Morrow, 2013.

John D. Gartner, *The Hypomanic Edge: The Link Between (A Little) Craziness and (A Lot of) Success in America*. New York: Simon & Schuster, 2005.

Charles Gasparino, *Bought and Paid For: The Unholy Alliance Between Barack Obama and Wall Street*. New York: Sentinel / Penguin, 2010.

Francis J. Gavin, *Gold, Dollars, and Power: The Politics of International Monetary Relations, 1958-1971 (The New Cold War History)*. Chapel Hill, North Carolina: University of North Carolina Press, 2007.

Timothy F. Geithner, *Stress Test: Reflections on Financial Crises*. New York: Crown / Random House, 2014.

Nicole Gelinas, *After the Fall: Saving Capitalism from Wall Street – and Washington*. New York: Encounter Books, 2011.

Pamela Geller and Robert Spencer, *The Post-American Presidency*. New York: Threshold Editions / Simon & Schuster, 2010.

Teresa Ghilarducci, *Guaranteed Retirement Accounts: Toward Retirement Income Security*. Washington, D.C.: Economic Policy Institute, November 20, 2007. URL: http://www.gpn.org/bp204/bp204.pdf

_____, *What You Need to Know About the Economics of Growing Old (But Were Afraid to Ask): A Provocative Reference Guide to the Economics of Aging*. Notre Dame, Indiana: University of Notre Dame Press, 2004.

_____, *When I'm Sixty-Four: The Plot Against Pensions and the Plan to Save Them*. Princeton, New Jersey: Princeton University Press, 2008.

George Gilder, *Knowledge and Power: The Information Theory of Capitalism and How It Is Revolutionizing Our World*. Washington, D.C.: Regnery Publishing, 2013.

_____, *Wealth and Poverty*. New York: Basic Books, 1981.

Jonah Goldberg, *Liberal Fascism: The Secret History of the American Left, From Mussolini to the Politics of Meaning*. New York: Doubleday, 2008.

_____, *The Tyranny of Cliches: How Liberals Cheat in the War of Ideas*. New York: Sentinel / Penguin, 2012.

David P. Goldman, *How Civilizations Die (And Why Islam Is Dying Too)*. Washington, D.C.: Regnery, 2011.

Jason Goodwin, *Greenback: The Almighty Dollar and The Invention of America*. New York: John Macrae / Henry Holt and Company, 2003.

William M. Gouge, *A Short History of Paper Money and Banking in the United States*. Auburn, Alabama: Ludwig von Mises Institute, 2011.

Charles Goyette, *The Dollar Meltdown: Surviving the Impending Currency Crisis with Gold, Oil, and Other Unconventional Investments*. New York: Portfolio / Penguin, 2009.

Michael Grabell, *Money Well Spent? The Truth Behind the Trillion-Dollar Stimulus, the Biggest Economic Recovery Plan in History*. New York: PublicAffairs / Perseus Books Group, 2012.

David Graeber, *Debt: The First 5,000 Years. Brooklyn, New York: Melville House Books, 2012*.

Thomas Greco, *The End of Money and the Future of Civilization*. White River Junction, Vermont: Chelsea Green Publishing, 2009.

_____, *Money: Understanding and Creating Alternatives to Legal Tender*. White River Junction, Vermont: Chelsea Green Publishing, 2012.

Andy Greenberg, *This Machine Kills Secrets: How WikiLeakers, Cypherpunks, and Hacktivists Aim to Free the World's Information*. New York: Dutton Adult, 2012.

Alan Greenspan, *The Age of Turbulence: Adventures in a New World*. New York: Penguin Books, 2007.

William Greider, *Secrets of the Temple: How the Federal Reserve Runs the Country*. New York: Simon & Schuster, 1989.

G. Edward Griffin, *The Creature from Jekyll Island: A Second Look at the Federal Reserve*. Third Edition. Westlake Village, California: American Media, 1998.

Alexander Hamilton, James Madison and John Jay, *The Federalist Papers*. New York: Mentor Books / New American Library, 1961. For an online version of James Madison's Federalist Paper No. 44, go to this URL: http://www.constitution.org/fed/federa44.htm

Bob Harris, *The International Bank of Bob: Connecting Our Worlds One $25 Kiva Loan At A Time*. New York: Walker & Company, 2013.

Keith Hart, *Money in an Unequal World*. New York: Texere, 2001.

David Harvey, *Seventeen Contradictions and the End of Capitalism*. Oxford: Oxford University Press, 2014.

Friedrich A. Hayek (Editor), *Capitalism and the Historians*. Chicago: Phoenix Books / University of Chicago Press, 1963.

_____, *Choice in Currency: A Way to Stop Inflation*. London: Institute of Economic Affairs, 1976. This can be downloaded from the Internet at no cost from http://www.iea.org.uk/sites/default/files/publications/files/upldbook409.pdf

_____, *The Counter-Revolution of Science: Studies On The Abuse of Reason*. New York: The Free Press / Macmillan / Crowell-Collier, 1955.

_____, *The Constitution of Liberty*. The Definitive Edition, Edited by Ronald Hamowy. Chicago: University of Chicago Press, 2011.

_____, *Denationalisation of Money: The Argument Refined: An Analysis of the Theory*

and Practice of Concurrent Currencies. Third Edition. London: Institute of Economic Affairs, 1990. This can be downloaded from the Internet at no cost from http://mises.org/books/denationalisation.pdf

_____, *The Fatal Conceit: The Errors of Socialism*. Chicago: University of Chicago Press, 1991.

_____, *The Road to Serfdom*. Chicago: Phoenix Books / University of Chicago Press, 1944.

Henry Hazlitt, *The Failure of the "New Economics": An Analysis of The Keynesian Fallacies*. New Rochelle, New York: Arlington House, 1959.

_____, *From Bretton Woods to World Inflation: A Study of Causes & Consequences*. Chicago: Regnery Gateway, 1984. This can be downloaded from the Internet at no cost from http://mises.org/books/brettonwoods.pdf

Robert L. Hetzel, *The Great Recession: Market Failure or Policy Failure? (Studies in Macroeconomic History)*. New York: Cambridge University Press, 2012.

_____, *The Monetary Policy of the Federal Reserve*. New York: Cambridge University Press, 2008.

David Horowitz and Jacob Laksin, *The New Leviathan: How the Left-Wing Money-Machine Shapes American Politics and Threatens America's Future*. New York: Crown Forum, 2012.

Philip K. Howard, *The Rule of Nobody: Saving America from Dead Laws and Broken Government*. New York: W.W. Norton, 2014.

Timothy Howard, *The Mortgage Wars: Inside Fannie Mae, Big-Money Politics, and the Collapse of the American Dream*. New York: McGraw-Hill Education, 2014.

Glenn Hubbard and Tim Kane, *Balance: The Economics of Great Powers From Ancient Rome to Modern America*. New York: Simon & Schuster, 2013.

Michael Hudson, *The Bubble and Beyond: Fictitious Capital, Debt Deflation and Global Crisis*. ISLET / Open Library, 2012.

W.H. Hutt, *The Keynesian Episode: A Reassessment*. Indianapolis: LibertyPress, 1979.

Bob Ivry, *The Seven Sins of Wall Street: Big Banks, Their Washington Lackeys, and the Next Financial Crisis*. New York: PublicAffairs Press / Perseus Group, 2014.

Andrew Jackson and Ben Dyson, *Modernising Money: Why Our Monetary System Is Broken and How It Can Be Fixed*. Positive Money, 2013.

Steven H. Jaffe, Jessica Lautin and the Museum of the City of New York, *Capital of Capital: Money, Banking, and Power in New York City, 1784-2012*. New York: Columbia University Press, 2014.

Simon Johnson and James Kwak, *13 Bankers: The Wall Street Takeover and the Next Financial Meltdown*. New York: Pantheon Books, 2010.

Robert Kagan, *The World America Made*. New York: Vintage / Random House, 2012.

Craig Karmin, *Biography of the Dollar: How the Mighty Buck Conquered the World and Why It's Under Siege*. New York: Crown Business, 2008.

Margrit Kennedy, *People Money: The Promise of Regional Currencies*. London: Triarchy Press, 2012.

Charles R. Kesler, *I Am the Change: Barack Obama and the Crisis of Liberalism.* New York: Broadside Books, 2012.

John Maynard Keynes, *Essays in Persuasion.* New York: W.W. Norton, 1963.

_____, *The General Theory of Employment, Interest, and Money.* New York: Harcourt, Brace & World, 1935.

Charles P. Kindleberger and Robert Z. Aliber, *Manias, Panics and Crashes: A History of Financial Crises (Sixth Edition).* London: Palgrave Macmillan, 2011.

Arnold Kling, *The Case for Auditing the Fed Is Obvious.* (Monograph / Briefing Paper). Washington, D.C.: Cato Institute, April 27, 2010. URL: http://www.cato.org/pubs/bp/bp118.pdf

Knowledge @ Wharton and Ernst & Young, *Global Banking 2020: Foresight and Insights.*

Gabriel Kolko, *Railroads and Regulation 1877-1916.* New York: W.W. Norton, 1970. Originally published in 1965 by Princeton University Press.

Laurence J. Kotlikoff, *Jimmy Stewart Is Dead: Ending the World's Ongoing Financial Plague with Limited Purpose Banking.* Hoboken, New Jersey: John Wiley & Sons, 2011.

Laurence J. Kotlikoff and Scott Burns, *The Clash of Generations: Saving Ourselves, Our Kids, and Our Economy.* Cambridge, Massachusetts: The MIT Press, 2012.

_____, *The Coming Generational Storm: What You Need to Know About America's Economic Future.* Cambridge, Massachusetts: MIT Press, 2005.

Paul Krugman, *The Return of Depression Economics and The Crisis of 2008.* New York: W.W. Norton, 2009.

Stanley Kurtz, *Spreading the Wealth: How Obama Is Robbing the Suburbs to Pay for the Cities.* New York: Sentinel / Penguin, 2012.

Joel Kurtzman, *The Death of Money: How the Electronic Economy Has Destabilized the World's Markets and Created Financial Chaos.* New York: Simon & Schuster, 1993.

Kwasi Kwartyeng, *War and Gold: A Five-Hundred-Year History of Empires, Adventures and Debt.* London: Bloomsbury Publishing, 2014.

Arthur B. Laffer, Stephen Moore and Peter J. Tanous, *The End of Prosperity: How Higher Taxes Will Doom the Economy – If We Let It Happen.* New York: Threshold Editions / Simon & Schuster, 2008.

Arthur B. Laffer, Stephen Moore, Rex A. Sinquefield and Travis H. Brown, *An Inquiry into the Nature and Causes of the Wealth of States: How Taxes, Energy, and Worker Freedom Change Everything.* Hoboken, New Jersey: John Wiley & Sons, 2014.

Arthur B. Laffer and Stephen Moore, *Return to Prosperity: How America Can Regain Its Economic Superpower Status.* New York: Threshold Editions / Simon & Schuster, 2010.

George Lakoff, *The Political Mind: A Cognitive Scientist's Guide to Your Brain and Its Politics.* New York: Penguin Books, 2009.

George Lakoff and Elizabeth Wehling, *The Little Blue Book: The Essential Guide to Thinking and Talking Democratic.* New York: Free Press, 2012.

John Lanchester, *I.O.U.: Why Everyone Owes Everyone and No One Can Pay.*

New York: Simon & Schuster, 2010.

David S. Landes, *The Wealth and Poverty of Nations: Why Some Are So Rich and Some So Poor.* New York: W.W. Norton, 1998.

Vincent Lannoye, *The Story of Money For Understanding Economics.* Seattle: CreateSpace Independent Publishing / Amazon, 2011.

Jonathan V. Last, *What to Expect When No One's Expecting: America's Coming Demographic Disaster.* New York: Encounter Books, 2013.

Adam Lebor, *Tower of Basel: The Shadowy History of the Secret Bank that Runs the World.* New York: PublicAffairs / Perseus Group, 2013.

Lewis E. Lehrman, *Money, Gold and History.* Greenwich, Connecticut: The Lehrman Institute, 2013.

_____, *The True Gold Standard – A Monetary Reform Plan Without Official Reserve Currencies.* Greenwich, Connecticut: The Lehrman Institute, 2011.

Gwendolyn Leick (Editor), *The Babylonian World.* London: Routledge, 2009. See chapter "The Egibi Family" by Cornelia Wunsch.

George Lekatis, *Understanding Basel III: What Is Different After March 2013.* Washington, D.C.: Basel III Compliance Professionals Association (BiiiCPA), 2013.

Lawrence Lessig, *Republic, Lost: How Money Corrupts Congress – and a Plan to Stop It.* Twelve / Hachette Book Group, 2011.

Louise Levathes, *When China Ruled the Seas: The Treasure Fleet of the Dragon Throne, 1405-1433.* Oxford: Oxford University Press, 1997.

Hunter Lewis, *Crony Capitalism in America: 2008-2012.* Charlottesville, Virginia: AC2 Publishing, 2013.

Michael Lewis, *Boomerang: Travels in the New Third World.* New York: W.W. Norton, 2011.

_____, *Flash Boys: A Wall Street Revolt.* New York: W.W. Norton, 2014.

_____, *Panic: The Story of Modern Financial Insanity.* New York: W.W. Norton, 2009.

Naphtali Lewis and Meyer Reinhold (Editors), *Roman Civilization: Sourcebook II: The Empire.* New York: Harper Torchbooks, 1966.

Nathan Lewis and Addison Wiggin, *Gold: The Once and Future Money.* Hoboken, New Jersey: John Wiley & Sons, 2007.

Qiao Liang and Wang Xiangsui, *Unrestricted Warfare.* Panama City, Panama: Pan American Publishing Company, 2002.

Bernard Lietaer and Stephen Belgin, *New Money for a New World.* Qiterra Press, 2011.

Bernard Lietaer and Jacqui Dunne, *Rethinking Money: How New Currencies Turn Scarcity Into Prosperity.* San Francisco: Berrett-Koehler Publishers/BK Currents, 2013.

Charles A. Lindbergh, Sr., *Lindbergh on the Federal Reserve* (Formerly titled: *The Economic Pinch*). Costa Mesa, California: Noontide Press, 1989.

Julia Lovell, *The Great Wall: China Against the World, 1000 BC-AD 2000*. New York: Grove Press, 2007.

David Lukas, *Whose Future Are You Financing? What the Government And Wall Street Don't Want You To Know*. Little Rock, Arkansas: Race Publishing, 2014.

Deirdre N. McCloskey, *Bourgeois Dignity: Why Economics Can't Explain the Modern World*. Chicago: University of Chicago Press, 2010.

Heather MacDonald, *The Burden of Bad Ideas: How Modern Intellectuals Misshape Our Society*. Chicago: Ivan R. Dee, 2000.

Robert D. McHugh, *The Coming Economic Ice Age: Five Steps To Survive and Prosper*. London: Thomas Noble Books, 2013.

Bethany McLean and Joe Nocera, *All the Devils Are Here: The Hidden History of the Financial Crisis*. New York: Portfolio / Penguin, 2010.

Michael Magnusson, *The Land Without A Banking Law: How to Start a Bank With a Thousand Dollars*. York, England: Opus Operis Publishing, 2013.

_____, *Offshore Bank License: Seven Jurisdictions*. York, England: Opus Operis Publishing, 2013.

Michael P. Malloy, *Principles of Bank Regulation, 3rd (Concise Hornbook)*. Eagan, Minnesota: West Publishing/Thompson Reuters, 2011.

Felix Martin, *Gold: The Unauthorized Biography*. New York: Knopf, 2014.

James A. Marusek, *Solar Storm Threat Analysis* (Monograph). Bloomfield, Indiana: Impact, 2007. URL: http://www.breadandbutterscience.com/SSTA.pdf.

Karl Marx and Friedrich Engels, *The Communist Manifesto*. London: Penguin Classics, 1985.

Philip Matyszak, *Ancient Rome on 5 Denarii a Day*. London: Thames & Hudson, 2008.

John Mauldin and Jonathan Tepper, *Code Red: How to Protect Your Savings From the Coming Crisis*. Hoboken, New Jersey: John Wiley & Sons, 2013.

_____, *Endgame: The End of the Debt Supercycle and How It Changes Everything*. Hoboken, New Jersey: John Wiley & Sons, 2011.

Martin Mayer, *The Fed: The Inside Story of How the World's Most Powerful Financial Institution Drives the Markets*. New York: Free Press, 2001.

Michael Medved, *The 5 Big Lies About American Business: Combating Smears Against the Free-Market Economy*. New York: Crown Forum, 2009.

David I. Meiselman and Arthur B. Laffer (Editors), *The Phenomenon of Worldwide Inflation*. Washington, D.C.: American Enterprise Institute, 1975.

Mary Mellor, *The Future of Money: From Financial Crisis to Public Resource*. London: Pluto Press, 2010.

Gavin Menzies, *1421: The Year China Discovered America*. New York: Harper Perennial, 2002.

_____, *1434: The Year a Magnificent Chinese Fleet Sailed to Italy and Ignited the*

Renaissance. New York: Harper Perennial, 2009.

Atif Mian and Amir Sufi, *House of Debt: How They (and You) Caused the Great Recession, and How We Can Prevent It from Happening Again*. Chicago: University of Chicago Press, 2014.

Norbert J. Michel, *The Financial Stability Oversight Council: Helping to Enshrine "Too Big to Fail"* (Monograph / *Backgrounder*). Washington, D.C.: The Heritage Foundation, April 1, 2014.

Willem Middlekoop, *The Big Reset: War on Gold and the Financial Endgame*. Amsterdam: Amsterdam University Press, 2014.

James D. Miller, *Singularity Rising: Surviving and Thriving in a Smarter, Richer, and More Dangerous World*. Dallas, Texas: BenBella Books, 2012.

Terry Miller, Anthony B. Kim and Kim R. Holmes, *2014 Index of Economic Freedom*. Washington, D.C.: Heritage Foundation / *Wall Street Journal*, 2014. URL for free download: http://www.heritage.org/index/download

Gregory J. Millman, *The Vandals' Crown: How Rebel Currency Traders Overthrew the World's Central Banks*. New York: Free Press, 1995.

Brendan Miniter (Ed.), *The 4% Solution: Unleashing the Economic Growth America Needs*. New York: Crown Business / George W. Bush Institute, 2012.

Hyman P. Minsky, *John Maynard Keynes*. New York: McGraw-Hill, 2008.

_____, *Stabilizing an Unstable Economy*. New York: McGraw-Hill, 2008.

Ludwig von Mises, *The Anti-Capitalist Mentality*. Princeton, New Jersey: Van Nostrand Company, 1956.

_____, *Human Action: A Treatise on Economics*. Third Revised Edition. Chicago: Contemporary Books, 1966.

_____, *On the Manipulation of Money and Credit*. Dobbs Ferry, New York: Free Market Books, 1978.

_____, *The Theory of Money and Credit*, New Edition. Irvington-on-Hudson, NY: Foundation for Economic Education, 1971.

Frederic S. Mishkin, *The Economics of Money, Banking and Financial Markets: The Business School Edition, 3rd Edition*. New York: Prentice-Hall, 2012.

Kelly Mitchell, *Gold Wars: The Battle for the Global Economy*. Atlanta, Georgia: Clarity Press, 2013.

Stephen Moore, *How Barack Obama Is Bankrupting the U.S. Economy* (Encounter Broadside No. 4). New York: Encounter Books, 2009.

_____, *Who's the Fairest of Them All? The Truth About Opportunity, Taxes, and Wealth in America*. New York: Encounter Books, 2012.

Charles R. Morris, *The Trillion Dollar Meltdown: Easy Money, High Rollers, and the Great Credit Crash*. New York: Public Affairs/Perseus, 2008.

Alan D. Morrison and William J. Wilhelm, Jr., *Investment Banking: Institutions, Politics, and Law*. New York: Oxford University Press, USA, 2008.

Warren Mosler, *Soft Currency Economics II: What Everyone Thinks That They Know About Monetary Policy Is Wrong*. Seattle: Amazon Digital Services, 2012.

Cullen Murphy, *Are We Rome? The Fall of an Empire and the Fate of America*. Boston: Mariner Books/ Houghton Mifflin, 2007.

Robert P. Murphy, *The Politically Incorrect Guide to Capitalism*. Washington, D.C.: Regnery, 2007.

Charles Murray, *Coming Apart: The State of White America, 1960-2010*. New York: Crown Forum, 2012.

_____, *What It Means to Be a Libertarian: A Personal Interpretation*. New York: Broadway Books, 1997.

Ralph Nader, *Unstoppable: The Emerging Left-Right Alliance to Dismantle the Corporate State*. New York: Nation Books, 2014.

Andrew P. Napolitano, *Lies the Government Told You: Myth, Power, and Deception in American History*. Nashville: Thomas Nelson, 2010.

Sylvia Nasar, *Grand Pursuit: The Story of Economic Genius*. New York: Simon & Schuster, 2011.

R. Nelson Nash, *Becoming Your Own Banker (Sixth Edition). Infinite Banking Concepts, 2012*.

Paul Nathan, *The New Gold Standard: Rediscovering the Power of Gold to Protect and Grow Wealth*. Hoboken, New Jersey: Wiley & Sons, 2011.

Karen Rhea Nemet-Nejat, *Daily Life in Ancient Mesopotamia*. Ada, Michigan: Baker Academic Publishing, 2001.

Maxwell Newton, *The Fed: Inside the Federal Reserve, the Secret Power Center that Controls the American Economy*. New York: Times Books, 1983.

Johan Norberg, *Financial Fiasco: How America's Infatuation with Home Ownership and Easy Money Created the Economic Crisis*. Washington, D.C.: Cato Institute, 2009.

Grover Norquist and John R. Lott, Jr., *Debacle: Obama's War on Jobs and Growth and What We Can Do Now to Regain Our Future*. Hoboken, New Jersey: John Wiley & Sons, 2012.

Mancur Olson, *The Logic of Collective Action: Public Goods and the Theory of Groups*, Revised Edition. Cambridge, Massachusetts: Harvard University Press, 1971.

_____, *Power and Prosperity: Outgrowing Communist and Capitalist Dictatorships*. New York: Basic Books, 2000.

_____, *The Rise and Decline of Nations: Economic Growth, Stagflation, and Social Rigidities*. New Haven, Connecticut: Yale University Press, 1984.

Ronen Palan, Richard Murphy and Christian Chavagneux, *Tax Havens: How Globalization Really Works*. Ithaca, New York: Cornell University Press / Cornell Studies in Money, 2009.

Scott Patterson, *Dark Pools: The Rise of the Machine Traders and the Rigging of the U.S. Stock Market*. New York: Crown Business / Random House, 2012.

Ron Paul, *End The Fed*. New York: Grand Central Publishing / Hachette, 2009.

_____, *Liberty Defined: 50 Essential Issues That Affect Our Freedom*. New York: Grand Central

Publishing / Hachette, 2011.

_____, *Pillars of Prosperity: Free Markets, Honest Money, Private Property.*
Ludwig von Mises Institute, 2008.

_____, *The Revolution: A Manifesto.* New York: Grand Central Publishing / Hachette, 2008.

Ron Paul and Lewis Lehrman, *The Case for Gold: A Minority Report of the U.S. Gold Commission.*
Ludwig von Mises Institute, 2007. This can be downloaded from the Internet at no cost from http://
mises.org/books/caseforgold.pdf

John Peet and Anton La Guardia, *Unhappy Union: How the Euro Crisis – and Europe – Can Be Fixed.*
London: Economist Books, 2014.

Michael G. Pento, *The Coming Bond Market Collapse: How to Survive the Demise of the U.S. Debt Market.* Hoboken, New Jersey: John Wiley & Sons, 2013.

Peter G. Peterson, *Running On Empty: How the Democratic and Republican Parties Are Bankrupting Our Future and What Americans Can Do About It.* New York: Farrar, Straus and Giroux, 2004.

Kevin Phillips, *Bad Money: Reckless Finance, Failed Politics, and the Global Crisis of American Capitalism.* New York: Viking Press, 2008.

_____, *Boiling Point: Democrats, Republicans, and the Decline of Middle-Class Prosperity.*
New York: Random House, 1993.

Thomas Piketty, *Capital in the Twenty-First Century.* Cambridge, Massachusetts: Harvard University Press, 2014.

Federico Pistono, *Robots Will Steal Your Job, But That's OK: How to Survive the Economic Collapse and Be Happy.* Seattle, Washington: CreateSpace / Amazon, 2014.

Lowell Ponte, *The Cooling.* Englewood Cliffs, New Jersey: Prentice-Hall, 1976.

Richard A. Posner, *The Crisis of Capitalist Democracy.* Cambridge, Massachusetts: Harvard University Press, 2010.

_____, *A Failure of Capitalism: The Crisis of '08 and the Descent into Depression.*
Cambridge, Massachusetts: Harvard University Press, 2009.

Virginia Postrel, *The Future and Its Enemies: The Growing Conflict Over Creativity, Enterprise, and Progress.* New York: Free Press, 1998.

Sidney Powell, *Licensed to Lie: Exposing Corruption in the Department of Justice.* Dallas: Brown Books Publishing, 2014.

Eswar S. Prasad, *The Dollar Trap: How the U.S. Dollar Tightened Its Grip on Global Finance.*
Princeton, New Jersey: Princeton University Press, 2014.

Nomi Prins, *All the Presidents' Bankers: The Hidden Alliances That Drive American Power.* New York: Nation Books, 2014.

John Quiggin, *Zombie Economics: How Dead Ideas Still Walk Among Us.* Princeton, New Jersey: Princeton University Press, 2012.

Raghuram G. Rajan, *Fault Lines: How Hidden Fractures Still Threaten the World Economy.* Princeton, New Jersey: Princeton University Press, 2010.

Joshua Cooper Ramo, *The Age of the Unthinkable: Why the New World Disorder Constantly Surprises Us And What We Can Do About It.* New York: Little Brown / Hachette, 2009.

Ayn Rand, *Capitalism: The Unknown Ideal (With additional articles by Nathaniel Branden, Alan Greenspan, and Robert Hessen).* New York: Signet / New American Library, 1967.

Carmen M. Reinhart and Kenneth S. Rogoff, *This Time Is Different: Eight Centuries of Financial Folly.* Princeton, New Jersey: Princeton University Press, 2009.

James Rickards, *Currency Wars: The Making of the Next Global Crisis.* New York: Portfolio/Penguin, 2011.

_____, *The Death of Money: The Coming Collapse of the International Monetary System.* New York: Portfolio / Penguin, 2014.

Jeremy Rifkin, *The Age of Access: The New Culture of Hypercapitalism, Where All of Life Is a Paid-for Experience.* New York: Jeremy P. Tarcher/Penguin, 2000.

_____, *The Zero Marginal Cost Society: The Internet of Things, the Collaborative Commons, and the Eclipse of Capitalism.* New York: Palgrave Macmillan, 2014.

Barry Ritzholtz with Aaron Task, *Bailout Nation: How Greed and Easy Money Corrupted Wall Street and Shook the World Economy.* Hoboken, New Jersey: John Wiley & Sons, 2009.

Keith Roberts, *The Origins of Business, Money and Markets.* New York: Columbia University Press / Columbia Business School Publishing, 2011.

Wilhelm Roepke, *A Humane Economy: The Social Framework of the Free Market.* Chicago: Henry Regnery Company, 1960. This can be downloaded from the Internet at no cost from http://mises.org/books/Humane_Economy_Ropke.pdf

Murray N. Rothbard, *America's Great Depression.* Fifth Edition. Auburn, Alabama: Ludwig von Mises Institute, 2000. This can be downloaded from the Internet at no cost from http://mises.org/rothbard/agd.pdf

_____, *The Case Against the Fed.* Second Edition. Auburn, Alabama: Ludwig von Mises Institute, 2007. A version of this book can be downloaded from the Internet at no cost from http://mises.org/books/Fed.pdf

_____, *A History of Money and Banking in the United States: The Colonial Era to World War II.* Auburn, Alabama: Ludwig von Mises Institute, 2002. This can be downloaded from the Internet at no cost from http://mises.org/Books/HistoryofMoney.pdf

_____, *The Mystery of Banking.* Second Edition. Auburn, Alabama: Ludwig von Mises Institute, 2010. This can be downloaded from the Internet at no cost from http://mises.org/Books/MysteryofBanking.pdf

_____, *What Has Government Done to Our Money?* Auburn, Alabama: Ludwig von Mises Institute, 2008. This can be downloaded from the Internet at no cost from http://mises.org/Books/Whathasgovernmentdone.pdf

_____, *For a New Liberty: The Libertarian Manifesto* (Revised Edition). New York: Collier Books / Macmillian, 1978.

Michael Rothschild, *Bionomics: The Inevitability of Capitalism.* New York: John Macrae / Henry Holt and Company, 1990.

Nouriel Roubini and Stephen Mihm, *Crisis Economics: A Crash Course in the Future of Finance*. New York: Penguin Books, 2010.

Robert J. Samuelson, *The Good Life and Its Discontents: The American Dream in the Age of Entitlement 1945-1995*. New York: Times Books, 1995.

_____, *The Great Inflation and Its Aftermath: The Transformation of America's Economy, Politics and Society*. New York: Random House, 2008.

Peter D. Schiff and Andrew J. Schiff, *How an Economy Grows and Why It Crashes*. Hoboken, New Jersey: John Wiley & Sons, 2010.

Detlev S. Schlichter, *Paper Money Collapse: The Folly of Elastic Money and the Coming Monetary Breakdown*. New York: John Wiley & Sons, 2011.

Peter H. Schuck, *Why Government Fails So Often: And How It Can Do Better*. Princeton, New Jersey: Princeton University Press, 2014.

Peter H. Schuck and James Q. Wilson (Eds.), *Understanding America: The Anatomy of an Exceptional Nation*. New York: PublicAffairs / Perseus Books Group, 2009.

Robert L. Schuettinger and Eamonn F. Butler, *Forty Centuries of Wage and Price Controls: How NOT to Fight Inflation*. Washington, D.C.: Heritage Foundation, 1979. This can be downloaded from the Internet at no cost from http://mises.org/books/fortycenturies.pdf

Barry Schwartz, *The Paradox of Choice: Why More Is Less*. New York: Ecco / Harper Collins, 2004.

Peter Schweizer, *Architects of Ruin: How Big Government Liberals Wrecked the Global Economy – and How They Will Do It Again If No One Stops Them*. New York: HarperCollins, 2009.

James C. Scott, *Seeing Like A State: How Certain Schemes to Improve the Human Condition Have Failed*. New Haven, Connecticut: Yale University Press, 1998.

George Selgin and others, *Has the Fed Been a Failure?* Revised Edition. (Monograph). Washington, D.C.: Cato Institute, 2010.

Hans F. Sennholz (Editor), *Inflation Is Theft*. Irvington-on-Hudson, New York: Foundation for Economic Education, 1994. A copy of this book may be downloaded at no cost from FEE's website at http://fee.org/wp-content/uploads/2009/11/InflationisTheft.pdf See also: Hans F. Sennholz, "Inflation Is Theft," *LewRockwell.com*, June 24, 2005. URL: http://www.lewrockwell.com/orig6/sennholz6.html

Judy Shelton, *Fixing the Dollar Now: Why US Money Lost Its Integrity and How We Can Restore It*. Washington, D.C.: Atlas Economic Research Foundation, 2011.

_____, *Money Meltdown: Restoring Order to the Global Currency System*. New York: The Free Press / Macmillan, 1994.

Amity Shlaes, *The Forgotten Man: A New History of the Great Depression*. New York: Harper Collins, 2007.

_____, *The Greedy Hand: How Taxes Drive Americans Crazy And What to Do About It*. New York: Random House, 1999.

Fred Siegel, *The Revolt Against the Masses: How Liberalism Has Undermined the Middle Class*. New York: Encounter Books, 2014.

Julian L. Simon, *The Ultimate Resource*. Princeton, New Jersey: Princeton University Press, 1981.

Chris Skinner, *Digital Bank: Strategies to Launch or Become a Digital Bank*. Singapore: Marshall Cavendish International (Asia-Singapore) / Times Publishing, 2014.

_____, *The Future of Banking in a Globalised World*. Hoboken, New Jersey: Wiley Finance Series, 2007.

Mark Skousen, *Economics of a Pure Gold Standard*. Seattle: CreateSpace, 2010.

_____, *The Making of Modern Economics: The Lives and Ideas of the Great Thinkers*. Second Edition. Armonk, New York: M.E. Sharpe, 2009.

Craig R. Smith, *Rediscovering Gold in the 21ˢᵗ Century*. Sixth Edition. Phoenix: Idea Factory Press, 2007.

_____, *The Uses of Inflation: Monetary Policy and Governance in the 21ˢᵗ Century* (Monograph). Phoenix: Swiss America Trading Corporation, 2011.

Craig R. Smith and Lowell Ponte, *Crashing the Dollar: How to Survive a Global Currency Collapse*. Phoenix: Idea Factory Press, 2010.

_____, *The Great Debasement: The 100-Year Dying of the Dollar and How to Get America's Money Back*. Phoenix: Idea Factory Press, 2012.

_____, *The Great Withdrawal: How the Progressives' 100-Year Debasement of America and the Dollar Ends*. Phoenix: Idea Factory Press, 2013.

_____, *The Inflation Deception: Six Ways Government Tricks Us...And Seven Ways to Stop It!* Phoenix: Idea Factory Press, 2011.

_____, *Re-Making Money: Ways to Restore America's Optimistic Golden Age*. Phoenix: Idea Factory Press, 2011.

Helen Smith, *Men on Strike: Why Men Are Boycotting Marriage, Fatherhood, and the American Dream – and Why It Matters*. New York: Encounter Books, 2012.

Roy C. Smith, Ingo Walter and Gayle DeLong, *Global Banking* (Third Edition). Oxford: Oxford University Press, 2012.

Vera C. Smith, *The Rationale of Central Banking and the Free Banking Alternative*. Indianapolis, Indiana: Liberty Press / Liberty Fund, 1990.

Jacob Soll, *The Reckoning: Financial Accountability and the Rise and Fall of Nations*. New York: Basic Books, 2014.

Guy Sorman, *Economics Does Not Lie: A Defense of the Free Market in a Time of Crisis*. New York: Encounter Books, 2009.

George Soros, *The Age of Fallibility: Consequences of the War on Terror*. New York: Public Affairs, 2007.

_____, *The Bubble of American Supremacy: the Costs of Bush's War in Iraq*. London: Weidenfeld & Nicolson, 2004.

_____, *George Soros on Globalization*. New York: Public Affairs, 2005.

_____, *The New Paradigm for Financial Markets: The Credit Crisis of 2008 and What It Means*. New York: Public Affairs, 2008.

_____, *Open Society: Reforming Global Capitalism*. New York: Public Affairs, 2000.

_____, *The Soros Lectures at the Central European University*. New York: Public Affairs, 2010.

Thomas Sowell, *Basic Economics: A Common Sense Guide to the Economy*. Third Edition. New York: Basic Books/Perseus Books Group, 2007.

_____, *A Conflict of Visions: Ideological Origins of Political Struggles*. New York: William Morrow, 1987.

_____, *Dismantling America*. New York: Basic Books, 2010.

_____, *Economic Facts and Fallacies*. Second Edition. New York: Basic Books, 2011.

_____, *The Housing Boom and Bust*. Revised Edition. New York: Basic Books, 2010.

_____, *Intellectuals and Society*. New York: Basic Books/Perseus Books, 2009.

_____, *Marxism: Philosophy and Economics*. New York: William Morrow, 1985.

_____, *On Classical Economics*. New Haven, Connecticut: Yale University Press, 2007.

_____, *The Quest for Cosmic Justice*. New York: Free Press/Simon & Schuster, 1999.

_____, *The Vision of the Anointed: Self-Congratulation as a Basis for Social Policy*. BasicBooks/HarperCollins, 1995.

Dimitri Speck, *The Gold Cartel: Government Intervention on Gold, the Mega Bubble in Paper, and What This Means for Your Future*. New York: Palgrave Macmillan, 2013.

Paul Sperry, *The Great American Bank Robbery: The Unauthorized Report About What Really Caused the Great Recession*. Nashville, Tennessee: Thomas Nelson / HarperCollins Christian Publishing, 2011.

Henry William Spiegel and Ann Hubbard (Editors), *The Growth of Economic Thought (3rd Edition)*. Durham, North Carolina: Duke University Press, 1991.

Mark Steyn, *After America: Get Ready for Armageddon*. Washington, D.C.: Regnery, 2011.

_____, *America Alone: The End of the World As We Know It*. Washington, D.C.: Regnery, 2008. *[Full Disclosure: Steyn quotes Lowell Ponte in this book.]*

Joseph E. Stiglitz, *Freefall: America, Free Markets, and the Sinking of the World Economy*. New York: W.W. Norton, 2010.

_____, *Globalization and Its Discontents*. New York: W.W. Norton, 2002.

David A. Stockman, *The Great Deformation: The Corruption of Capitalism in America*. New York: PublicAffairs/Perseus Books Group, 2013.

Paola Subacchi and John Driffill (Editors), *Beyond the Dollar: Rethinking the International Monetary System*. London: Chatham House / Royal Institute of International Affairs, 2010. URL: http://www.chathamhouse.org/sites/default/files/public/Research/International%20Economics/r0310_ims.pdf

Cass R. Sunstein, *A Constitution of Many Minds: Why the Founding Document Doesn't Mean What It Meant Before*. Princeton, New Jersey: Princeton University Press, 2011.

_____, *Simpler: The Future of Government*. New York: Simon & Schuster, 2013.

Ron Suskind, *Confidence Men: Wall Street, Washington, and the Education of a President*. New York: Harper Collins, 2011.

Bob Swarup, *Money Mania: Booms, Panics, and Busts from Ancient Rome to the Great Meltdown*. London: Bloomsbury Press, 2014.

Charles J. Sykes, *A Nation of Moochers: America's Addiction to Getting Something for Nothing*. New York: St. Martin's Press, 2012.

Nassim Nicholas Taleb, *Antifragile: Things That Gain from Disorder*. New York: Random House, 2012.

_____, *The Bed of Procrustes: Philosophical and Practical Aphorisms*. New York: Random House, 2010.

_____, *The Black Swan: Second Edition: The Impact of the Highly Improbable: With a New Section: "On Robustness and Fragility."* New York: Random House, 2010.

_____, *Fooled by Randomness: The Hidden Role of Chance in Life and in the Markets*. New York: Random House, 2005.

Peter J. Tanous and Jeff Cox, *Debt, Deficits and the Demise of the American Economy*. Hoboken, New Jersey: John Wiley & Sons, 2011.

Daniel K. Tarullo, *Banking on Basel: The Future of International Financial Regulation*. Washington, D.C.: The Peterson Institute for International Economics, 2008.

Richard H. Thaler and Cass R. Sunstein, *Nudge: Improving Decisions About Health, Wealth, and Happiness*. New York: Penguin Books, 2009.

J.A. Thompson, *The Bible and Archeology*. Grand Rapids, Michigan: William B. Eerdmans Publishing, 1962.

James Turk and John Rubino, *The Money Bubble: What to Do Before It Pops*. Moscow, Idaho: DollarCollapse Press, 2013.

Walter Tyndale, *Fundamentals of Offshore Banking: How to Open Accounts Almost Anywhere*. Seattle, Washington: CreateSpace/Amazon Publishing, 2009.

United States Government Accountability Office, *Offshore Tax Evasion: IRS Has Collected Billions of Dollars, but May be Missing Continued Evasion* (Report). Washington, D.C.: GAO, March 2013. URL: http://www.gao.gov/assets/660/653369.pdf

Richard Vague, *The Next Economic Disaster: Why It's Coming and How to Avoid It*. Philadelphia: University of Pennsylvania Press, 2014.

Johan Van Overtveldt, *Bernanke's Test: Ben Bernanke, Alan Greenspan and the Drama of the Central Banker*. Chicago: B2 Books/Agate Publishing, 2009.

Harry C. Veryser, *It Didn't Have to Be This Way: Why Boom and Bust Is Unnecessary – and How the Austrian School of Economics Breaks the Cycle*. Wilmington, Delaware: ISI Books / Intercollegiate Studies Institute, 2012.

Damon Vickers, *The Day After the Dollar Crashes: A Survival Guide for the Rise of the New World Order.* Hoboken, New Jersey: John Wiley & Sons, 2011.

William Voegeli, *Never Enough: America's Limitless Welfare State.* New York: Encounter Books, 2010.

M.W. Walbert, *The Coming Battle: A Complete History of the National Banking Money Power in the United States.* Chicago: W.B. Conkey Company, 1899. Reprinted by Walter Publishing & Research, Merlin, Oregon, 1997.

David M. Walker, *Comeback America: Turning the Country Around and Restoring Fiscal Responsibility.* New York: Random House, 2009.

Jude Wanniski, *The Way the World Works.* New York: Touchstone / Simon & Schuster, 1978.

Jack Weatherford, *The History of Money: From Sandstone to Cyberspace.* New York: Crown Publishers, 1997.

Carolyn Webber and Aaron Wildavsky, *A History of Taxation and Expenditure in the Western World.* New York: Simon & Schuster, 1986.

Janine R. Wedel, *Shadow Elite: How the World's New Power Brokers Undermine Democracy, Government and the Free Market.* New York: Basic Books / Perseus Books Group, 2009.

Eric J. Weiner, *The Shadow Market: How a Group of Wealthy Nations and Powerful Investors Secretly Dominate the World.* New York: Scribner, 2010.

David Wessel, *In Fed We Trust: Ben Bernanke's War on the Great Panic: How the Federal Reserve Became the Fourth Branch of Government.* New York: Crown Business, 2009.

Diana West, *American Betrayal: The Secret Assault on Our Nation's Character.* New York: St. Martin's Press, 2013.

_____, *The Death of the Grown-Up: How America's Arrested Development Is Bringing Down Western Civilization.* New York: St. Martin's Press, 2007.

Drew Westen, *The Political Brain: The Role of Emotion in Deciding the Fate of the Nation.* Washington, D.C.: PublicAffairs / Perseus Books Group, 2008.

R. Christopher Whalen, *Inflated: How Money and Debt Built the American Dream.* Hoboken, New Jersey: John Wiley & Sons, 2010.

Lawrence H. White, *The Clash of Economic Ideas: The Great Policy Debates and Experiments of the Last Hundred Years.* Cambridge: Cambridge University Press, 2012.

_____, *Is The Gold Standard Still the Gold Standard among Monetary Systems?* (Monograph). Washington, D.C.: Cato Institute, February 8, 2008. URL: http://www.cato.org/pubs/bp/bp100.pdf

Meredith Whitney, *Fate of the States: The New Geography of American Prosperity.* New York: Portfolio, 2013.

Peter C. Whybrow, *American Mania: When More Is Not Enough.* New York: W.W. Norton, 2005.

Addison Wiggin and William Bonner, *Financial Reckoning Day Fallout: Surviving Today's Global Depression.* Hoboken, New Jersey: John Wiley & Sons, 2009.

Addison Wiggin and Kate Incontrera, *I.O.U.S.A.: One Nation. Under Stress. In Debt.* Hoboken, New Jersey: John Wiley & Sons, 2008.

Benjamin Wiker, *Worshipping the State: How Liberalism Became Our State Religion.* Washington, D.C.: Regnery, 2013.

Aaron Wildavsky, *How to Limit Government Spending...*, Berkeley, California: University of California Press, 1980.

John Williams, *Hyperinflation 2012: Special Commentary Number 414. Shadow Government Statistics (Shadowstats)*, January 25, 2012. URL: http://www.shadowstats.com/article/no-414-hyperinflation-special-report-2012

Jonathan Williams (Editor), *Money: A History.* New York: St. Martin's Press, 1997.

David Wolman, *The End of Money: Counterfeiters, Preachers, Techies, Dreamers – and the Coming Cashless Society.* Boston: Da Capo Press / Perseus Books, 2012.

Thomas E. Woods, Jr., *Meltdown: A Free-Market Look at Why the Stock Market Collapsed, the Economy Tanked, and Government Bailouts Will Make Things Worse.* Washington, D.C.: Regnery Publishing, 2009.

_____, *Nullification: How to Resist Federal Tyranny in the 21ˢᵗ Century.* Washington, D.C.: Regnery Publishing, 2010.

_____, *Rollback: Repealing Big Government Before the Coming Fiscal Collapse.* Washington, D.C.: Regnery Publishing, 2011.

Thomas E. Woods, Jr., and Kevin R.C. Gutzman, *Who Killed the Constitution?: The Federal Government vs. American Liberty From WWI to Barack Obama.* New York: Three Rivers Press, 2009.

Bob Woodward, *Maestro: Greenspan's Fed and the American Boom.* New York: Simon & Schuster, 2000.

_____, *The Power of Politics.* New York: Simon & Schuster, 2012.

L. Randall Wray, *Modern Money Theory: A Primer on Macroeconomics for Sovereign Monetary Systems.* London: Palgrave Macmillan, 2012.

_____, *Understanding Modern Money: The Key to Full Employment and Price Stability*. Northampton, Massachusetts: Edward Elgar Publishing, 2006.

Pamela Yellen, *The Bank On Yourself Revolution: Fire Your Banker, Bypass Wall Street, and Take Control of Your Own Financial Future*. Ben Bella Books, 2014.

Fareed Zakaria, *The Future of Freedom: Illiberal Democracy at Home and Abroad*. New York: W.W. Norton, 2003.

_____, *The Post-American World*. New York: W.W. Norton, 2009.

Luigi Zingales, *A Capitalism for the People: Recapturing the Lost Genius of American Prosperity*. New York: Basic Books / Perseus Books Group, 2012.

Todd J. Zywicki, *The Economics and Regulation of Network Branded Prepaid Cards* (Working Paper). Arlington, Virginia: Mercatus Center / George Mason University, January 2013. URL: http://mercatus.org/sites/default/files/Zywicki_Prepaid_v2.pdf